CW00550841

Praise for *The Writers' Room Survival G*

"Niceole combines years of writing experience with wit, humor, and elegance. A die-hard fan of TV and film, her knowledge comes from a deep love of entertainment, and her insight into our business is invaluable. It's not only an educational read, but a hell of a lot of fun as well."
— Akela Cooper, screenwriter, *Malignant*

"If you want to understand how to create a writing career with longevity, this book is for you. Niceole Levy is raw and honest with what she reveals about the process of being in a writers' room and what it takes to survive. I love her truth. Niceole knows what it is to start at the staff level and rise to the top. I love that she interviews writers at all levels anonymously to gain insight. She also points out what works and doesn't work about the system. This book is a gift of information. I highly recommend it."
— Jen Grisanti, story/career consultant, writing instructor, speaker, and author

"Levy takes all the hard-won knowledge about working in TV writers' rooms that rookies used to kill for and veterans used to guard like nuclear codes and stitches it into a brisk, bouncy bible. I wish I had this kind of road map when I started out."
— Marc Bernardin, writer/producer, *Star Trek: Picard*

"With this book, Niceole provides not only a peek into the sacred writers' room, but also the tools on how to survive once you're there. I always say if you get the meeting, they like your writing, and now they just need to see if they like you. This inside look at how to survive a writers' room will help your showrunner know they made the right decision in hiring you."
— Karen Horne, senior vice president, equity & inclusion, Warner Bros. Discovery

"If you want to be a television writer, get this book. You'll find out in the time it takes to read it what it takes professional television writers years to learn. With honesty and humor, Niceole teaches you everything you need to know, including where to sit on day one, how a story gets broken in a room, exactly how to avoid unexpected pitfalls like getting embroiled in room politics, and the all-important inside information on how to make sure you get asked back for the next season. They should hand out this book to all new staff writers as soon as their deal closes."
— Carole Kirschner, career coach and author of *Hollywood Game Plan*

"Every once and a while, a how-to book comes along that you didn't know you needed until you needed it: Syd Field's *Screenplay*, William Goldman's *Adventures in the Screen Trade*, Stephen King's *On Writing*, Julia Cameron's *The Artist's Way*, and Robert Del Valle's *The One-hour Drama Series: Producing Episodic Television* all come to mind. Niceole Levy's *The Writers' Room Survival Guide* will soon join their ranks. It isn't a book about writing as much as it's a book about people—how to navigate all the good, bad, and ugly personalities—and the scenarios they can create. I can't emphasize enough how essential it will be to anyone coming up in a writers' room and trying to make sense of it."
— Cheo Hodari Coker, creator, executive producer, and showrunner of Marvel's *Luke Cage*; and writer/producer, *SouthLAnd*, *NCIS: Los Angeles*, *Almost Human*, and *Ray Donovan*

"This is truly the book every TV writer should own. Not just aspiring TV writers—all TV writers. It is overstuffed with valuable information and advice I wish I'd had when I was starting out, and what I now need to remind myself how to be a good writer and showrunner."
— Mike Royce, co-creator/showrunner, *Men of a Certain Age* and *One Day at a Time*

"Niceole's book is not only an expert guide for aspiring and new TV writers, it's invaluable for showrunners, directors, actors, and executives to learn what we do, what we are up against, and how we do it. An essential read for anyone in or near television and film."
— Christine Boylan, co-executive producer on *Avatar* for Netflix and *Poker Face* for Peacock

"This is bound to become the one dog-eared bible all aspiring TV writers keep with them."
— Eric Heisserer, showrunner, *Shadow and Bone*

"Such an incredibly valuable resource. Mandatory reading for all new TV writers and all up-and-comers. The book lays out all the dos and don'ts, everything you need to know to set yourself up for success in a business that only has one rule: The show must go on. *The Writers' Room Survival Guide* demystifies the process with wit, honesty, and practical knowledge."
—Glen Mazzara, executive producer/showrunner, *The Walking Dead* and *The Shield*

"If you have half a toe in the door of the TV industry, you must get *The Writers' Room Survival Guide*. Niceole has done her time in every kind of room, and she's exhaustive about telling you how you can thrive in the often-puzzling world of TV."
—Ben Blacker, TV writer and host of *The Writers Panel* podcast

"If you're looking for a book that includes candid insight on success strategies and methods to avoid screwing up in a TV writers' room, this is that book. Intelligent research and anecdotes prove essential reading for anyone choosing the writer's journey—beginners and pros alike."
—Aaron Rahsaan Thomas, writer/producer, *S.W.A.T.*

"Wonderfully comprehensive. Niceole sets the layout, ground rules, and navigational tools for any writer as a collaborator in this unique setting. She coaches and inspires. Read this and you are ready to take the plunge into and succeed in this creative landscape."
—Dave Watson, founder and editor, Movies Matter, davesaysmoviesmatter.com

"Niceole Levy has written a fast-paced, information-packed book that is a master class on what to expect when you cross the threshold into the writers' room. You'll learn what to do and what *not* to do. Even if you are just curious as to what it's like, you will enjoy this read. This truly is a survival guide for anyone who wants to become a writer for a TV show."
—Forris Day Jr., co-host, *Get Real: Indie Filmmakers* podcast and contributor to *Hitch 20* on YouTube

"Whether you're a first-time staff writer, a writers' assistant, or a PA, or a college student wondering if the job's for you, Niceole Levy gives you the real lowdown on the expectations and etiquette of the writers' room from the point of view of a real working TV writer, something I don't think you'll find in any other book."
—Bob Shayne, writer, *Simon & Simon, Magnum P.I., Hart to Hart, Whiz Kids*

"Every wannabe writer, working writer, and showrunner should read this book! Niceole provides a road map to navigate your way through showrunner styles, destructive room dynamics, and even toxic environments, while modeling the mentoring and good communication that should be the foundation of every writers' room. Niceole is very vulnerable about her own mistakes and challenges, sharing how she overcame them and what she learned. I've interviewed more than 140 TV writers and showrunners and read more than 40 books on film and TV writing and have never come across such a comprehensive guide to the writers' room."
—Gray Jones, TV editor/writer, host of the *TV Writer Podcast*, partner of *Script Magazine*, and author of *How to Break In To TV Writing: Insider Interviews*

"I wish I had this book when I was thrown into the *Family Guy* room with zero comedy writing experience. Navigating the personalities in a room is crucial, and Niceole lays out perfectly how to do exactly that. I can't recommend this book enough if you're someone who is mentally unstable enough to consider a career in TV writing."
—Damien Fahey, co-executive producer, *Family Guy*; radio host; former *MTV* VJ

"Writing is the easy part. Dealing with humans is harder. Niceole Levy has written an essential guide for beginners trying to get into or find their way around their first writers' room. Her book offers clear, concise help on how to handle not just deadlines, but also bosses, colleagues, and assistants. I just wish she'd written it when I was starting out."
—Guy Nicolucci, writer, *Late Night with Conan O'Brien, Daily Show with Jon Stewart*

THE WRITERS' ROOM
SURVIVAL GUIDE

Don't Screw Up the Lunch Order
and Other Keys to a Happy Writers' Room

NICEOLE LEVY

MICHAEL WIESE PRODUCTIONS

Published by Michael Wiese Productions
12400 Ventura Blvd. #1111
Studio City, CA 91604
(818) 379-8799, (818) 986-3408 (FAX)
mw@mwp.com
www.mwp.com

Cover design by Johnny Ink
Copyediting by Elizabeth Kennedy

Manufactured in the United States of America
Copyright © 2022 by Niceole Levy
First Printing 2022
All rights reserved. No part of this book may be reproduced in any form or by any means without permission in writing from the author, except for the inclusion of brief quotations in a review.

Library of Congress Cataloging-in-Publication Data
Names: Levy, Niceole, author.
Title: The writers' room survival guide : don't screw up the lunch order
    and other keys to a happy writers' room / by Niceole Levy.
Description: Studio City, CA : Michael Wiese Productions, [2022] | Summary:
    "You're about to embark on a journey to an unknown land, into the
    writers' room of a television show. This is not like writing alone. It
    is a place with new people, new traditions, and new language. Going in
    blind could end badly. An experienced guide can help you succeed. Use
    this book to build skills to thrive, and to help avoid traps to survive.
    Writers' rooms can be a heaven or hell, depending on a few things. The
    best rooms foster inclusive and productive creative flow. The worst
    create a toxic stew of bad feelings and doubt. Both kinds and everything
    in between require basic knowledge of how the room works. These
    fundamentals are best learned before you go in. The mystery box of the
    writers' room need not stay sealed shut forever. Consider this book your
    crowbar"-- Provided by publisher.
Identifiers: LCCN 2022002720 | ISBN 9781615933464 (trade paperback)
Subjects: LCSH: Television authorship--Vocational guidance--United States.
    | Television writers--Professional relationships--United States.
Classification: LCC PN1992.7 .L48 2022 | DDC 808.2/25--dc23/eng/20220708
LC record available at https://lccn.loc.gov/2022002720

Contents

Foreword

When Niceole Levy interviewed for the ViacomCBS Writers Mentoring Program in 2011, her writing sample included a supernatural short story that I loved. It was unique and original, just like Niceole. The fact that she'd watched 700 shows (and kept a meticulous record of it!) demonstrated her love of, and commitment to, television. Plus, she was just fun to meet.

Inviting Niceole to be part of the program was one of the smartest things we did. Not only has she gone on to have an impressive television writing career, but she's one of our most dedicated and generous program alumni, always available to help those alums coming up behind her. She cares deeply about writers and is committed to helping them learn to navigate this complicated business. She also does that with younger writers on all the shows she works on. She's the ally you want in the room.

And now, she's put it all into an exceptional book. If you want to be a television writer, get this book. You'll find out in the time it takes to read it what it takes professional television writers years to learn. With honesty and humor, Niceole teaches you everything you need to know, including where to sit on day one, how a story gets broken in a room, exactly how to avoid unexpected pitfalls like getting embroiled in room politics, and the all-important inside information on how to make sure you get asked back for the next season. They should hand out this book to all new staff writers as soon as their deal closes.

Because she has the experience to know what's needed in a story break or a room dynamic, Niceole is one of the most in-demand television writers. She always moves the ball forward. Her experiences—having worked on ten seasons of television, written nineteen episodes, and sold a pilot—gives her the insight and credibility to teach newcomers how to launch a successful television career. She has the heart of a teacher and mentor. You're in for an enlightening and entertaining trip into the world of the television writers' room.

—Carole Kirschner, career coach and author of *Hollywood Game Plan*

How to Get Talked into Writing a Book 101

"I think it should be you."

With those words, Carole Kirschner got me into yet another fine mess.

You know how it is, right? There's always that one person, the one you can never say "no" to? Carole's that person for me. But with good reason.

When I went in for my interview for the ViacomCBS Writers Mentoring Program back in 2010, Carole was the person I spoke with. She made me instantly comfortable, and I was able to deliver on the promise I'd made to myself: *Be you, no matter what.*

I got into that program, and since my first day, Carole has been one of the captains of Team Niceole. She helped me by giving notes on early samples. She referred me for jobs. She joyfully called to tell me I had gotten into the Showrunner Training Program at the Writers Guild of America (WGA) — a program she co-runs — and she's always a source of guidance, be it in whether or not to stay with a project or with thoughts on how to strike a better work-life balance.

So one day, Carole told me she'd talked to her publishers about a book on life in the writers' room, and that someone needed to write it.

"I think it should be you."

I wanted to say no because I had so much on my plate, and who had time to write a book? But I didn't say no. . . because Carole was asking, and because I love teaching and haven't had the time to do it lately. So this book would be a way to teach and mentor without having to do it in person in a classroom.

So that's why I wrote this book.

I'm writing it from my POV of writers' rooms and some of the collective experience of my friends. But by no means is it the sacred tome on writers' rooms. In the same way that every writer's story of how she or he got her or his start varies widely, so do room experiences. But this will, I hope, provide some insights for those looking to get into or about to join their first rooms — ways to find your comfort zone, build your skill set, create strong relationships, and build a successful career.

I'm also writing this from the POV of a writer who has worked in drama rooms. I will reference differences in comedy rooms when I can, based on anecdotes from my comedy-writing friends, and I will include some of their experiences in the anonymous stories that you'll find at the end of the chapters. The nuts and bolts of how to survive a room apply to all writers' rooms, but there are some cultural differences in comedy, so if you're pursuing it, you'll definitely want to take what I give you here and compare notes with someone with real-life time in a comedy room.

Not all my tips will be right for you. But it's a place to start when you're swimming in waters that feel a lot like the Bermuda Triangle meets Sharknado and all you want to do is keep your job and write some TV.

I hope this book will also shed some light on the process for TV fans who wonder how, exactly, their favorite shows get

made. So you'll find out how writers' rooms, showrunners, studios, and networks all work together (or at cross-purposes) when it comes to creating episode after episode of the TV you love.

Mostly, I hope this book reminds anyone who has a bad day in the room: You are aren't alone. It happens to *all of us*. And I hope it teaches you to celebrate the good days. Because those happen, too.

I'd be remiss if I didn't thank some people who are a big reason why I have the career experience to even attempt this book. Carole Kirschner, obviously. Jeanne Mau and Tiffany Smith-Anoi'a, who were my gateway into the business via the ViacomCBS Writers Mentoring Program. And Karen Horne, Jennifer Grisanti, and Julie Ann Crommett, who were my guides through NBC's Writers on the Verge (now NBC Launch). Without those programs, I might still be beating my head against the wall, trying to get someone to let me in.

You'll find that I discuss your personal network a lot in this book. Here's why. . . these are some amazing writers who have helped me get jobs, given me advice, or just been awesome friends through this process: Nkechi Okoro Carroll, Nichelle Tramble Spellman, Terence Paul Winter, Cheo Hodari Coker, Charles Murray, Aaron Rahsaan Thomas, Brian Anthony, Amy Pocha, Seth Cohen, Dennis Saldua, Isaac Gonzalez, Debby Wolfe, Ryan Harris, Omar Ponce, Leonard Chang, Marcos Luevanos, Steve Harper, Ken Sanzel, Rashad Raisani, John Glenn, Joe Pokaski, Christine Boylan, J. Holtham, Allie Kenyon, and Pornsak Pichetshote. I could go on. . . but there's only so much room in this thing.

Thank you to all the friends who kept me going when I was ready to give up. You were right. It worked out. Resa, you've been on the ride the longest. . . thanks for hanging in there! Special mention to my L.A. found family, especially the Marcuses (Zoe, Peter, Eli, and Charlie), and Diane and Bill Robinson, who make sure I know I'm loved at all times.

To the Vacation Friends. . . thank you for your friendship, even when it was hard. You make me laugh and you make my heart sing, and I adore you.

Thank you to Joyce Burditt, an amazing writer who gave of her talent and friendship and good heart and pushed me to keep writing samples until the last spec was really the last spec.

Thank you to Amanda Green and Tracy George, who read all the words I type, listen to my freak-outs, love me through my faults, and make me certain I will always have someone at my back when the world feels like it's falling apart.

The inspiration for everything I do is my family, who have been there from my start as a chubby-cheeked TV fan straight through to now. It wasn't always an easy dream to believe in, but they believed in me. And because my most important job in life is "World's Greatest Aunt," I need to say to Madison, Will, Thayne, Madden, Jackson, Cole, and Quinn. . . you make the world brighter, always.

Okay, enough with the mushy stuff. . . on to the book.

And if you think this book is unhelpful or boring, blame Carole. She made me do it. 😉

This Is Not a Book about Breaking into the TV Business...

But since that's always the first question anyone wants to ask when I sit down for a chat with an up-and-coming writer — How do you break in? — let's tackle it.

There's no one-size-fits-all answer, and we'll discuss some of the ways people get that first staff job when we talk about the role of support staff in the writers' room, because that's a big one and it involves a lot of different steps and combinations of job duties. . . or it requires one season working for the right showrunner who recognizes your brilliance immediately. See? Already a wide swing in how one route can work and we're just getting started.

But here's the best thing anyone ever told me about trying to break in to writing for TV. . .

Just don't give up.

Really. Sometimes that's the biggest part of it. Persistence is your friend. You will see some people get a staff job at twenty-three. Great for them. That's their path. Some people work and work and take this production assistant (PA) gig and this assistant gig and get staffed in their thirties. Again great for them. And some people. . . some people decide the career they thought would make them happy for life isn't really what they want to do and transition into writing in their thirties, forties, fifties. . . and their life experience is often the calling card that gets a room door to open for them. And some of us just take longer to get started than others. I was one of those. I wrote and wrote but didn't have any real connections for a long time. And once I started to develop helpful relationships, it still took more time to finally find the path in that was *my* path.

Some people, including me, break in via the network/studio writing fellowships offered by ViacomCBS, NBC, Disney-ABC, HBO, WB, and Nickelodeon. There are also great opportunities to be found with the National Hispanic Media Coalition (NHMC), the Coalition of Asian Pacifics in Entertainment (CAPE), Film Independent, Final Draft, Humanitas, Sundance Screenwriters Lab, and the Austin Film Festival, and there are multiple ways to utilize The Black List to get your material read or put up for consideration with their partners.

If you have some strong feature samples and think that's your way in, look at the Academy Nicholls Fellowship or the Universal Writers Program.

Some people start as actors and transition into writing. Some start in theater. Some are novelists who make the jump. Sometimes you hear stories about that unknown writer who wrote a pilot that actually sells. (This is way more complicated than it sounds and something we'll talk about in detail later — spoiler: You're almost never going to be the showrunner of that show if this is how you break into the business. But even this rule has exceptions.)

One thing we all have in common, no matter what our path was, is that we did the work. We watched countless hours of TV (and movies), read thousands of pages of scripts, wrote thousands and thousands of our own pages, and built our skill set up to make certain we were ready when someone finally said "yes" and gave us an opportunity. If you haven't done that work, in my opinion, you aren't ready yet. So start doing it. Ask people what their favorite pilots are; then watch them and read them. Find a show you love, read anything you can about how that show was made, study it. Then watch episodes again and see what you can learn about how to shape a series arc and long-term character arcs. Find other writers you trust to read your work and read for other writers — learning to give and take notes is also a huge part of the job, and that's a perfect way to start.

But when I say, "Don't give up," that doesn't mean you can't decide this isn't for you. Because some people do. The ten years it can take to break in (if you're me) can be debilitating emotionally and financially. You have to know what you really want for your future. If it's a home and a family and a way to pay a mortgage without stress, it may be time to look at the other things in life you love to do and make a career of that. And that's fine. Choose that. Because this life is fun and artistic and sometimes amazing. . . but it can be hard, and it's okay to want something else.

I almost went with my something else. I started a baking business because. . . *ten years*. . . and I was starting to wonder if maybe, just maybe, the writing game wasn't going to work out. And then it did. I always joke that the universe was like, "Damn, she's too good at this baking thing. We better get her a break as a writer, STAT!" And my career has been on a steady rise since (she writes, knocking on a little bit of wood).

If you're staying in, just know what your lines in the sand are. What I mean by that is decide what you really need to make your life work, and then make a plan to obtain/maintain/or work toward it. Again, if it's a relationship you want, you have to prioritize finding that relationship or you may look up and five years have gone by with your head in the ten scripts you were writing and you're like, "Oh, man. . . I meant to fall in love by now." If you live to travel, know that your vacations and your friends' will almost never line up once you start working in TV. Most of the world takes off in the summer, but you will likely be working every summer. So how do you slot in your global adventures in the downtime between seasons and still get to see the people you love? Dream of being a home-owner? Decide how much monthly debt you can carry while possibly being out of work for six to twelve months because it happens, and you need to be able to keep yourself afloat without massive amounts of stress when it does.

I know it might sound like I'm trying to scare you off. I'm not. I just want everyone who gets into this business to come in eyes open, the way I thankfully did because my mentors were honest with me, gave me truthful, helpful advice, and talked to me about things bigger than writing. . . like carving out time for myself, the need for downtime, and the financial realities of being a working writer.

If you do hang in there. . . you'll get a job and join the Writers Guild of America, either West or East. And when you go to your new member orientation, you'll hear someone talk to you about what an amazing accomplishment it is to become a part of the union. You might think they're exaggerating. *They are not.* When I went to my new member orientation, showrunner David Shore (*House, The Good Doctor*) told us that approximately fifteen hundred people are drafted by Major League baseball each year. *The WGAW (my coastal side of the WGA) admits about three hundred members annually.*

So yes, it's hard and competitive, but it's achievable. Just be honest with yourself about what you need to be happy. And if it's writing TV for a living? Be real with yourself about what that means for your day-to-day life, your financial future, and your family life.

And then. . . don't give up.

And once you're in the writers' room? Well, *that* is what this book is for. So read on and hopefully you will find some tips and solutions that help you avoid some of the rough spots and land mines other first-time writers have stumbled upon in their first jobs, including me.

1.

The People Part
of the Writers' Room

**Who does what, what the titles mean,
and how to get the lay of the land**

It's easy to be so excited about finally getting a job as a TV writer that you basically can't think about anything but the fact that you're now *an actual working TV writer*. But unlike writing pilots, specs, and features alone in your office or your bedroom — or in my case, on the sofa in front of the TV — TV writing is a team sport. I'll say that a lot in this book because it's the fundamental truth of making TV. No one person can do everything. Even if you wrote every script for a series, you'd need help from directors and talented producers and production staff and crew to make the show.

But very few writers are David E. Kelley, busting out whole series alone on their computers, which means our main job as TV writers is to tell stories in concert with other writers. To take our best ideas and theirs, weave them together, and present the showrunner with the best possible version of each episode. That takes teamwork and compromise; it takes a room of people who can disagree and move on; it takes the humility to always remember that until you're the showrunner, *it's not your show:* Your job is to support the showrunner's vision. It

I

feels like a small miracle that most shows successfully assemble a room full of hypertalented people who can manage this, yet it happens over and over again, every year.

Joining any writers' room, let alone your first, will feel significant. Unless you're one of the people who moves from show to show with a friend who's an executive producer (EP)/showrunner, you're almost always walking into a roomful of strangers. And given how most writers feel about social interaction (meaning we'd all rather swallow nails), meeting anywhere from four to twelve new faces is *a lot*. So here are some key things to think about regarding the people and personalities you're about to join, and you should start thinking about them before you ever step foot into the room.

Do your due diligence. They're vetting you, but vetting is a two-way street. Hopefully this process started before you accepted the job. When you booked your showrunner meeting, you should have run through every person you know and come up with any adjacent contacts to the person who might be giving you a job so you can ask how that person is to work with. Even if a friend of yours was a PA two seasons ago on a show the showrunner worked on, call that friend. Get info on what it was like to be in a room with him or her, even if the person wasn't the boss then. You will learn things about this showrunner as a person and you might find out something incredibly useful, like *"Oh, and he/she loves this random comic book character or movie or book"* and you know that same random piece. Now you have something you can mention in conversation during your meeting that gives you common ground.

You may also get insights into that person's process: how best to break story and how to pitch. Does the showrunner like to run the board, does the Number Two run it, or is each writer responsible for doing his or her own? Ask about things like the response when writers request time off (*Yes, you can ask for time off, especially for medical stuff*), room culture (*Is it a good work environment or are people pitted against each other?*), and what kind of hours should you expect to work (*You want a showrunner who likes to go home!*). All these details will help you in your showrunner meeting. And when you book the job, they'll help you figure out how to function in the room your new boss is going to run.

You'll also hear about this person's humanity. Is the person supportive? Does he or she cater to upper-level writers and ignore lower levels? Is this person inclusive of everyone or does he or she have favorites or cliques? How does the showrunner treat the assistants: Are they emerging writers who are allowed to participate in the room or stenographers and gophers expected to remain silent and work all hours of the day?

One thing to know going in — *you may hear bad stuff about some showrunners; that doesn't necessarily mean they are bad showrunners.* Not everyone loves every person at work, so even if your showrunner is a decent person, you may run into a writer who didn't get along with a showrunner and has some opinions. Or you may be getting an opportunity on a show with a showrunner who's notorious in this town for mistreating people in the room. The more people you can speak with, the better. Sometimes your reps can help you. They may know people who have worked with the showrunner who are willing to talk to you. But your network of contacts is your best resource. Writers try to save other writers from bad experiences — or at least send you in with your eyes wide open about what to expect.

So what's truly "bad" behavior and what falls under the "someone just didn't like this person" header? Did you hear that the showrunner can be a little abrupt and gives lots of notes? That he or she takes scripts away from lower levels pretty quickly? Writers aren't allowed to leave the room for scripts, so they have to write on nights/weekends? That stuff is stylistic — the specific way some showrunners like to have things done. Everyone can be abrupt. . . if it's not targeted or habitual, don't let that worry you. Lots of notes are the way some shows operate: It's their process. So buckle up and get ready for the ride. And that thing about having to sometimes write on nights/weekends instead of getting days out of the room? It's truly showrunner dependent, but it's also highly doable. As many writers will tell you when it comes to those nights and weekends: *That's what the money's for.*

If that's pretty normal behavior, what's truly bad? Well, first things first — *any showrunner who creates a culture where a staff member doesn't feel safe has stepped across a line.* We'll discuss this kind of situation in depth later, but when I say that I mean — sexually harassing people, harassing someone based on their race/gender/religion/sexual orientation/disability, or being physically abusive or intimidating. We've seen this manifested the past few years with reports of male showrunners putting hands on female staffers, showrunners who were verbally abusive/belittled writers of color and women — and the people who tried to defend them — and showrunners who have refused to listen to writers of color over culturally sensitive story points. And P.S., These showrunners aren't always men.

Because it can't be said enough, I'll say it here: This kind of behavior is *NEVER* okay. It should be reported immediately, and if you don't feel safe reporting it, please 1. reach out to another member of the staff that you trust, preferably someone of higher rank than you, 2. contact a writer outside of your show to ask for guidance on how to file a complaint, or 3. contact the WGA and ask for assistance in navigating things. *It's scary and awful to have to step forward, but every person in the writers' room deserves to feel safe.* So it is more than okay to ask for help if you run into one of these showrunners or, frankly, any member of your staff whose behavior is creating an unsafe work environment.

I know you're wondering how someone with that type of reputation is still running a show in the first place. It's because it takes time and reporting parties to get abusive showrunners fired. . . more time than it should, more reporting parties than we'd like — but there is a process. And for every person who speaks up, there are probably multiple who did not feel safe and chose to keep their own counsel. When a showrunner has a reputation for success or has created the big new thing that everyone's tweeting about, studios and networks will try to solve problems without upending their creative team — meaning sending the showrunner to counseling or training or bringing in additional upper-level creatives to change the culture. So someone who's been a hitmaker or who just made the big hit, they're going to get more rope. . . which isn't right, but it's reality. The more people who set off alarm bells, the more studios and networks are spurred to step in and take action.

Now there are people who become notorious as "bosses you don't want to work for" who aren't "monster" showrunners. Some people aren't outright bullies — they simply make life miserable every day. Like showrunners who take the script you spent days on, read ten pages, and decide to rebreak the whole episode without finishing the read. It leaves the room in constant chaos, forces nonstop rewrites, and usually means scripts are late to production, which means production is always scrambling, too. And FYI, usually you end up using 50 to 75% of that original script once all the dust settles — not that your showrunner will know you cut and pasted the original scenes back in because he or she never read them.

Or there's the showrunner who waits until five o'clock to come into the room after the writers have been working all day and blows up legit everything on the board, then expects people to stay late and fix it instead of coming in refreshed the next day with new ideas. That sort is usually the showrunner who basically never wants to go home for whatever the reason, so writers are kept late, making "ordering dinner" a routine, disrupting the home lives of their staff even though it's not increasing the quality of the show or the writing. And there's the showrunner who thinks you work for them literally 24/7, who doesn't have any respect for family/private time. (*Yes, grateful as you are to have this job, you still get to have a life outside of work. Please don't ever let anyone make you forget or doubt that.*)

If you're lucky like I've been, most of the feedback you hear about your future showrunner will be good. Stuff like "fair, will give lots of notes, but will give you a real shot to succeed," or "really good human who likes to go home at the end of the day and treats the people on the team like adults," or "runs such a good room, I learned so much about how to break story." And that's the kind of stuff that should make you doubly excited to have gotten this particular gig. You're set up for success and to learn a lot. And later, I'll discuss how to maximize that opportunity. But if the feedback you hear feels stilted or rehearsed or cautious, there's probably a problem and the writer you're speaking to likely doesn't feel comfortable sharing details. Try to find someone else who will, talk to your reps, and do what you can to find out what the issues are on the show before you join.

If you find out your potential showrunner is one of the notorious ones, you have a choice to make — knowing what you now know, how badly do you want this job? It's not fair, but it's honest to say that getting your first job is tremendously difficult. Chances are you were up against a dozen other writers, at least, who sat down with the showrunner for that precious staff writer spot (*and that's after the stack of literally a hundred-plus scripts was thinned out to the frontrunners*). So is it worth walking into a bad/notorious/toxic situation just to get your first credit? The only person who can answer that is you. Every single one of us has to make those choices for ourselves. But I will tell you this in case it helps. . . *everyone in town knows who those showrunners are*. That's why you'll find people willing to talk to you and warn you about what you're getting into. That's why you'll already have tips on how to navigate land mines in the room. And that's why little of what happens on that show for the time you're there will follow you. There was a showrunner in town who was so notorious for going through staff writers that reps would tell their clients, "It's okay, everyone gets fired from that show. Go make some money and get your first script." And people did it. . . made some money, got their first script, got to be part of building a season of TV, and then were able to go out for other shows with that all-important first credit under their belt. I know most of them would tell you it wasn't easy, but it paved their way into better jobs with better showrunners.

But the only person who has to live with your choice is you. So be honest with yourself. Lots of us survive bad jobs. But one problem in this town is that we all tell our war stories, as if you have to endure something terrible to succeed. *You do not.* You can hope for and believe in good room experiences — and most of my friends, like me, have had more good ones than bad. It's part of why I've encouraged people lately to talk more about their good rooms — what made them great, why they would love to work with certain people again. To remind us all that *that* should be the expectation, not the bad stuff.

The Rest of Your Writers' Room

After you've gotten the lowdown on your new showrunner (*and accepted the job!*), you'll be in a little bit of a holding pattern, waiting for the all-important "start email." This usually comes from the showrunner's assistant or the writers' assistant with details like what day the room starts, what time to meet up, where the room is, what parking info you need, how to get your IDs, and any specific information the showrunner wants you to have (*research to get a jump on, ideas you need to be thinking about, etc.*).

That email is usually sent to the staff at large, which means you now have the names of all the other people you'll be working with in the room. And the next thing you should do is Google/IMDB them all and find out who they are and what they've worked on.

Part of that is just getting to know people. You may not remember every name of every writer from that show you loved six years ago, but then lo and behold, you see on IMDB that one of your co-EPs worked on that show. For example, on my first show, *Ironside*, I discovered that one of our consulting producers worked on a little three-season show I adored. We ran into each other in the kitchen one day, and I mentioned how much I loved the show, which he appreciated. It gave me a way to strike up a conversation with someone I barely knew, and most people will respond well to having you mention something they worked hard on.

Or maybe someone on staff worked with a mutual friend, which you'll realize when you scan their IMDB page and see a show you knew writers on. You can 1. reach out to your friend and say, "Hey, I'm going to be working with X!" and see what their response is — you can learn a lot from that — and 2. if the response is something like "OMG, I love them so much! You're going to have the best time!" then you can introduce yourself to that writer with a mutual connection, "Oh, you're friends with X, too, right?" and start to build a bridge on day one. (If the response feels tepid or cautious in any way, it usually means there was an issue between your friend and this writer, so probably better to not mention the connection.)

I know it might sound — and feel — a little stalkery. But the truth is, *building relationships is one of the key components of writers' room survival.* You're going to be spending anywhere from eight to twelve hours a day with these people, and the quicker you get to know everyone's personalities and create at least small connections, the quicker you'll have people you can rely on when you have questions about process or the schedule or anything you don't want to bother the boss with — and the sooner you'll know whom to steer clear of unless it's absolutely necessary.

Remember, TV is a team sport — so make it a priority to be part of building the team. And yes, even as a staff writer, you can take part in team building. You'll find moments when the room desperately needs someone to pitch something stupid for a laugh, or when someone suggesting the showrunner's favorite lunch spot (*more on this later*) takes the edge off a tough day, or if you're me, you bring in homemade cookies for the other writers. (*Hey, it works!*) But the bigger point is, this is your new TV family. Do what you can to care for them. Sometimes that's as simple as stopping by to say good morning to your upper levels, see how their families are, ask if you can help with anything. You'd be amazed how often an EP or co-EP has work on his or her desk that can easily be passed on to you. Stopping by and offering can prompt them to say, "Actually, can you write these log lines for marketing?" and not only have you added to your value, you're helping someone check a box on their to do list, and they'll remember you for the effort.

Hierarchy: What It Is, What It Means

One of the things you'll have to manage in your writers' room is the idea of hierarchy. And believe me, even if your show-runner is one of those awesome people who says, "Hierarchy doesn't matter here; I just care about getting the best idea," *someone* in that room cares about it. So here's what you need to know about what the titles are and what they mean:

Showrunner. At the end of the day, the showrunner wins all the fights. This is clear cut, unless, of course, you have co-showrunners. That usually happens because 1. a writing team created/runs the show or 2. because a writer without showrunning experience created the show and an experienced showrunner was brought on. In those situations, you'll have to learn the vibe of the relationship. Sometimes it's clear who gets the final say; sometimes it's not. That's when those bonds you've been building in the room can come in handy. Sometimes a more experienced writer can help you figure out who exactly is at the top and whom to defer to — and help you navigate the tricky politics of multiple showrunners.

The Number Two is usually a co-executive producer (co-EP) but can also be an executive producer (EP). Most upper levels in this role have one key job: run the room. The showrunner will have a million things to do during the day — coming in and out, leaving directives, or asking the room to work through some ideas. The Number Two keeps the room moving, getting pitches on the board, helping to craft beats to pitch when the showrunner returns.

The Number Two may also be the designated lower-level mentor, keeping tabs on the lower-level writers on staff, which ranges from check-ins to offering to read early pages and give feedback on documents before they have to be turned in to the showrunner. If this person exists on your staff, *please use him or her.*

(*Sometimes it's another co-EP, often referred to as the Number Three.*) Not every show has this person, and that's a shame, because it's a focused way to cultivate talent and build a writer's skill sets. This person usually has a mentorship-filled heart and wants to help you succeed. When the room mentor gives you notes, tells you to speak more in the room, or tells you to speak less, listen and do that. This person knows you've got little to no experience in the room and is trying to help you. Let that happen.

The Number Three. This isn't always an official designation, but rather something that happens by default. If there's another co-EP in the room besides your Number Two or an experienced supervising producer, that person is usually the one who jumps in and takes charge when both the showrunner and Number Two are out of the room. The Number Three will keep the train running, pushing the story break forward.

This may also be that designated mentor. Again, if you have one, seize the opportunity. This can also be a great person to run a pitch by before the room if you want to try it out in front of one person rather than twelve.

Supervising producer. This person can be a Number Three, sometimes acts as a Number Two, and will also step in when needed to run the room. Generally, to get to this level, you're talking about a writer who has worked on about six seasons of TV if not more — so when you have questions, the supervising producer is a great source of knowledge and may be a little less intimidating than a co-EP who's been doing this for twenty years.

Producer. A writer who has reached the top of mid-level status.

Co-producer. Welcome to mid-level status! This is where your on-screen credit moves to the front of the show and you start to get more responsibilities.

Executive story editor (ESE). Pending any title repetition, this is usually your third season or so of TV. So you're starting to know a good amount about how it all works, but there is a lot more to come.

Story editor. Generally, this is the first year when you'll receive script fees on top of your weekly salary as a writer.

Staff writer. Staff writers typically work on a WGA minimum salary and do not receive script fees but will receive residuals for any episode they write/co-write. There is some variance on this — some studios will make you repeat staff writer with something called a "hybrid" deal where you receive a 10% raise over minimum and script fees, but you don't get a bump in title.

So why do all those titles matter? They do and they don't. They are a way to note someone's time in. . . that they've worked their way up the ladder, season after season, and to indicate who has more experience and go-to knowledge when questions or problems arise. But it doesn't always mean their ideas are better. Which is why some showrunners, during their day one "welcome to the room" speech, will say, "Hierarchy doesn't matter here; I just care about the best idea." And the person usually means it. But then you come across the co-EP who has a chip on his shoulder because it took him eighty-eight episodes to get to producer and someone else on staff got there in forty. *That guy,* he cares about hierarchy, and he'll let you know it. Maybe not in the room, but when he co-writes with people or when he gives notes or when he quashes someone's pitch because he's more experienced and must be right. When you encounter this, recognize that's who this person is, use whatever allies you have in the room to survive it, and move on. You are there to do your job, not to give this person someone to lord their title over or to put yourself at risk by fighting with him.

Hierarchy also matters because as you rise up the ranks, you'll likely be given more responsibilities, depending on the culture of your show. You may be asked to take passes on early documents or script drafts, take part in more casting sessions or prep meetings, spearhead conversations with consultants who will come in to speak with the room, or cover extra episodes on set. Basically, as the showrunner recognizes your ability to manage more than yourself, you'll find more work coming your way — sometimes work that feels above your level. I was asked to take over the room in my third staff writer year. . . talk about feeling intimidated! But my co-EP believed I could keep us on task and get the pitches we needed, so I did it.

When it comes to hierarchy, though, it's important to remember that whole "team" concept. Even as a staff writer, if you're on a show where there's more than one of you at that level, reach out to the other staff writer(s). You're not competing against each other for survival. If you're both great writers, your boss will be thrilled. If one of you is stronger, you were always stronger, and that's just how things worked out. But rather than be against one another, you can be each other's trusted sounding board.

As you continue to move up the title ladder, your job as a good writer human is to reach back. . . help the new staff writers, mentor the rising new ESE who just joined the show and feels a little lost. If you see someone's behavior in the room is upsetting the showrunner, you can be part of the solution. . . take that writer for a walk, say something like, "Hey, I noticed that the boss seems to get a little steamed when you do X" and just give the person a chance to fix the behavior independently. Again, team sport. . . if your team is healthy and functioning, everything is going to work better, and you can do your part to help create that reality.

Support Staff: Writers' Assistants, Script Coordinators, and PAs

The first and most important thing to know about the support staff of your show is that they work *with* you, not *for* you. They are there to support the show. I know that seems self-explanatory, but you'd be amazed how writers can start to treat support staff like personal assistants, *and that is definitely not their jobs.* So I'll run down what everyone does and then discuss how you can be a vital support component for them, making your team even stronger.

Showrunner's assistant. This person works directly for the showrunner; if you need to grab a minute to ask the boss for time off, this is the person you ask. If you wonder when you might get notes on something, stop by this desk. But remember, the job is basically managing the showrunner's life — so be respectful of his or her time.

Writers' assistant. This is the person who will legit type every word the room says all day long and turn it into coherent notes you can all write from. It is heroic work. And writers' assistants are often aspiring writers themselves. Depending on the rules of your room, they may be allowed to pitch ideas, and hopefully they will be co-writing a script or getting a solo episode.

Script coordinators (SCs). This proofreading god or goddess is the person who will make you look better than you really are when they send out your scripts by catching the typos you missed and fixing your broken formatting. Script coordinators track who has the script files, due dates for drafts, and paperwork that helps you get paid for writing your documents. They almost always have templates created for story documents, outlines, and scripts — so ask them for it if it hasn't been distributed yet; it will make your life easier! Script coordinators will also be the conduit by which "clearances" work *(for those who don't know, these are legal checks on names of people, places, and things in scripts to make sure we can actually use them).* Most SCs are also aspiring writers. Not all of them participate in the room, but when they are able to, they may pitch, and often are also getting a co-write or a solo episode.

Production assistants (PAs). Usually there's at least one PA for the writers, sometimes more than one. Production assistants manage the financial life of the room: They get a budget from the studio for snacks, beverages, supplies, and lunches, and then handle ordering, shopping, and picking up or delivering lunch every day. They have to process receipts for accounting and also perform a variety of other duties to support the showrunner, showrunner's assistant, and other writers on staff. In recent years, PAs have endured a lot of stress because as studios cut budgets for writer lunches and snacks, PAs have sometimes been left holding the financial bag when writers insist on getting X item and the studio won't pay for it. Please *do not* let this happen. Keep in touch with your PAs, make sure they're not having accounting issues, and help solve the problem if they are. On one of my shows, we each gave the PA a hundred dollars in cash to use for overages on our lunch orders, and he'd let us know if we ran through our cash so we could re-up. *It is never your PA's job to cover expenses out of his or her own pocket.*

Working with Your Support Staff

Like I said, they work with you, not for you — but that doesn't mean you can't ask them for help. The support staff is a resource and always happy to pitch in. If you don't know how the show refers to something already established, your writers' assistant or script coordinator most definitely will — or they'll find you an answer. If you're moving into your office and need some help, the PA will be more than happy to lend a hand. If you have a special request for a meal because you're not feeling well but you have to get some work done, one of those wonderful people will probably help you out. Just remember, ask nicely and say thank you. You'd be amazed how many people forget that.

When it comes to writing stuff — you can also utilize this team to ease your workload and give them some valuable work experience. Almost every episode of TV you write will require additional written material: Did you put in a close-up of a newspaper? That newspaper needs text. Are we looking at police reports in files? They all need content. Multiple social media screens? They need to get filled up with realistic looking posts. You can ask your support staff to pitch in on these materials, giving them some guidelines for what you need: a Twitter feed about a boy band written by a teenage girl, a newspaper article about the fire that destroyed a landmark, etc. They'll be thrilled to pitch in, and it will help you stay focused on your script or prep meetings.

But please: Give them credit. Be free in saying things like, "X and Y really pitched in and created all those social media posts. It was such a help." Say it to your boss, so he or she knows the support staff are being team players and that they've contributed material to the show.

Support staff can also save your life while you're on set. Last-minute changes to script pages? Sometimes you can call those in to your script coordinator, and they'll type them up and get the pages to the showrunner while you're moving locations. Need notes from a day in the room for the episode you're writing on set and don't have them? Your writers' assistant has your back.

Because the team will always support you, be sure you support the team. Mentoring isn't just for writers on staff; it's for future writers. *Everyone working in these support jobs wants to be you: a working TV writer.* So as you have time, talk to them, find out what they're interested in writing, offer to read their material, and be a sounding board for their ideas. This is the start of your learning to be a good "boss," by looking after the people who work tremendously hard every day to keep the room running. Be good to them, and it will only make you better.

TRUE TALES OF LIFE
INSIDE A WRITERS' ROOM

MALE UPPER-LEVEL BIPOC DRAMA WRITER
ON PITCHING IN YOUR FIRST ROOMS

Early in my career, I was in a room where lower-level writers were encouraged to speak, but not expected to add much to the process, so hearing positive feedback on a pitch or even receiving eye contact from higher-level writers was rare. I've also been in rooms where an idea pitched by a lower-level writer gets little overt support, but when the exact same idea is pitched by an upper-level writer, it is enthusiastically embraced. My advice for lower-level writers in those instances is to stay positive. The good news is that your idea is right on track. Keep pitching ideas, and eventually you'll find yourself in a position where either the show you're on, or the next show, will openly recognize the value you bring to the room.

FEMALE DRAMA WRITER ON DEALING WITH A ROOM BULLY

I was in a room with a very talented producer who was also very mean to me. They felt that because I came through a diversity program that I hadn't paid my dues. The meanness I could take. Not a problem. I've been around mean people, but the staff was afraid of the producer. Everyone was afraid of them! So because they didn't like me, whenever they were around, no one really spoke to me or gave me space in the room. If this producer liked to talk about something, you couldn't talk about it because it was "their thing." And they had lots of things: film, television shows, books, travel, sports, food, etc. Still, that wasn't the bad part. The bad part was that they had been around for so long that they knew and were friends with everyone in Hollywood. Everyone! This producer was a perfect example of building a great network. Their friendships and connections crossed cultures, religions, and networks. So I had nowhere to run because they were one degree separated from nearly every production in Hollywood. No exaggeration. It was difficult and stressful, and if you asked this person or any of the people who ostracized me, they'd say, "I never knew there was a problem." I was seriously beginning to hate the very thing that I had worked so hard for, for so long.

How I handled it:

I CHOSE TO DIG IN and hold my peace! I made a decision that I was going to buckle down and stand it. That even though this producer was mean, I would learn from their talent. It was hard, but two things helped. One was another producer who never failed to support me and include me, in the room and out. The other was the pandemic shutting the room down. When we came back to the room, the world was a different place and the producer was a different person. What's sad about this story is that it wasn't unique. I learned from other junior writers that we all had hateful, asshole people in our rooms who were allowed to do and say things that were really awful because they were talented and considered indispensable to the production.

The Quickstart Guide

**Logistics and other stuff that
comes before the actual work**

On the day I reported to the Universal lot for my first day as a staff writer on *Ironside*, I was, to put it mildly, a wreck. I was nervous about going to the wrong gate (even though I'd been to this lot easily fifty times). I was worried about parking in the wrong spot (there was no assigned parking for lower levels, but we did get to park in the covered structure — you just had to 1. not steal anyone's designated spot and 2. beat the *CSI* crew in before they took all the parking). Once I survived the gate and parking, it was time to make it to the right office door and then find the lovely human being who'd been communicating information to me via email for days: the showrunner's assistant.

I went in happy to be there and happy to go where I was told to go. When I was walked to my very own office, it was nothing fancy: some used furniture that had *Desperate House-wives* paperwork stuck in the desk drawers. . . because all studio furniture is basically recycled show to show. . . a semi-uncomfortable chair, a couch, a whiteboard, a corkboard. That was basically it. But to me, it was literally the greatest place I'd ever seen. Because this was the office where someone was paying me to write TV. . . like, that was *my job* now.

There were logistics to deal with before there was work, though. . . start paperwork, getting an ID, parking pass paperwork, scouting out where the bathrooms were, and figuring out where the lot restaurants were in case I didn't want what we were having for lunch that day. And of course scouting out the cool spots on the lot that I couldn't wait to visit when I had some free time to wander around (hello, Bates Motel and Jaws!).

But the truly big — and most important — part of the day was meeting the other people. Being brave enough to walk up to a stranger's office door and say "Hi, I'm Niceole, one of the staff writers." And so I put on my big girl pants and did just that. As you saw in Chapter 1, the relationships you make with your fellow writers and support staff can make or break a show experience. If the show is dysfunctional, those bonds give you safe harbor in the storm; if the show is functional, you get a lovely family-feeling unit to hang out with every day. And if you're truly lucky, as I was, you get a group of people who *want* you to succeed, who see your passion and your talent and your work ethic and decide to invest in you. A lot of that comes from your willingness to start conversations. Get to know your fellow writers as people so you can ask about their lives outside of work. It will help you build kinship that comes in handy when you need an ally or advice.

Once all the introductions are done and you know where you're going to be working from for the next ten to forty weeks, and you have your shiny new ID badge and parking pass, well, then it's time to figure out how this whole writers' room thing works. So let's dive in.

The Basics of How a Writers' Room Works.
We'll Get Into Specifics Later.

There are no hard and fast rules here. That's the first rule. And yeah, I know. *Annoying!* But truthfully, it depends so much on the personality of your showrunner, the type of show, and if it's a new show or a returning show. But there are some things that come up in every room that I can lay out so you'll have a reference point when it's your turn.

As noted in Chapter 1, your room will generally be run by your showrunner or your Number Two (and if you split into multiple rooms, sometimes your Number Three also runs a room).

Running the room means the person who keeps beats going up on the board, discussion flowing, and work getting done. You'll find a room quickly develops its own rhythm — some are super serious with little chitchat and a hard press toward the work. Some are looser with tangents breaking the workflow. This tone is largely set by your showrunner and echoed by your Number Two. The best showrunners will chat with you on day one about the way they like things done, what their pet peeves are, and how they like things to flow. But there are a lot of little logistical things you probably haven't even thought about that can be minefields. . . so let's run them down.

Where to sit. Yes, this is a real consideration. I know. This seems silly already. But it's important to think about. . . and scope out before you claim your seat in the room. Again, some showrunners will tell you how they feel about this from day one. But some won't, and you'll have to figure it out. If you're on a returning show, then you can simply ask one of those returning writers you've been introducing yourself to if there's a pecking order in seating. If it's a new show, the best plan is usually to hang back a bit and see how things shake out.

Why? Hierarchy plays a part. . . some showrunners like having upper-level writers close to them, which means you need to know where the showrunner is sitting first (always) to see if their co-EPs and company take seats nearby. Some of it's about your personality/needs. If you know you are a person who fidgets a lot, don't sit near your showrunner. It is the type of thing that can drive a boss crazy, and you may not be able to tone your fidgeting down, but you can put distance between you and the person who decides if you keep your job or not. Need to go to the restroom a lot? See if you can snag a seat near the door so you can slip in and out without much disruption.

One of the things that varies room to room is "same seat every day" vs. "mix it up and sit anywhere you want." I am a 100% proponent of the "same seat every day" approach. It's not just because I happen to be a creature of habit who likes to not have to think about where to sit after the first day. It's also because I am a huge germaphobe, and well, writers' rooms can get gross. People snack at the table all day. Drinks get spilled. And then there's the thing no one will be allowed to do in my rooms but that happens in lots of them and makes me insane: People put their feet on the table.

I know. I know. You're like, "Niceole, big deal, I like to sit with my feet on the table." Sure. I don't mind doing it at home when it's my space and my table. But here's why I beef it at work: You very often eat at that table. And I don't just mean snacks. Many rooms require writers to eat together in the writers' room, and if someone else's feet were anywhere near my section of table. . . well, that's just gross.

I'll be super frank: this is my biggest pet peeve in a room. People don't get why it bothers me quite so much, but even in a pre-COVID world, it drove me crazy. The bathrooms we use at work are public, and your shoes walk those floors multiple times a day. And that's just a huge no for me when it comes to those shoes then touching down where I eat food and drink sparkling water and write notes all day.

So yeah, that's why I'm all about the same seat every day. Side-note: The best writers' PAs are the ones who know they need to Lysol the table at the end of every day without being asked (largely because of the feet thing, but also just because people are slobs). If you ever realize it's not being done, please help-fully suggest that they start.

If you end up in a "mix it up and sit somewhere else every day" kind of room, well, you have two choices. You can go with the flow, which will definitely make your life easier. Or you can be me and say, "Y'all sit where you want. But I'm staying here." I've only had one showrunner really make a fuss about it, but I stuck to my guns. Now, to be fair, this wasn't when I was still at staff-writer level. Then I would have put up with it and stayed quiet. But when it finally did come up, I knew myself in the room well enough to know that I was going to hate moving all over, and so I just politely took my seat every day and didn't say anything about where anyone else went.

Oh, and one super important, not to be forgotten thing: *Your showrunner's seat is your showrunner's seat.* That doesn't mean no one else will ever sit there. If the boss isn't in the room, you can sit there. Sometimes you're working on a break and it's easier to see the board from his/her seat, so someone moves there for a little while. But when your showrunner comes into the room, you need to move back to your regular space. You should never assume that the showrunner is okay sitting somewhere else. If he or she sees you moving and says, "No, it's fine," it proba-bly is. But the better part of valor is picking up your stuff and vacating the seat.

And this goes for whether you're sitting in your own seat or temporarily borrowing someone else's: Mind your table space. Imagine trying to fix a story problem as someone's sea of empty snack wrappers and dirty paper towels spills on to your notebook. Yeah, not so much. Clean up after yourselves, and don't become the person other writers exchange looks about because you're the Pigpen of the writers' room.

And for goodness' sake, never change the settings on someone's chair if you are temporarily sitting in their spot. Seriously. . . I've worked with upper-level writers who would breathe fire at you if you messed up their chair. Move your chair and use it if you need it set a certain way.

Whew! Yeah, that's a lot about where you sit. But it's all come up in my real writing life. And even stranger things may come up in yours. Now on to a new topic.

Why is lunch such a big deal? a.k.a., Don't be the person who makes lunch difficult — so you know how there are universal jokes about some jobs, like cops and doughnuts? Well, this is a universal truth about TV writers: Hungry writers are no fun. Seriously, we are dreadful when we're hungry, like little starving toddlers on the verge of a tantrum. And the writers' PA who has to make sure we're all fed every day has a truly important job: Get the lunch order early, get it correctly, and get it to the room on time. For those who don't know, lunch is often provided in writers' rooms. Not guaranteed, and there's usually a maximum amount you can spend per day, but it's more common than not. On *Ironside*, because we shot locally, we used the catering that the crew used several times a week and ordered in on the other days. Usually it's ordering in from a variety of local restaurants or food spots on the lot.

Rooms handle the lunch order differently, but it's key in every single one of them. Some rooms create a binder of menus that people can flip through to choose from day to day with a rotation of who gets to choose the lunch spot. This rotation can be random, it can be predetermined, or it can literally be decided by drawing names out of a hat. But if your room starts at 10 and no one has started a lunch order by 10:30, be sure to ask "Hey, what's for lunch today?" because the choice will always steal time from the room and the later the order is taken, the later it shows up.

Some rooms eat at a set time every day. My latest room (even over Zoom) basically always broke at noon for lunch. (And yes, in the Zoom world, you have to wrangle your own lunch; but on the plus side, no one orders from a place you hate.) Some rooms vary from day to day depending on when the order was taken or what the showrunner's schedule is.

The key to all this is: Don't be the person who makes lunch difficult. If it's your turn and you don't want to pick, pass immediately to the next person. If you know several people dislike a certain spot that you love, don't pick it every time you're up. When it's not your turn, it's fine not to like the place someone else picks. When that happens, say you can grab your own lunch that day. I've done this repeatedly. I just walk to the lot café or a local spot nearby and grab my own food. Yes, that means I paid for it. But I also didn't have to eat food I didn't like. (P.S., Working writers can afford to buy their own lunch. Assistants and support staff, get all the free lunches you can. Seriously. And writers, make sure your assistants eat!)

My POV is this: The studio offered to buy me lunch, and I wanted something else. So it doesn't bother me to grab it myself.

I've worked with PAs who will insist you take the P-card (the show credit card) to pay for your lunch if you're grabbing it yourself so long as you can wait for them to get back with everyone else's food. If it works out, great — if it doesn't, I try not to ever let the PAs sweat it.

And unless your showrunner is making your PA go to more than one location to pick up food, *please, please, please do not ever ask your PA to make a second stop for you.* Even if they offer, they have to get food for four to ten other people. Don't hold up everyone else because the PA is trying to be nice to you. If the showrunner got lunch from somewhere else, and if you can order from that place, then fine. The showrunner gets to ask for that — it's his or her show.

An addendum to this — coffee runs. On a lot of shows, in the afternoon, the PA will come in and ask if anyone wants a coffee run, or someone in the room will suggest it. A lot of studios no longer cover this expense, so either the showrunner treats or someone in the room will. As a lower-level writer, you will likely never be able to pick up this tab. You can offer, but any well-trained writer who outranks you will not let you pay. You'll pay later when you get to those higher titles. (Or you can treat the assistants to something the way the upper levels treat you.) It will probably make you uncomfortable, but it's simply the good people etiquette of our business. "Senior writer pays" is a lesson I learned quickly.

I know this will come as a shock after my admitting my pickiness over where I sit and what I eat for lunch, but I'm also super snobby about my coffee. So when the run is to Starbucks, I politely decline. As an upper-level writer, I offer to treat on some runs and suggest we go to Coffee Bean or Peet's or whatever better coffee spot is nearby. Lots of people like Starbucks, and I don't have to be a judgy asshole — I can just not get coffee those days and enjoy it on the days we go other places. (*A lot of being in the room boils down to not being an asshole. I will repeat that a lot. But you'd be surprised how many people need to hear it again and again and again.*)

Okay, now that we've covered all those personal/personality/logistics things, let's get into some broad strokes on the creative.

Have good handwriting? You may have just found your way to be invaluable. One of the things my mentor, the amazing Carole Kirschner, drilled home for us in the ViacomCBS Writers Mentoring Program is that *your job as a staff writer is to make yourself invaluable.* We'll hit on this idea in numerous sections because there are different ways it applies. Here in the Quickstart Guide, that way is handwriting. Yep, I said "handwriting." Because if you have good, legible handwriting and volunteer to take on writing cards (if you're in an index-card room) or writing on the board, your room will *love* you. Especially people like me, who a) have terrible handwriting and hate writing on the board, and b) don't like writing on the board during the break of their own episode.

It doesn't have to be calligraphy. . . just neat, readable handwriting that people don't have to squint to see or constantly say "what's that word?" I know it seems simple, but this is one of those little things that can slow down a room or derail a great story break. So if you have the penmanship, raise your hand and offer.

Sidenote: Even if you don't have great handwriting, like me, sometimes there's a moment where no one will offer to write on the board. So offer. When I end up on board duty, I remind people that "I have worse handwriting than most doctors, but someone's gotta do it." This gets the work going in the room and often limits how much board writing I have to do in the future because I am not exaggerating. My handwriting is NOT good. But your ego is less important than the collective production of the room. So when everyone else is too shy or just doesn't want to do it, go up there and write your messy words on the board and know you've done your part to get the work done. And while we're on the topic of writing on the board. . .

Whiteboards vs. index cards vs. the combo. . . and what about magnetic cards? This has become one of the most critical pieces of information in any room I've been in because there are definitely differences in story breaks depending on the methodology. I'll be frank. I'm a girl who likes a combo: I like to do initial work on the whiteboard, then transfer beats to cards and blend them as a room before the final pitch to the showrunner. To me, it's the most effective method I've seen. You can start big picture on the board and work pretty free-form: what do we owe this episode, what do we need to set up. Then you throw up specific moves your characters need to make on the board, break out the individual beats in their story order, then move to cards to develop the scene order of the acts and episode.

But I have also worked on shows that are whiteboard only. This method is still highly effective, but it requires a lot of board clean-up. You'll end up breaking beats, pitching them, then drawing arrows as the showrunner says, "I think this beat belongs in act two, not act three," and making notes on adjustments on the fly because there simply isn't time to rewrite it in the moment when you have thirty minutes to pitch an entire episode. After the pitch, then someone — the episode writer, writers' assistant, or PA — will need to rewrite the board before work starts the next day with those adjustments in place so that the room can pick up and move on.

The compromise I hear about most — and have worked with once — is a set of whiteboards used with magnetic cards. People who have worked with them generally seem to really like it. . . the combination lets you have the portability of cards with the erasability of whiteboards. So when you need to change one beat, you only have to rewrite that one magnetic card, not the whole shebang.

My only experience with them was not my favorite. Oftentimes, our room came to a standstill while the showrunner stood at the board "studying" beats in a way that didn't allow for good brainstorming or interaction. But again — at the end of the day, it's the showrunner's show. So if that's how he or she likes to do things, your job is to adapt and figure it out. (And take notes on what you like and don't like for when you're running a room someday!)

One thing that plays into a story break regardless of whether you use cards or whiteboards is a concept one of my mentors refers to as "short boarding" vs. "long boarding." So I want to walk you through that a little bit here.

Basically, as you break story in a room, writers pitch more and more detail that lands and sounds great for the scene. You (or whoever is writing on the board) will incorporate those details in the summary of the scene on the board. This often includes how we get in and out of the scene, any specific dialogue that has to be covered, clue trails/plot details that are needed to move the story along, and references to personal relationships between the characters and/or emotional moves of the scene.

As you can imagine, that can make a pitch for a scene go from a few lines that describe the basic idea of the scene (your short board) to a detailed, almost ready for the outline version (your long board).

For example, a long-board version of a scene:

INT. BULLPEN

Castle and Beckett talk about the case. New information in from a C.I. – a witness saw the crime but is too scared to come into the station. Beckett is going to meet them in a safe location. Castle wants to go, but their earlier fight makes him hesitate. Ryan and Esposito observe in the background, their bet on how long the fight will last hanging in the balance. Beckett is tempted to leave Castle behind, but instead, she says having him along might make the witness more comfortable. They walk to the elevator, carefully avoiding their earlier disagreement, but both know that eventually they'll have to talk about it. As they exit, Ryan tries to call the bet, but Esposito says Castle and Beckett haven't made up. . . game is still on.

You can see how this gives the writer a great roadmap when they go off to outline, laying out the important bits of the scene, key character interactions, background action with the supporting characters, and the emotional through line of Castle/Beckett's personal story.

Now imagine pitching all of that to your showrunner, who is coming in at the end of the day to hear the pitch of the episode. It's a lot! So that's why it's helpful to know how to write up the short-board version.

The short board of the "Castle" scene I just wrote up is essentially the brief version that conveys the important stuff in the scene without giving the showrunner every single detail.

So. . . the short board:

INT. BULLPEN

Castle/Beckett still tense after fight. She gets a tip on a witness from a CI. Castle lags back, but Beckett invites him to go. They'll talk about their issues later. Esposito and Ryan realize that their bet on when the partners will make up remains unresolved.

Fewer words, same basic ideas, but the long board provides details that will fill in your outline and let you write your description more easily in script. It's great information to have for the writer of the episode, but it's not necessary to pitch every move of the scene to the boss. This is a great skill to start honing from day one. It will help you with pitches in the room, and if you are the person writing on the board or writing cards, it will allow you to start writing the beats in either form yourself without someone dictating them to you word for word.

The real trick here: Some showrunners will want you to have the long-board version on the board but to pitch them the short-board version. The good part about this is, if they ask questions, you'll have all the answers there right in front of you to reference. In the current virtual space, when we're sharing pitch boards on screens, it's really helpful if they're concise but you can fill in details as you move through the pitch when asked. So that's another reason why knowing how to form the shorthand is essential.

Screenwriting software wars. A key piece of information that will come in the early weeks of the room, if not on day one, is what program the show is using. I am here to tell you that there are times this will make you literally want to scream bloody murder because we all like or hate the main ones. There's usually no gray area — it's either like (no one loves any of them) or hate.

The majority of rooms still use Final Draft (FD). Some will require you to have the most current version, while others don't care which version you use. And this is mostly for script writing, though some also craft outlines in FD as well. (Most of my shows have used Microsoft Word for story areas and outlines, then switched to FD for script.)

But there's also Movie Magic Screenwriter (MMS). And the people who like it like it a lot. Those of us who hate it *hate it*. Like, we hate it *so* much. Part of that is probably coming up on FD and being used to it, and so MMS doesn't feel intuitive after that. And some of it is just that the crashes and disasters we've suffered on MMS are way worse than anything we've experienced on FD. So it's just a personal preference — for the showrunner. You can keep writing your own stuff in whatever program you want. But for the show, the default is the showrunner's favorite. (And if you don't have that program, buy it and don't complain about having to spend money you can deduct from your taxes. It's a business expense and your support staff doesn't have to spend hours trying to get the studio to send you a free license.)

The past few years, new programs have come along, and some showrunners like them. One of my favorite showrunners asked us to use this thing called WriterDuet. If Movie Magic Screenwriter makes me shout obscenities at the screen, WriterDuet made me want to throw my computer across the room. But I figured it out and got my work done. And hopefully I will never have to use it again.

Differences in broadcast/basic cable vs. premium cable/streaming rooms. I get asked this question a lot on panels, so thought it worth a discussion here. There are some subtle differences in episode breaks if you're on a broadcast or basic cable show vs. a premium cable or streaming show. Though most are logistical, some have long-term ramifications on your skill set, so you should be aware of them as you consider job opportunities.

First of all, the big difference in breaking episodes is commercials or no commercials. But hopefully it's only a difference in how you get in and out of some scenes and not in how you actually break the episode.

People will disagree with this, but for my money, *every show should break their episodes like they have act outs even if they don't take commercial breaks.* Why? Simple. Shows that don't do this often feel flat and monotone. In a fifty-minute episode, it seems like they've wasted forty minutes with little happening, then suddenly *everything* happens in the final ten minutes. Breaking as if you have act outs keeps the show building a natural ebb and flow. You have mini climaxes throughout the episode and create big emotional moments. I know it seems like that should happen regardless, but I bet if you think about it, you can name several shows you've watched on streaming platforms or premium cable that felt like they moved too slow for large portions of the episodes. I don't know for a fact those shows were broken without act breaks — but I'd bet on it in Vegas.

So great. You're on a streaming or premium show, and you're going to run your break as if you have act breaks. What's the difference? Aren't you just breaking it with them but not typing them in the script? Not exactly. There are tricks we use when we have actual commercials that you can't use or can't use as easily on a show without ads. For instance, a show builds to a huge action set piece that ends on a crash or an explosion, then commercial break! Post all those ads, we're back in the show, deep in the aftermath of said crash or explosion. . . minutes if not hours of story time jumped during the commercial break. You can still utilize time jumps in streaming and premium cable, but sometimes it requires more finesse. It may force you to "end an act" on the board in that set piece but then act in on a different story so you can buy time to get to that aftermath. This is especially true if you need another character to show up and react to what's happened. You can't play that they found out off-screen nearly as easily as you can with that handy commercial break.

Some of the tricks we use in broadcast and basic cable are also harder to do without causing confusion when you can't anchor them to commercial breaks. On *Cloak & Dagger*, for instance, we liked to mess with our format a lot. We were constantly wondering how to make an episode different so we didn't fall into a hard routine pattern. We did one episode where we alternated who each act was about until finally all three stories came together. We did another where each act started with a scene from one particular story. We did a time-loop episode where the action kept restarting. This can all be done without the commercial break, but it's a lot more challenging and requires the room to decide how to keep the audience following the story threads without getting that rhythm of, "Oh, okay, after every commercial, they're doing this. Got it." It's all manageable but worth thinking about when you're looking at what beats are missing on the board at the start and end of each day in the room.

In terms of the other differences, these mostly fall into how the work for the show is structured. On a traditional broadcast show and on a lot of basic cable shows, you're writing scripts and still breaking episodes when production starts. That can mean that you'll get a pick-up past your initial twenty weeks to work through the rest of the season (which is what you're working so hard for). That can also mean, depending on the show, that you get the chance to cover or shadow on set and potentially to participate in post-production, depending on the showrunner's attitudes on including lower-level writers in those activities.

On a streaming or premium cable show, your room could be a mini-room, which can be as little as four weeks (the shortest I've heard) up to sixteen weeks (the longest I've heard that isn't a traditional room). The biggest issue for you as a lower-level writer in this type of room situation will be that the room ends once all the episodes are broken/written, generally long before production begins. That means that very few writers, if any, will be going to cover set. It's an issue a lot of us are bringing up with showrunners and with the WGA because it means there's a lack of training available for writers to learn to produce their episodes. There are writers making it to the upper levels, even becoming Number Twos, who haven't produced an episode of TV because they're moving from streaming show to streaming show and not being held for production.

Working in rooms where the writers are let go before production also affects your ability to shadow in post-production. A lot of showrunners aren't great about including lower-level writers in the editing room, but when they are willing, the time observing and watching how the edit is put together is incredibly valuable. Even though I was able to stay on for part of production on my first streaming show, I wasn't able to participate in post at all. It was a real disappointment, but it's kind of the norm.

None of that means those aren't great jobs. They are, sometimes, the jobs that make you a hot commodity in a way a broadcast show never will. But just know that it will be on you to find a way to develop the skills that the show may not provide for you. Because you'll need that production and post knowledge when you work your way up to showrunner.

Paper teams: what they are, why they happen. Paper teaming has a terrible reputation in our business because people know it's unfair and unethical, but that doesn't mean it doesn't still happen. Each studio tells a showrunner how much money there is to hire a staff. And because a staff is usually hired top to bottom, that means that by the time the showrunner is looking to bring in one or two staff writers, money is tight, sometimes too tight to hire two writers. But say the showrunner really needs two writers to get the number of voices he or she wants in the room.

So that's when the idea of paper teaming comes up. It means that even though you and another writer are both solo writers who do not work in a writing team, the studio will make you a writing team on paper so you can split one writer's salary, the same way writing teams do. For the studio, it's a way to get two writers for the price of one. It's often justified because it lets shows give two writers an opportunity when they can really only afford one.

You might be saying, "Well, what's so bad about that? We'll still get paid, and we both get to write on a TV show." Yes, you do, and that's why most people say yes to the arrangement even if they don't love it. It's your big break, you still get paid, and you still get to join the WGA. . . so it's got a silver lining.

But you aren't in a real partnership with someone you want to build a career with. You're in a partnership on paper that means you're making half the money and only getting to write half a script when you are a solo writer who intends to move on to your next gig as a solo writer. It's frustrating and not in the spirit of what WGA minimums are meant to do for writers, which is guarantee them fair pay for their work. But it happens. So be aware of what it is and why someone may someday mention it to you, even though the WGA is doing everything it can to rid our business of this practice forever.

Paper teaming is different than being assigned to co-write a script during the season. You've still been hired as a lower-level solo writer, not as a part of a team, so you're receiving your full weekly salary. When you get assigned to co-write a script, it does mean splitting the script fee — if you're getting script fees (most staff writers do not, another thing we're trying to fix in the WGA). This is a common practice on some shows. Certain producers love the idea of people pairing up to write episodes. It's not my fave, but I got to write a lot of TV episodes because I was on multiple shows that did this, and it means your name comes up in the rotation quickly and more often than on shows with lots of solo episodes. (And even on the episodes where you don't get script fees, you'll still get residuals for the episodes. . . so it's not all bad.)

Devices: cellphones, tablets, and all the gadgets. Hopefully your show-runner will make the rules about electronic devices clear on day one. But even if you're technically allowed to bring a cell phone or iPad into the room, my advice is: *Don't.* It's too easy to be tempted to zone out when the writer you don't like is talking, and it can distract other writers to see you on your device.

I know parents in rooms will say they need their phones for kid emergencies. I get that. Some bosses are cool with that, even if they have no cell phone policy. Some aren't. You can always give out the room's office number, and one of the support staff will come get you if a call comes in you need to take.

I had a family situation for a few seasons involving my mother's care and safety. I had historically been a "no phone in the room" person, even if it was okay. But with her situation getting more worrisome, I spoke to my Number Two and told him why I was suddenly going to start having my phone in the room. He was totally cool with it — and again, it was allowed — but it was a huge shift in my behavior, and I wanted him to understand why I was doing it.

So even if you have to bring your phone or tablet into the room to be available for family stuff, just remember to keep it in your pocket, on your lap, or in your seat — basically out of sight unless you have to take a call. (Then be sure to step outside. I know, you're thinking, "Duh, I know that." But you'd be surprised!)

Female mid-level writer
on the writers' room becoming a playground

Sometimes showrunners just have an attitude of "It's my room, and I can do what I want." In one room, the showrunner loved to throw a football around to the other guys on staff. Literally right over and past our heads. I hated it, and I felt like I couldn't say anything. But I was forever worried about getting beaned with that ball. And don't get me started about when he picked up a bat and swung it around like he was in a batting cage!

Male showrunner on "some advice I give
to all new staff writers"

A few things you can do to set yourself up for success are 1. read and research the show before you start (if you have time, start the day after you get the offer!). Get five nonfiction books on the topic or world and read them, keeping notes so you can add ideas, details, and lingo to room conversations. And 2. if it's a difficult room that disbands or collapses, don't despair. Keep going to work; keep smiling; keep reading the material and let your showrunner know you like the drafts; email concise, specific pitches to the showrunner for upcoming episodes (maybe from that reading you've done!). Basically just keep showing up. It pays off, trust me.

Showrunners may stop convening the writers' room for a variety of reasons — toxic personalities, schedule problems, production issues. This will make it more important than ever that you be present in the office, friendly and open to everyone you can be, and available for whatever work helps support the show.

FEMALE MID-LEVEL WRITER ON WRITERS BEING RUDE IN THE ROOM WITH THEIR DEVICES

I watched a lower-level writer basically glue his face to his iPad while our assistant was breaking their first episode of television. It was so disrespectful. I decided then and there that I was done with this person forever. And believe me, the showrunner noticed.

MALE DRAMA WRITER ON READING THE ROOM

One mistake I've definitely made: stepping into the fray. Be mindful when there's a dispute among other writers, especially if they outrank you. Often, there are dynamics in play that have more to do with underlying personal conflicts than they do with the story you're actually working on. In situations like this, emotions can be elevated, your voice is less likely to be heard, and the chance that weighing in will hurt you rather than help the situation can be high. This is a good time to watch, listen, and learn.

3.

There Is No One Way to Run a Writers' Room

I mean, it sure would be nice if there were, but. . .

W HEN YOU THINK ABOUT THE JOB of showrunner, a lot of things may come to mind: the boss, watching every move on set, hanging out with actors, writing furiously into the wee hours getting scripts done on time, phone calls with studio and network execs or producers arguing why you know the show better than they do and to please trust that you and the writers know what you're doing, watching edits of three different episodes at various stages in one day, or picking music for one episode and locations for another. It's all that. And a million things I promise you've never thought about unless you've seen someone do the job up close and in person.

If you want an honest visual representation of the gig, well, imagine a cat wrangler wrangling two hundred cats. Some are small and cute and cuddly, some are grumpy, some hate every other living creature on Earth, and some are actually tigers armed with big claws, sharp teeth, and the ability to bring the show to a screeching halt.

That's the job many of us aspire to. And it's not as easy as I make it sound.

When it comes to the people who do the job, I genuinely wish I could nail it down for you, make a chart that says, "There are this many types of showrunners, this one is most common, etc." But the path to the job isn't a straight line, which means a lot of different writers with different experiences — good and bad — climb into the showrunner chair, and they bring all their baggage, good and bad, with them.

Most people who become showrunners have worked in a variety of rooms. And as I hope you will do in your career, they've absorbed the techniques they liked from those rooms and made a list of "hard no" styles they have no desire to repeat once they're the boss. I say "most" because this won't always be true. Some people get a room early in their careers or become co-showrunners early and haven't had a variety of showrunners to learn from; some come from features and have never worked in a writers' room but have enough buzz to get the showrunner or co-showrunner title. Hopefully those folks will talk to a lot of other people who have done the job and get ideas on how to best run a room. . . and then trial and error will help them to figure out what they like and don't like and to hone their process.

Whatever their origin, the truth is — *there are as many different ways to run a writers' room as there are showrunners.* People's personalities, their own training, their work habits, their family schedules — all of that and more will play into the rules your room operates under. So this isn't going to be a "this is how it works" guide. This is more of a "here's a lot of the ways it can work" guide.

I realize that in the preceding paragraphs, I didn't mention the *other* kinds of showrunners, the ones who either come into the business full of bad character or who learn unprofessional and/or abusive behavior in their early rooms — and instead of deciding they never want to behave that way, that's the style they emulate. We're going to talk about these toxic showrunners in depth in Chapter 12 because the more stories that come out about them, the more the conversation deserves its own space.

But I want to be sure to say this next thing out loud: *Even the best showrunner can have a truly awful day.* They might snap and yell at the room because they feel like the work they needed done didn't get done, they might force people to stay late when you don't understand how it's helping, or they might call someone out for bad research or a crappy pitch in front of the room. *It can and probably will happen because good humans have bad moments.* So don't think the world is shifting beneath your feet if that boss you've adored for weeks suddenly gives someone hell for not getting a shot on set. The job of showrunner is hard. . . damn near impossible. . . and even though all two hundred of those cats, you included, want the show to be good and get made on time and on budget, sometimes things go wrong, and sometimes good bosses will have bad days. That's not being a bad boss; that's being a human being. Try to focus on all the days they get the job right and let it go.

But now we'll talk about how different people approach running a room or, as was the case with my first job, running a show that does not utilize a writers' room.

But I thought that "room" thing was literal. . .

If you've been through one of the network writing programs, worked with a Hollywood-based career coach, or listened to one of the several outstanding podcasts that are out there on being a working writer, you've heard stories about the writers' room. But if you've read or listened to *me* talk about this, you know that my first show didn't actually have one.

It's not a common occurrence, and it's primarily used on shows that are more procedural in nature. . . or where the showrunner is the person who maintains the overall serialized elements of the show. But it does happen, usually because the showrunner simply doesn't like being in the room or finds it to lack economy when it comes to their time.

On my first show, our boss said we didn't have a writers' room, we had a writers' hallway, the long corridor that all our offices branched off of. And the truth was, that's exactly how it functioned. It just took a little extra effort on all our parts.

Instead of saying hello to everyone when I got into the room every day, I had to make a point of seeking out my fellow writers, say good morning, ask how their evenings were, or see if anyone needed a hand on whatever they were working on. This is essentially the same type of conversation that starts the day in the room. It was just happening on an individual basis. If one of my co-EPs was breaking an episode, I'd drop by and ask if any research was needed or if there was anything I could help pitch on. When my fellow writers were on outline or script, I'd offer to read early drafts if it was helpful or be there for them when they needed to talk through a spot that wasn't quite working. And when one was in production, I'd text them some supportive messages and ask if there was any way I could help.

This not only allowed me to build relationships with the rest of the staff, it gave me opportunities to pitch in on multiple episodes. I helped rebreak stories when studio or network notes upended it; I gave notes that helped streamline some scenes when writers were trying to get to a proper page count; and I found with research that helped writers come up with clues, set pieces, and other possible story ideas.

And really, that's the job when you're on staff — pitching in. I know you'll be excited about breaking and writing an episode that's going to have your name on it, but honestly, it's about being part of *every* episode. That way everyone else will be engaged and excited to pitch clues, fixes, and cool moments in yours.

This methodology means that you'll come up with story ideas on your own, pitch them to the showrunner (or a co-EP, depending on how your boss likes to run things), and get feedback, and if you're a newer writer, you'll have a more senior writer assigned to help you break your story. Then you'll pitch the break to the boss and get adjustments before you head to outline.

All room, all the time

This is the most common type of room you'll encounter, at least in my experience. Typically, on a super functional show, your hours will be something like ten to six with an hour lunch. That varies by showrunner. Some like an earlier start and finish, and some think nothing good gets done after 5 p.m. (It rarely does, for the record.) But in general, your workday every day is spent in the writers' room working on stories as a group. This means the showrunner can come and go as his or her schedule dictates, and provide adjustments along the way, and then the whole room is there for support when the episode is pitched in its entirety so the showrunner can approve it and send the writer off to outline.

That standardization of room hours doesn't mean there aren't other tricky bits you'll have to figure out how to navigate here. Some things that come up in all-day rooms:

Bathroom breaks. Yes, I'm serious. Most showrunners will just say "go when you gotta go," but sometimes you get people who want to schedule breaks and only have people leave the room during those breaks. Be sure to ask what the rule is if no one's made it clear. . . and yes, I know how ridiculous that sounds. But the last thing you want to do is get up to go to the bathroom while your showrunner's talking if they're the type of person who's going to flip out about it.

Lunches. Is the time yours or theirs? The majority of my rooms have considered lunch time free time. You can eat with your fellow writers, you can go to your office alone, or you can head off campus for meetings — whatever you want to do with that hour. But occasionally you run into the philosophy that if the studio is paying for lunch, then lunch is still technically work time. So all the writers will be expected to eat together in the room, maybe talking about work, maybe talking about other stuff, but the expectation is that you will be there. That usually means you get fifteen to thirty minutes of your own time to go make calls, take a walk, whatever you can squeeze in. I'm not a fan of this, but it has happened to me. I think the best strategy is to give your writers their hour of time — and if they gravitate to eating together, great, but usually, even if I love my fellow writers, I just need some time to myself to recharge for the afternoon.

Writing time. If you're just starting out on staff, you might hear some of the upper-level writers talking about "writing from home." Whether or not that's even an option depends on how your showrunner does things. In many rooms, once your episode is broken, you go off to outline, then write your script, and only come back to the writers' room once you're finished writing. (It's not as long as you probably think. . . but more on turnaround times later.)

Some showrunners hate to spare people from the room because you never know who's going to have the best idea in a tricky spot of the episode break. So they'll ask you to write around the room. . . meaning mornings, evenings, and weekends. I'd say this is more commonly my experience as a writer, and frankly, I prefer it. I *hate* not being in the room. It makes me feel disconnected to the episodes being broken when I'm not around. Other people hate having to write in their "off" hours — but a gentle reminder: That's why they pay you so well, to make up for the hours you're working when you're not "working."

One final note on this: even if you are able to leave the room to write, *write at the office.* Even if people tell you it's okay to write from home. You will have questions and problems on outline and in script, and it's much easier to wander down to someone's office and talk it out than it is to try and catch people out of the room on the phone. Also it keeps you present and connected to the show — if a problem comes up that everyone needs to pitch in on, you can go back into the room and participate and not hear about it after. Later in your career, writing from home is a fine option if you prefer it — but starting out, you want to be in the office with your room full of resources as much as possible.

Room splits. Some showrunners find it more effective to split larger rooms (with staffs of ten or more people) into smaller rooms. This is especially common in comedy rooms where duties are split up — i.e., one is the punch-up room, one is the rewrite room, etc. In an hour-long drama, this usually is about trying to get ahead of the writers' schedule. Why? If you're on a traditional schedule where production starts as you're writing, that moving train comes for your script drafts faster than you can imagine. So breaking two episodes over a week instead of just one means two episodes are already being outlined and you can move on to the next two.

Again, this is not my fave for the same reason I stated above regarding leaving the room to write: I'm a room person. I love being part of building all the stories, and being kept out of half of them makes me a little twitchy. But it definitely helps the show move faster. And it gives you a chance to develop your room pitching skills quickly because instead of nine or eleven or thirteen other writers speaking up and giving you some room to hide, you're in a room of five or six, and everyone has to contribute more to get the work done. So to me, that's the plus side, especially for newer writers.

The John Wells method

If you've ever been lucky enough to hear John Wells talk about his showrunning philosophy, one of the things he does that clearly works well for him is limit and block out room hours. What does that mean? It means that the writers' room always meets, say, Monday, Wednesday, and Friday from ten to two, and during those hours, no one is allowed to interrupt John's room time. That means that the room always knows it has its showrunner during those hours, barring a "the house is on fire"-type emergency.

This helps the room target its work so that the team knows how to prioritize the time when the showrunner is in. It doesn't mean that you won't be working on story beats on those alternate days or having mini-rooms with other writers trying to solve story problems — it just means that you never have to wonder when the showrunner is coming in to hear the pitch or answer questions.

This also helps solve the problem of writing time. When the room meets limited hours or days, it means writers on outline or script are free to use those down days and non-room hours to write so you don't end up writing on weekends or late into the evening.

I recently finished my first room of this type, and I have to say, it does a lot to create work-life balance. It lets you schedule things in your normal life on weekdays because you know when you absolutely have to be in the room — and you can plan your writing schedule accordingly.

Now that we've discussed some of the most common writers' room structures, here are some more critical pieces of information you'll need to know to help navigate your first room.

What's a Number Two? What does he or she do?

The Number Two, a role we briefly introduced in Chapter 1, is likely to be an EP or co-EP level writer (though sometimes it may also be a supervising producer, depending on your room makeup). This person is tasked with keeping the room moving when the showrunner isn't present. That happens more than you might imagine because showrunners are constantly pulled away for meetings and phone calls and casting and production and post. So your Number Two is the lieutenant who keeps the board marching forward and who can answer outline and script questions for writers.

Depending on how your showrunner likes things done, the Number Two may also be the designated pitcher in the room. That means when the showrunner is there to hear what the room's been working on, the Number Two is the one passing on that information. Typically, the staff will chime in to help add details as the Number Two needs them, but he or she is the main voice in the room during the pitch. This isn't how all showrunners like things done — in some rooms, the writer of each episode runs the board and pitches the varying iterations to the showrunner. That's really just something you'll have to figure out on a show-by-show basis.

In my opinion, the best Number Twos also make themselves available to the staff as the designated helper, not just with the work but also with the work environment. A good Number Two will offer to read early drafts and pass on notes before you turn in documents to the showrunner, and if the Number Two doesn't have time, he or she will pick someone on staff who does to set up the newer writers for real success. A good one will also talk to lower-level writers and writers with limited set and post experience about how to handle these job duties if they're expected on a particular show.

And, of course, a Number Two should be a safe place for people to come and report inappropriate behavior from anyone on staff or in production, showrunner included.

Breaking the season arc or prepping the network pitch

This is the first task of a room, be it a first season show or a returning one. Studios and networks like to know the plan for the season. So this typically involves the showrunner coming in with some solid tentpoles and "musts" for the season that the writers' room can then build on to sketch out how the eight, thirteen, or twenty-two episodes are going to play out.

This is a lot of broad strokes stuff. It's easy to get in the weeds on details, and you'll be tempted to pitch cool smaller ideas, but the truth is — save them. Write them down for yourself so when you're breaking a specific episode you can remember that awesome interaction you wanted to pitch. Your job here is to come up with a shape and an overview of the season.

An example of this I can relate is our work on *Cloak & Dagger*. Each season, our showrunner Joe Pokaski had some big ideas he brought into the room on day one. So in season one, for example, he knew he wanted Ty and Tandy to spend time together by episode three or four, he knew he wanted both of them to learn new aspects of their powers by episode five, and he knew how he wanted the season to end. We wrote all that up on the board in a general episode grid and then started pitching other stories that could fill in the rest of the episodes. Again, this was broad stuff like "What if Ty runs into his brother's old friend and finds out something about his brother's death?" or "What if Tandy lets her boyfriend take the fall for her crimes, then comes back to him later for help?"

Those pitches start out general and everyone contributes, and then the showrunner will like some, throw out others, and before you know it, you'll have episode ideas for each week. Not full episodes, just an idea of what we need to do with our characters week in and week out.

Generally, the staff will be assigned sections of the arc or pitch document to write that the showrunner then compiles and rewrites as needed. On a rare occasion, I ended up actually being included in one pitch — five of the writers joined the showrunner for the network pitch. It's not something most junior writers will ever have to do, but it was definitely an experience!

Once the studio and network give adjustments and sign off on the direction of your season, it's time to start breaking episodes.

The worst thing that can happen to a room is that you sit down for the first few days of this season story conversation and your showrunner basically has no thoughts about what he or she wants to do. It seems impossible, I know, but it happens and it's awful. The only thing you can do in this situation is pitch your heart out — talk to other writers about ideas you love and that they love and present a unified front on things that can get the work moving forward. Because whether the showrunner has ideas about what happens next or not — the studio and network are expecting someone to tell them what the season is about. Thank goodness you have a room full of talented folks to help figure it out.

Different story breaking strategies: "A" story first? Characters first?

That whole thing about how there are as many different ways to run a room as there are showrunners? I'm starting to think there are as many different ways to break story as there are showrunners, too. But there are some basics that should help you get started no matter what strategy your showrunner likes best.

"A" story. This is the main story of your episode. It will generally be tied to your lead character(s) but not always. In a procedural show, this is usually your main case — the ins and outs of the clue trail, the people we meet, and the resolution of the story.

"B" story. This is anywhere from one to three smaller stories focused on series regulars who aren't your leads. This is where the supporting characters get to shine. You may also have a B story featuring your lead(s) because they have more than one story in an episode (one romantic, one work driven, say) or if you're A story is focused on a different cast member.

"C" story/runner. C story and runner are things you may hear used interchangeably. It's basically a three-beat story that plays through the episode. Sometimes it's comic relief. Sometimes it's setting up something you'll come back to in a later episode. Sometimes it's a way to tie up a story from prior episodes. If

you have one or two cast members who are great at one liners and awesome expressions, you'll think of a lot of C stories for them because they do so much work without a lot of screen time.

Some shows prefer to focus on the A story itself first. What are the moves of the big story in the episode? Some prefer to do this from a character place first. Both will get you where you're going. It's really just a style preference.

For example, on *Cloak & Dagger* we usually started our breaks with what we owed or needed to set up for Ty and Tandy. Then we would sketch out their beats and figure out where their stories intersected, and that would often create the spine of our episode.

On *S.W.A.T.*, we usually started with ideas for the A-story case (loglines, really) and then pitches on what the character B stories could be. Once we had sign off on the general areas, then we'd get into the nitty-gritty of building the individual stories.

Other things you can think about at this stage are — what's a new, unusual way to open an episode? What's a cool location we haven't used? What's a fun place for an action set piece or a character conversation? Those ideas can often create a roadmap for an entire episode. So if you have ideas on those things, always bring them up — you never know what can shake out of a sentence like, "Have we ever done a scene in the loft of the church?"

This is where doing your homework outside of the room can really pay off. If you're on a police, medical, or legal show, what news stories can you bring into the room to spur episode ideas? What thoughts have you had about a particular character's development or a relationship on the show? Those things can also spark great B stories throughout a season. And if you're on a show where the weekly format is up for grabs —you can tell stories out of order, you can do multiple timelines, you can do flashbacks — think of a structure you want to play with and bring it to the room.

But one important caveat: *Just because you pitch it doesn't mean you'll get to write it.* And that's okay. Because you're helping the show succeed, and that's your job. Oftentimes the best way to help the room out of a tough break is pitching something you were holding on to for your own episode. It works here, you know it will fix the problem, so share it. Your showrunner will remember it, your fellow writers will remember it, and it will probably make your show better on the whole.

What do blending and weaving have to do with writing TV?

Blending and weaving are terms you'll hear used to describe the same thing — once your A story and B story and C story beats are laid out, you have to put them in order to complete your episode structure. So you'll "blend" or "weave" (or "smush," another favorite) the beats together on the board into whatever act structure you're using.

For those who aren't familiar with the various act structures in TV drama, you basically have teaser/four, five-act, and six-act structure. What are the differences? Teaser/four allows for longer teasers. A great example of this is *The Good Wife* — if you rewatch that show, they had some lovely luxurious teasers that set all the stories in motion before the title card into commercials. Five act has a short teaser at the top of act one, followed by opening titles, then the rest of act one. Both are preferable, in my opinion, to six act, but you'll find some networks love it. Six act means all your acts run at a more uniform pace — no longer/shorter acts really, and you'll find you have less time to make moves between act outs, so the plotting will feel tighter and faster than in the other structures.

And yes, I'm a broken record on this, but you should *always* be breaking episodes with act outs, even if you're on cable/streaming. Always. Trust me.

The process of blending or weaving depends on the room and how the Number Two or showrunner likes to do it. I've been in rooms where we start with the act outs and build backward and forward from there; I've been in rooms where it's a big collective project, and in ones where one or two people manage the blend and then the room reviews it. But by the time you're done, you'll have a whole episode of TV!

Room hours: Sometimes they're humane; sometimes they aren't.

So I mentioned three different types of room-running philosophies and that showrunner styles are as varied as the people who have the job. Most shows operate on a humane, "let's let everyone have decent quality of life" edict — at least most of the ones I've been on. But that isn't always true. This town is legendary for stories of notorious writers' rooms where people worked until 2 a.m. and had to be back at 9 a.m. the next day. Places that order dinner every night (trust me, that's not a good thing), and places that make writers work weekends and over holiday breaks.

The bottom line when you end up in a situation like this is, it sucks but there's probably not much you can do about it except survive. Some showrunners thrive on a sense of chaos or have personalities that say if you're not working all the time, then you're not working. You may get lucky and have a Number Two who understands this isn't good for everyone and pushes back a little, but chances are it will only help so much. So how do you get through it?

1. *Take care of yourself physically and emotionally.* Easier said than done, I know. But if you know taking a fifteen-minute walk at lunch will save your sanity, take your walk. If you need to bring your own food to make sure you're eating healthy, bring your own food. Whatever you have to do to buy yourself a little peace, you should do it.

2. *Take care of your fellow writers.* Everyone is going to get run down and exhausted and frustrated, maybe all at the same time, maybe in rotation. Be there for each other as much as you can. I am the queen of bringing treats into the room. That happens a lot more often when the room is under stress. That's my way of helping. Or find an inside joke that helps break the tension. Or just check in on people. Ask if they're doing their own self-care, and remind them that it's important.

3. *Remember — this job is not forever.* Money and credits are great motivators to stay at a job, but a job that's hurting your health and your mental well-being isn't worth it. When I found myself in this situation, I phoned my reps, told them what was going on, and said, "I can finish the season, but I don't want to come back." That gave them time to plan on getting me out for staffing but reassured them I was going to be able to walk away from the job cleanly without any "oh, she couldn't hack it" ridiculousness following me out the door.

4. *Boundaries — you can set them.* Yes, this is especially hard when you're a staff writer. But you still have a right to your life. If you have a big event planned on a weekend and your boss asks you to take a pass at

something over that same weekend — you can go to your event *and* get your work done. *You can. I promise.* It will feel like you should cancel and spend every hour of the weekend on the work. But you will do better work this weekend and every other day of the season if you do what matters to your life — and going to that event that's been on your calendar for months? That matters.

Zoom-rooming: What's different about rooming from home?

The pandemic opened up the world of Zoom-rooming, and it's unclear how many people may want to stay in that virtual space longer and how many rooms will be back in person fully in the next few seasons of TV (a lot of that hinges on whether studios are going to try to keep the money they've saved by not paying for physical office spaces, so TBD). But here's what I can tell you about things you should do if you're in your first room or you've just joined a new room and it's being conducted in a virtual space.

1. *Find ways to connect with other writers.* Start a text thread with a few or all of the writers in the room; email writers and start conversations that way; have phone calls. It's important to still feel like you have a relationship with your coworkers even though you can't be in their presence every day. Plus you want to be sure you've built a connection with these folks so they can help build your network of writer contacts.

2. *Don't be afraid to ask questions.* You don't have to do it on Zoom, but you can always hit someone up later and say, "Hey, did we get a schedule for this yet? I can't remember." Or ask for tips on navigating whatever digital board you're using. Or just double-check

about a pitch you want to make to see if another writer responds to it. Asking questions is an important part of learning as a staff writer, and you can't let the digital space limit your willingness to do it.

3. *Digital boards are not my fave. I will not lie.* But they are tools that help you get through a virtual room. It's fine not to be great at using them — just admit it, ask for help, and stay focused on the work. Miro, WritersRoom Pro, and just good ol' Google Docs are some of the things I've worked with. None is ideal, but they all help get the job done.

4. *The etiquette of the room is a little trickier* because it's harder to read people's body language over camera. It can be difficult to tell if someone got a joke or heard everything you said or liked/didn't like a pitch. Try not to get too anxious about it all. Everyone's trying to figure it out.

Every room is different until it's your room; a.k.a., adapt, adapt, adapt.

The one hard and fast rule about staffing is every show will be different. Even if you go to a show run by your former Number Two from a different show, that person will have slight tweaks on how things are done than the showrunner you both worked for. You adapt to the rules and the environment and get the job done.

But always be studying. What works? What doesn't? What do you love? What do you hate? Because someday, it'll be your room, and you'll set the tone for how the work gets done and the feel of the work environment based on what you've learned and, hopefully, what you know makes for a better, happier, more productive writers' room.

True Tales of Life Inside a Writers' Room

Male BIPOC Comedy Writer
on the Serious Work of Comedy Rooms

There's nothing funny about comedy rooms. It's a shark tank. You've got eight to fourteen (or more) insecure, well-read, smart, and truly competitive people fighting over every line of dialogue, whether the show be group-written or in a rewrite. The silence hurts. Pitching a joke and getting nothing. Or potentially worse, pitching a story turn that isn't even acknowledged as the room rolls on. It's a high-wire act where every participant is pretending it's just a stroll in the park. Flip side, when you kill it, it's undeniable. The room erupts. Audiences eat it up. You can point at the television and say, "I wrote that." Comedy rooms are serious business.

Your patience will be tried. The nature of trying to create a conflict, its resolution, and jokes that don't blow either out of the water means conversations go left. Like, way left. Your sensibilities will be tested. Your lines in the sand will be danced on and blown away. Hopefully those conversations are an honest exploration and not an ignorant declaration of "truth." Either way, you'll have to make choices on how to beat it, undermine it in the form of faux innocent analysis, or just roll with it.

Male Drama Writer on Different Room Structures

I'd just come off a show that was "all room, all the time" when I joined a new show that was the polar opposite. When I arrived, I was shown my office with a chair, desk, computer, and whiteboard, then left alone with the sentiment of "Do great things." We didn't even have a room to meet in collectively if we had wanted to. So I went from "all room, all the time" to "alone and unafraid" in a few short months. Adapt, adapt, adapt.

4

SURVIVING
THE STAFF WRITER YEAR

You worked so hard to get here.
Now how do you not screw it up?

S o you've done it! You wrote the right sample, got the
meeting(s), closed the deal, looked up info on all your fellow
writers so you know who they are and what they've worked
on. You made it to the room, even figured out where to sit.

Now what?

You dig in and do the hard work of keeping the job you prepared your whole life to get.

So how do you do that? Well, no one wants you to succeed
more than you do, even if you have one of those amazing
showrunners like I had early on who genuinely wants you to
do well. You have an opportunity and a responsibility to set
yourself up for success. But how?

Find out the rules of your room and what
the expectations for staff writers are.

This one seems easy. Surely someone's going to lay this all out
for you on day one, right? Not always. Hopefully you will
either have a showrunner who does point out their expectations

clearly and early, or you'll have an upper-level writer who steps in and gives you some guidance. Has someone on staff worked with your showrunner before? Maybe you can ask them if no one is volunteering the information.

But if all else fails, you may have to ask your Number Two for the standard operating procedure of the show. Is it a "staff writers speak only when asked to speak" room, or are you encouraged to pitch when you have a good idea regardless of level? Is it a room where the showrunner only likes to hear a group of organized pitches from the Number Two, or is everyone free to be in the discussion when the board is pitched? It's really important to know these things so that you don't get off on the wrong foot with your new boss because the way you perform at this first gig lays the groundwork for you to get the second one. (I know, no pressure. But that's reality. Your next showrunner will call the first one to ask how you were to work with.)

You may find out that staff writers don't get a script. It's not common, but it does happen. If that's the case on your show, hopefully you knew that coming in (because your showrunner made it clear in the meeting). But you'll probably be assigned other tasks — writing story areas, helping with outlines, writing sides or character breakdowns for casting. I know that's going to be a disappointment, but it doesn't mean you'll never get a script. So knock those other writing tasks out of the ballpark. It's going to help prove to the boss that if the show gets additional episodes, maybe you should write one after all, or at least it should guarantee you'll get a script the next season.

You may also find that staff writers on your particular show are assigned duties in the room, like writing on the board or writing index cards. There are showrunners who believe this helps the newer writers learn how to break story faster — so if you're asked to do it, do it with enthusiasm and try to be as helpful as possible during every break by keeping the board/cards neat and up to date.

And when your showrunner or Number Two lays out the rules of the room early on, be sure you follow them. If the room starts promptly at 10 a.m., then you are always in your seat ready to work at ten (or five till, if you're being really proactive). If you're asked to come back from lunch with ideas for a set piece, come back with at least one pitch. Again, I know this seems obvious, but I've seen writers self-sabotage by being late in the morning or after lunch and by being unprepared for a discussion we knew we were having. Small stuff, but it makes a huge difference in how your work experience goes.

Silence is not golden (unless you work in one of those rooms; see the above).

I have been lucky not to be in any of those rooms where staff writers are told to speak only when spoken to. It's my understanding that showrunners who prefer this think of it as a teaching tool. You're in the room, watching, listening to the experienced writers break story, and taking in how the process works. It's invaluable training, and then when the showrunner thinks you're starting to get the lay of the land, then maybe they'll ask for your thoughts and opinions on certain story points.

Most of my rooms have been rooms where showrunners wanted the best idea no matter who was pitching it. So everyone was free to speak up, pitch ideas, ask questions, and come up with solutions. This can put pressure on new writers who aren't used to the room environment. Sometimes that leads to paralysis. . . and a lot of silence from your spot at the table. And a staff writer who is too quiet in a room where there's freedom to speak may stand out as a potential problem.

One thing someone passed on to me that was incredibly helpful in my first room environment was this idea: *If you can contribute one thing before lunch and one after, you've had a good day.* Thinking of it in those terms can help you let go of the fear of having to have *all the things* to say. . . and let you focus in on one or two ideas that seem worth pitching. For instance, if you're talking about the main characters' relationship before lunch and you point out that there's something you've been thinking about in terms of developing their friendship/romance/conflict (depending on the type of show), that's a valid contribution, whether it lands or not. And say you know we're working on a heist beat after lunch. So you can brainstorm a few ideas for that and toss them out in the afternoon. Again, whether those things make the board or not isn't what matters. It's that you're participating, and sometimes your idea will spur other ideas that do solve a problem or lead to a great moment in the episode. But waiting until you have the perfect pitch could mean you'll miss your opportunity, and often you'll find that someone else pitches what was on your mind. Don't get upset about that. It's a good way to realize you were on the right track, and it teaches you to speak up sooner next time your gut says, "Pitch this!"

But don't talk unless you have something of value to say.

This means don't feel like you have to pitch constantly in the room to prove yourself. No one — and I mean no one — expects the staff writer to come in with whole episode breaks or full B-story arcs or frankly even great solutions to a problem in the break. Thinking about the show, trying to solve problems, trying to help generate story. . . that's the job. So if you find yourself just saying things to say them, stop. Take a break, listen to what everyone else is pitching, and maybe you'll land on a new solid idea that will actually move the conversation forward.

And when the room is on a tangent and people are relaying funny stories, it's fine to jump in with one of your own, but try not to be the person who takes everyone off on the tangent in the first place. And read the room. If you can tell by the Number Two's expression that it's time to get back on track, then save your story for another day.

One more important thing here. . . please never be afraid to pitch something crazy. Sometimes crazy gets you to the answer. Sometimes crazy breaks up the tension during a stubborn board day and lets the room laugh for a minute and move on. Every idea you pitch won't be the greatest idea ever. But every idea helps in some way to get the episode off the board, even if it's just to say "nope, we don't want to do that."

You don't get paid by the word, in the room or on the page.

This is different than talking too much in general in the room. This is about when you actually pitch and when you turn in written documents.

Being concise when you pitch is a skill set you'll have to likely develop over time. A helpful tip is to write down your pitches (on the notepad you should always have in front of you) before you pitch. That will help you deliver it in a short-and-sweet manner that will increase your chances of being truly heard and understood. We will all — even experienced writers — get our words twisted up in a pitch in the room and then have to explain what we really meant and then try to make our point again. It happens to everyone, even showrunners. But in order to build your confidence as a new writer, trying to pitch quickly and clearly will help you feel like you aren't vomiting words. And even when that happens, and it will, please remember. . . it happens to all of us!

When it comes to writing, pay attention to what you were asked to do. If you're asked to write a story area and the showrunner says one to two pages, don't deliver more than two pages. If you're assigned part or all of an outline, and the standard length on your show is ten pages, then you deliver a ten-page outline (or an appropriate number of pages for the section assigned to you). And if scripts are supposed to come in at forty-seven or fifty-two or fifty-five pages, that's the page count you hit. If you find you're over by a little bit, that's usually not the end of the world, but you definitely don't want to come in grossly over. I heard a story once about someone who turned in a seventy-five-page writer's draft on an hourlong show when fifty-five pages is usually a long episode. That person did not get a second script.

How to spot your allies

Allies in the room can be everyone from upper-level writers to your support staff. But learning to spot them can be tricky. Part of this will be people who just overtly offer support — but remember, that support goes both ways. In my rooms, I try to be sure the support staff knows I'm available to them as both a mentor and just a fellow teammate on the show. Sometimes your writers' assistant might want to ask you to confirm their take on something that was said in the room for their notes. Sometimes you'll have to huddle with your script coordinator to brainstorm names for clearances or copy for screens that are going to appear in an episode. And if you need a special assist from the writers' PA, well, it'll be helpful to have a great relationship with him or her. So talk to your PAs, be sure they know you're willing to answer questions for them on how you got to where you are, and offer to read their material.

Yes, I know, broken record on this point, but here's why: I've had issues in the room that I was trying to just tolerate and tough out. And then my showrunner came to me and said, "Hey, should we talk about what X has been doing in the room?" Because my support staff had seen the issue, and when the showrunner asked how things were going in the room, they were able to share because of their unique relationship with the boss. Many showrunners consider the support staff, especially the writers' assistant, to be their eyes and ears in the room. They have permission to be honest in a way you, as a writer, may not feel empowered to echo. This helps showrunners who care about room health to step in and fix problems before they become insurmountable. So yeah, you want the support staff on your side!

And P.S., If you need to talk to the showrunner about something, always go to the showrunner's assistant and say, "Hey, when the showrunner has a minute, I need to ask about X." The assistant will let you know when is a good time — because trust me, the last thing you want to do is to walk in and ask about time off after the showrunner's had a bad notes call with the network! (So always be nice to the showrunner's assistant because he or she is your gateway to the boss and someone you want on your side, too.)

Allies in upper-level ranks can be harder to spot. A good way to try to identify them is by finding ways to talk to them just as people. If you're in early in the morning (and you always should be), the coffee room is a great place to chat folks up. If you take a walk at lunch, extend the offer to anyone who wants to stretch their legs. Walks on the lot are a great opportunity to form relationships. If you can talk to them casually, you'll get a gut read on whether or not they're interested in answering your questions or supporting you. So you'll know whom to go to when you need help. You can also see how they respond to your offers of help. Just checking in with people to see if you can lend a hand can yield great relationship bonds. I do this frequently, still, and you'd be amazed how often someone says, "Actually, could you read this act and tell me if it makes sense?" Or they just want to talk through a story point with someone and you've just offered your time. Sure, sometimes the folks you're helping will not be the good mentoring/supportive types, but you do it for the good of the show, and people know you did it and will admire that you pitched in to help the jerk nobody likes.

In the room, you'll also be able to spot these allies because they're the folks who say things like "Niceole had a great pitch earlier" and give people credit for their ideas, and they'll jump in to support writers they know have a good idea but aren't as confident in their pitching, offering up a second on the idea and cueing the room to give it real consideration.

How to deal with saboteurs

Saboteurs can be harder to spot than allies. But sometimes they wave a flag that says, "I'm here to screw with people because I think it's fun." What does that look like? The person who cuts people off while they're pitching. The person who talks over other writers, which is usually done to women, underrepresented writers, and lower-level writers. The person who gossips about writers on staff to other writers on staff. The person who blatantly steals credit for someone else's idea. The person who is an outright asshole to the support staff and treats them like servants.

But there are more subtle forms of this, too. Sometimes lower-level writers are assigned to co-write with an upper-level writer. Usually that's a great mentoring opportunity where the upper level will explain changes they make or why they want to go this way when you suggest that way. But sometimes you get a person who makes it clear they get to make *all* the decisions and they kind of dare you to push back. This is much harder to wrangle. All you can really do is make your suggestions and then do what the upper level insists must be done. Because what you don't want is for this person to go to the showrunner and say, "Niceole is difficult. She won't take my notes, and she fights me on everything." That could be the kiss of death on getting your option picked up past your initial twenty-week contract. So even though you'll know in your gut you're right about something, you may have to let it go. I was in this position once, and every time I pitched a change based on our showrunner's notes, the upper level I was paired with overruled me. We ended up getting re-noted on the majority of those spots in the script and eventually my pitches made it in, but only after I basically made the upper level think they were their ideas.

Another thing that can happen is that someone you worked with earlier in your life becomes a problem. Maybe you were a writers' assistant in another room with a writer, but now you're staffed on a show with that person. He or she might still view you as an assistant, not a "writer," and may ask you to do things like help clean up the board with the writers' assistant after the showrunner gives out some adjustments. Technically, that's not your job (unless it's your episode and you want to be the one in control of the board). If this person is a co-EP or supervising producer, you have to be careful on pushing back. But if it happens too often, you need to speak to another upper level or get advice from a mentor on how to nip it in the bud. Once you become a staffed writer, being a team player is a great thing. . . but being pushed into a box by someone who doesn't regard you as a "real" writer yet? That's a problem.

Make yourself invaluable.

This is one of the core tenets I learned in the ViacomCBS Writers Mentoring Program, and it can take a lot of forms, but it results in one thing: Showrunners and upper-level writers who know that *you* are the person they can count on to get shit done.

I've mentioned some of this in other sections, but here's a list of ways you can pitch in to help your bosses that don't involve the writers' room:

- Story areas? I love writing story areas. Want me to take a first pass? (The answer will be yes because everyone hates doing these.)

- I can take an act (or more) of that outline if it will help? Outlining can be a huge time suck for writers at the co-EP/EP level who have lots of other responsibilities. So they may take you up on this offer.

- Character descriptions? I can write those up for you, if you'd like.

- Someone kvetching about writing sides for Casting? Ask if you can take a first pass.

- Episode loglines? Sure, I can crank those out.

- Homework is your friend. Do research on areas you know are being discussed in the room and bring in options. For instance, breaking in to a safe? Bring in three different ways to do it.

See? Lots of ways to be of help and support your show, and every single one will count when your showrunner and the upper levels decide whom to invite back for the next season or when someone calls to ask how you were to work with.

First in, last out: why it matters, how it helps you build a career

This one probably seems obvious, and I've said it in other parts of this book, but I cannot stress enough how important this is. *You want to beat your showrunner in if you can* (unless you have one of those bosses who gets up at 4 a.m.; then be the second person in), and you want to stick around, if not until your boss leaves (because again, there are people who work until midnight), at least until the rest of the writers have headed out.

Why is this important? *Because when your boss wants to talk through an idea he had and everyone else is gone, you're still there.* So you get direct facetime with the showrunner, and you maybe get to be helpful. There early? You can do some research to bring into the room if you didn't get to it the night before and be there if someone wants to have an early chat about story or a script problem.

Being around is important. . . and yes, you need to have boundaries and go home and sleep and eat and have a life. . . but if the room ends at six, you can probably handle hanging out until seven before you head out. . . and you never know what might come up in that hour. Room starts at 10 a.m.? Be there by 9:30 a.m. (at least) every day. . . that's your time for those coffee conversations and maybe to casually ask your awesome co-EP how you're doing in the room without feeling like you're being a pain.

Deadlines are not negotiable.

Well-run rooms have a writers' schedule that will make it clear when story areas, outlines, scripts, and revisions are due to the showrunner. Sometimes this is verbally stated. Sometimes the communication isn't clear and you're going to have to ask when something is due. But whatever the date is, *you must be ready on that date.* There is no, "I just need two more days." There's no, "I didn't get the chase written." There is no, "I'm not ready." Even if you aren't ready, even if you didn't get the chase written, even if you really do need two more days to turn your bad first draft of act five into a decent act five, you don't get it. You never, ever, *ever* get to miss a deadline.

TV is all about the deadlines. Not making a deadline is the fastest way to put your job in jeopardy. . . so never, ever, *ever* miss one.

Never.

Got it?

TV is a team sport: why you can never forget that

It can be so tempting to look at that other staff writer across the table (if there's more than one) and think of them as an adversary. If that writer gets to do something and you don't, doesn't that take away from you? If that writer gets a script first, is that a negative mark against you?

Do not go down that road. Every writer in that room is supposed to be there to help build a show that everyone wants to succeed. You're a team. A family. Sometimes a dysfunctional family with conflicts or a team that doesn't like each other off the court — but still, you're a unit trying to achieve the same goal.

Even if you are met with an adversarial attitude from other writers, read that as their own insecurity and try not to take the bait. If someone thinks you're a kiss-ass because you come in early and stay late, well, let 'em think it. And when you ask a fellow writer for help and are told, "I'm too busy," just move on about your business and don't grouse about it to other writers. You're doing your work; you're pitching in. And people who aren't? Trust me, *someone's* noticing.

The "I" and the "we": how to support writers in a pitch without taking credit

This will affect you less as a staff writer, but supporting other writers in the room when they're pitching something you believe in is an important part of the job. Sometimes that's just bringing up another reason it's a good idea beyond what the original pitcher stated. Sometimes it's about encouraging another writer who isn't sure about a pitch to at least give it a shot (or suggesting they ask an upper level privately if the idea is worth pitching).

But the longer you're in the room, the more you can do to encourage the sense of fair play there. If your writers' assistant says in passing, "Hey, you know that car chase? What if we found a way to jump the bridge into the LA River" — and you like that idea — then go back into the room and say, "Writers' assistant had a great idea for the car chase. Writers' assistant, you want to pitch it?" If the person defers to you and you pitch it, that's fine — but you've acknowledged the source of the idea — and that is being a good human, a good mentor, and a good room writer.

You'll see great Number Twos do this routinely. A writer I worked with, Rashad Raisani, has this ability to remember who pitched things five hours earlier and give them credit. It's amazing. And it's important for making sure the showrunner knows everyone is contributing.

Another way to foster that spirit is, if you think you're re-pitching something from earlier or another day, say, "Hey, I'm not sure who pitched this, but. . ." then give out the idea. Sometimes someone else will say, "Oh, that was Niceole's pitch!" Sometimes no one will remember. And sometimes the person will jump in and say, "Oh, yeah, I thought it might work because. . ." and you can team up to give the showrunner/ Number Two more detail on the idea.

Asking for time off: Yes, you really can, but know your moment.

Sometimes you had no idea you were about to book your dream job, and you already have tickets to go on a big family trip at the holidays and you need to leave two days before the room shuts down for the break. You will be *sorely tempted* to tell your family that you can't do it and you either have to come late or cancel. But please don't do this. Ask the showrunner's assistant to get you on the boss' radar, then go to them well in advance and say, "Hey, I'm so sorry, but my family planned this trip months ago, and is it okay with you if I miss these two days in the room? I'll be available via email, text, or Zoom if I can pitch in with anything that way." Most showrunners will say, "No problem," and you'll keep both show and family happy.

The more notice you can give a showrunner, the better — so if something's planned for right after the room starts, as soon as your deal is closed, you can reach out and start the conversation (again, via the showrunner's assistant!). If it's last-minute, just do your best to get them the info asap.

One thing you should definitely try to avoid is asking for time off when your episode is on the board. This is a time you probably have to yield and reschedule your plans and put work first. But once you know when your script is due, maybe you can reschedule and plan to take time off before you have another episode come up.

And what about medical stuff? Look, showing up when you're not feeling well isn't going to help anyone. So if you need to see a doctor or go to the dentist or get new glasses and you can't make it work outside of room hours, try to minimize the impact on the room, but schedule an appointment. I usually try to get the first appointment of the day, schedule at lunch when I might just be back late, or get the last appointment of the day so I can leave the room a little early. But you shouldn't be suffering with a bad tooth or straining to see the board because you can't make time to get yourself to a dentist or eye doctor to get them checked.

And if you're sick, email or text the showrunner, showrunner's assistant, Number Two, and writers' assistant and let them know you are sick as early as you can. Don't try to be tough and come in if you have something that's contagious or making you miserable. Showrunners are notorious germaphobes, and they will want to spray you down with Lysol if you show up sneezing or coughing. And if you're in pain, your mind won't be on the work; it'll be on how bad you feel. *It is okay to be sick.* Just let people know and be sure to read the notes from the day and be caught up when you come back in. (If you're sick and it's your episode, take advantage of our friend Zoom and ask if you can Zoom in. That way, you're present for the board discussion but not infecting the office with germs.)

Social media and the working writer: dos, don'ts, and why it matters

The most important thing to remember about social media is, once you are out there trying to get jobs in the business, people from the business may be paying attention to what you post. So if you've tweeted out long threads about why you hate such and such director's work, maybe think about deleting that. And don't slag on other people's shows. It's fine not to love everything, but maybe only post about what you *do* love or can't wait to watch and limit the negative stuff to private conversations.

I once did a podcast for a friend of mine and ranted a bit about how a particular showrunner had disappointed me. My friend, thankfully, didn't mind when I later asked her to please take it down because I had realized how that might look if someone from this showrunner's company/studio/network ever heard it. But it was a lesson learned for me. Don't say things you don't want out there forever.

But social media is a huge marketing tool for TV, and you can definitely pitch in and help support and promote the show either via your own accounts or with the show's official accounts. How?

Help create material for the show social media accounts. Fun trivia, short profiles on cast/crew/writers, behind-the-scenes photos you get from other writers on set or your own visits there (if you get to go to set). . . all of this makes people excited for upcoming episodes. P.S., If you're good at this, you may get roped into running the writers' room Twitter account. But there are worse things.

For example, at the premiere party for *Cloak & Dagger*, my boss was replying to fan tweets. Someone asked if we could have a writers' room Twitter account — something no Marvel show had done thus far. My boss replied that he didn't know, but he'd ask, and if we could, he'd assign me to run it. CUT TO: Me, running the writers' room Twitter account throughout season one!

Live tweet your episodes or support your release date if it's a streaming show. Fans love engagement with the people who make their shows. If you're working on a show that's releasing episodes weekly, pick the East or West Coast airing and live tweet reactions and fun commentary during it, hashtagging your show. If your show is on a streaming platform that does full-season releases, share some funny anecdotes or photos you know are okay to share to help celebrate the day your show drops. (If you're not sure if something is okay to share, either don't share it or ask someone first. Better safe than sorry!)

But definitely realize that not everyone is going to respond positively to everything you do or say, and remember, this is your professional self you're putting out there. I once upset the fandom on a show I was on and had to bite my tongue every time someone tweeted something at me about it. But you want to be sure the engagement with fans stays positive — and sometimes you can keep it positive for them by not answering; maybe less positive for you, but that's the gig.

And hopefully after you learn to pitch confidently, become invaluable, meet all your deadlines, kill it on social media, and make friends with your writers' room, you'll not only get your twenty-week option picked up, you'll get an invite back for the next season!

True Tales of Life Inside a Writers' Room

Male drama writer on that first room experience

Being staffed for the first time was an incredible experience and personally a life goal ever since I was a kid. But then you have to go to work, and while equally exciting, that's when imposter syndrome can really rear its ugly head. Especially if you're a few years younger than the rest of the room. You want to prove yourself worthy of the hire while, at the same time, knowing your role, which is a very complicated balancing act. Having spent time working my way up as a writers' PA, assistant, and script coordinator, the day-to-day of a writers' room was something I was privy to, but what was jarring to me was how "in my head" I was getting.

The slightest bit of undetected sarcasm or pregnant pause after a pitch could send me spiraling. It's a special kind of hell. But that was all internal, self-inflicted. I was actually quite lucky that my first room as a writer was filled with some of the most caring individuals I have come to meet in this business (believe me, I'm well aware of how rare that is). They made me feel like I could "hang," and eventually, that feeling of inadequacy waned. Though, I wouldn't say it went away completely. It probably shouldn't either. I'm a firm believer that if you think your shit never stinks, you suck as a human.

Female drama writer on getting your first script

On my first show, I wasn't guaranteed a script as a staff writer. I went in knowing I might not get one. At a point when we had a two-week writing break, the showrunner asked me to shape our IP source material into a mini arc. I took that job very seriously and made a document, and the showrunner responded to it really positively. A few weeks went by, and I went up to our Number Two and asked if I was going to get a script — I just wanted to know once and for all. *The next day, the answer came: yes. Because I'd proven myself with that document, they had confidence in me to take on an episode.*

FEMALE BIPOC DRAMA WRITER
ON NAVIGATING THE HIGHS AND LOWS

Being a TV writer is not a zero-sum game. You'll have W's and take a few L's, especially when it comes to pitching. Try not to get caught in the weeds when a pitch doesn't land, and you feel like you're the dumbest person in the room. Shake it off. The great thing about finally getting in the room is living to fight another day. Stay alert. Sharpen your listening skills and put your ego on the shelf. A mentor once said that being in a writers' room is like being on a life raft with other castaways. At some point, you'll hit rough currents, but you're on a team. Always look to see where you can help plug up a dam and be prepared to do that over and over again.

FEMALE DRAMA WRITER ON HOW TO HANDLE
ON-SET DISASTERS

Whoever said "everything that can go wrong will go wrong" certainly got it right about that first year on the job. In my case, seven weeks into the job, I found myself alone on set dealing with a cast walk-off at 3 a.m. With the showrunner unavailable, it was my 1st assistant director's advice (this person is your friend!) and a very strategic and purposefully flattering conversation with my leading actor "to save the crew" that brought everyone back to work and got the day's work done. I survived and my glorious reward was imminent: Three weeks later I was sent to set again. This time, to produce an episode without a script, while — on my way to the airport — my showrunner was let go from my show. So week ten on the job, "producing" an episode of TV without a script, in the middle of a political gossip- and shitstorm, while nobody knows who's in charge, that was my next task. How fun!

Joking aside, while I hope that my trial by fire was an extreme one, I have seen time and time again that extreme situations can offer opportunities for staff writers to shine. . .or perish. The practical ability to become part of the solution and keep up the morale (and schedule), often being the deciding factor. If your show has fallen way behind or finds itself in any crazy spot, your showrunner's hair is likely on fire while your upper-level staff members are either stretched thin working themselves to the bone, or have lost faith in the leadership and are in the process of gossiping and clocking out. Now, as a staff writer there are a couple of ways this could go for you.

You could: 1. decide to deal with the tremendous pressure by going on a cruise. (I'm not kidding. I've seen a staff writer decide to go on a cruise while his episode was dying on the board.) You might imagine, this is not the ideal choice. 2. decide to deal with the uncomfortable pressure and tensions by vanishing into your chair. While not the most offensive choice, it's also not going to earn you any gold stars. 3. get on board with the room gossip! That might create a sense of camaraderie to make you feel better, but let me reassure you that it will backfire hard. I've seen a staff writer get fired for complaining about working over a holiday weekend. Or you could 4. keep focused on the work ahead, do your best to be cheerful, and keep the morale up. This, I promise you, will be the greatest contribution you can make to this room. Upper levels will appreciate the hustle and even though — as a staff writer — it is not your responsibility to pull any carts out of the mud, you might just manage to become a part of the solution.

In my case, on set without a script, a person in charge, or any clue what I should do: I first and foremost focused on not getting pulled into set gossip. Then I went into triage mode, asking questions and trying to get the production team the immediate answers they needed to keep the cameras rolling. I focused on bolstering morale and rallying upper levels, cast, director, AD, and other creative partners around me. We made it through, and even though the very showrunner who hired me was no longer around, the lore of my on-set abilities reached my incoming next commander in chief before he ever met me. I'm pretty sure it was because of that that I was kept on staff where I continued to work for him. . . until he got fired for very different reasons. Not without irony, the news came down once again while I was on set. But, hey, at least on this go-around, it wasn't my first time producing an episode in the middle of a political shit- and gossip storm without anyone in charge.

FEMALE BIPOC COMEDY/DRAMA WRITER
ON THE BEST ADVICE SHE GOT IN HER FIRST ROOM

Here's something from my very first gig at staff writer, advice from the late great Michael Ajakwe Jr. This was 2005.

I had been hired to be a staff writer on a multicam comedy and had never been in the room before. Needless to say, I was terrified. Happened to tell Michael, and he said, "Don't worry, you'll be fine." What do you mean? What do I do? How do you know that? He said, "Look, you're a staff writer, so no one expects anything from you. Just have something to say every twenty minutes, and you'll be fine." I was like. . . WHAT!? Just say something every twenty minutes? And he says, "Yeah. Have something to say every twenty minutes. No more, no less."

So I started my gig and used his rule. Every twenty minutes. And I was a hit!!! Got a couple big jokes in that people liked. Suddenly, I started feeling myself. Talking a lot more. And then I got cracked on by an upper level. A smackdown. A joke was told at my expense. That's when I realized I had stepped outside of what Michael said. Every twenty minutes. And I went back to that strategy. And it worked well for me in the room.

Later the showrunners came to me to talk about a script and told me how well I was doing in the room. They said, "You know, usually when staff writers start their first job, they talk too much or too little. But you speak up just right." And I owe that success and bit of advice I now tell other staff writers to follow Michael Ajakwe!

And just a coda on that. Looking back, I now realize what was happening. As a first timer, you can't know what you don't know. Having something to say every twenty minutes gives you time to pick from your best thoughts to pitch (which makes you look good). It also keeps you from pissing off upper levels by stepping on what they were going to say or getting on their nerves (which also makes you look good). And it also gives you time to sit back and learn how a room works with no pressure. Michael was right; no one expected anything of me. So this was not the time to try and lead; this was the time to revel in being a follower. At least until your acumen for the job could be assessed and understood and until your value to the room could be determined and mined. So relax! Every twenty minutes will keep you gainfully employed. (Now, should your showrunner come to you and give you specific orders of what to do, that takes precedence over this.)

5

The Writing Part of Being in the Writers' Room

**This isn't you at home in your pajamas
writing in the dark. Embrace the process.**

W E ALL HAVE OUR WAY WE like to do things when we write our own projects. I still prefer note cards because I'm a note card girl. I have whiteboards for when I need to make sidenotes on things. I mostly outline my own work but occasionally just write from the pitch document because I like to live dangerously. I have all my own style quirks I prefer to use in a script. And I write 90% of my pages on my couch in front of my TV. That's the freedom of writing your own pieces. You get to do it all your way.

Once you're staffed on a show, you have to do things the boss's way. Some showrunners will let you write from home; some will ask that everyone works in the office. Sometimes you get to leave the room to write; sometimes you have to write at night and on weekends around your work in the room. And even if you do a standard process — come up with a story area, break the episode, outline the episode, turn in a writer's draft, etc. — there are quirks that can pop up at each stage of that process that will probably feel very different than what you're used to when you work on your own time. So this is where we talk about some of the things you'll encounter on staff when it comes to the writing. . . things that break from your individual writing routine.

Researchers and consultants: who they are, how to use them, what the rules are

Depending on the type of show you work on, there may be times when an expert could really benefit the storytelling. Examples of this: on *Ironside*, when I was trying to figure out how a bomb would blow up a building, our police consultant put me in touch with a bomb squad officer to answer questions; on *Allegiance*, I spoke routinely with the FBI consultant who liaisons with Hollywood to get answers to questions about the intelligence community; on *Cloak & Dagger*, when we decided to do stories about the Mardi Gras Indians of New Orleans and, in season two, discussed human trafficking, we consulted experts in both areas so that we were certain we were writing honest, genuine stories.

You're always free to do your own research on topics that are either already in play in the room or areas you might want to cover in an upcoming episode. I Googled a lot about how to build improvised explosive devices, or IEDs, before I had to worry about where the bombs went in that episode of *Ironside* — so I had a good idea of the type of bomb I wanted to use. On *Allegiance*, we needed to pull off a huge theft from a supposedly impenetrable safe, so I did a lot of research on how thieves defeat those massive lockboxes to make sure our explanation was believable.

Sometimes, though, as I noted above, the type of show you're on requires you to speak to outsiders: people who don't work on the show, at your studio, or at your network. So if you're going to do that, first of all, *be sure that your showrunner is cool with it and see if there are any rules you need to follow*. One of the things showrunners worry about is people expecting to get payment or credit for story help. Newsflash: That's pretty rare. Usually we're asking a few questions and thanking that person for their service, and that's that. At *Cloak & Dagger*, because it was a Marvel show, our experts had to be cleared by the studio first before we could talk to them due to security concerns. So I initiated the conversation with the studio (at my showrunner's request) and helped steer them to the human-trafficking experts we were most interested in speaking with.

If you have someone in your life who is a personal source and is an expert, it's absolutely fine to ask them questions; just try to avoid giving them story details. I have nurses, doctors, cops, firefighters, criminologists, psychologists, musicians, and athletes in my family and circle of friends, and I've asked them all for their help on specifics for stories before. An example of this: When I was working on *S.W.A.T.*, I asked my nephew, a police officer, to give me some gun options for a few different types of scenarios. He sent me links, and I was able to look at the guns and decide which ones I wanted to include. Just remind these folks that, like experts out in the real world, we're grateful for their help, but we can't promise them any payment or credit. Always cover that base to avoid any future trouble.

This feels like a good place to mention that, once you become a working writer (if it doesn't already happen to you), everyone — including your consultants — might try to pitch you ideas for episodes or scripts they think should get written. *You cannot hear those pitches.* You have a built-in saving grace in your contract, which is that you aren't allowed to hear those pitches per the studio. So you can sidestep without being a jerk. But it's really important not to let people constantly throw ideas at you for "the episode you guys should really do" because if an episode similar to that gets pitched, written, and shot by sheer coincidence, that person can claim it was their idea and you stole it. And nobody wants to deal with that.

Story areas: what they are and how to be good at the thing everyone hates doing

Story areas are the written mini-pitches a writers' room does to float episode ideas past the studio and network for approvals before a writer starts writing a script. The reason for them? If a studio or network blows up an idea (and it happens), then at least you aren't on page forty-five of a fifty-two-page script when things go kaboom. P.S., You'll also hear people call these "story arenas." It's the same thing, just different terminology used in the industry depending on where you came up. *You'll find samples of these at the end of the book on p. 273.*

Sometimes you're writing these from a full break, so it's easy to see what all the important beats are. Sometimes, after a room discussion to brainstorm some episode ideas, you have a few big moments, a great guest character, and an awesome ending, and so you're selling those elements to get the story cleared before the room invests time and energy into a full break of the episode. How story areas get done, however, differs on every show — and sometimes you don't actually do them. (I know, confusing!) So here are some things to remember:

The mini-story area. On *Ironside*, my boss liked us to write what was essentially a paragraph-long synopsis of the episode idea. This is basically a detailed log line with a few extra bits — maybe a line about a B story or two to give readers a rounded view of the episode.

The one- to two-pager. This is the most standard version of the story area I've encountered. This is a document that hits the big beats of the teaser, the story highlights, the big emotional arcs for the characters, and the culmination of the episode. It's finding the most important details of the episode and giving it a little sales magic to try and get the studio and network excited.

The episode synopsis. This is a system some showrunners use when they don't like handing in outlines. This is usually done after a full episode break because you're sidestepping a major part of the writing process by skipping the outline. There are different ways to do this, but in short, you're probably doing about five to six pages that sum up the episode's emotional arcs for your main characters, the A or main story, and the B or secondary stories. Since this is post-break, you can sell some big moments, like your leads rushing into a building where you know a serial killer is holding a woman at knifepoint and it's a desperate race to save her life.

The trick to all of these, whether it's a paragraph or six pages, is to really think about the information you need to sell the story. *That's what this document is: a sales document.* And that's why you don't want to fill it with dialogue you love or get into the details of a scene you can't wait to write. *Give them the big idea:* "We go on an epic high-speed chase through downtown Los Angeles, putting civilians in peril to catch a killer." Because if you get into the nitty-gritty — you want to do a motorcycle jump and crash through a building window — they might ixnay that in the area when they'd go for it once they see it written in script. Sometimes someone's read three high-speed chase ideas that week and yours is number three and they'll just be in the mood to kill a chase. So save the detail, put it in the script, and convince them a chase is exactly what you need. The danger with dialogue? If you write a line they fall in love with, you may be stuck with it in script even if *you* don't love it. Or worse, you love it, but they kill it before you get to script.

Use active, vibrant verbs and adjectives; make sure you're clear to whom you're referring throughout (pronouns can get dicey in these); underline, italicize, or bold things for emphasis (probably dependent on your showrunner's style preference); and have fun with it. Yes, people hate writing them — but if you're good at writing them, especially if you're on one of those shows where staff writers don't get a script, you'll still feel like you're contributing to the show, making everyone else's life easier, and you'll be learning the pithy sales style of writing you'll need when you transition to writing pitch documents, which are literally *all about sales.*

Outlining: Everyone hates this, too. Here's how to conquer the demon.

Before I got into the ViacomCBS Writers Mentoring program, I hadn't outlined a writing project since graduate school and was proud of it. I hated writing them. So why bother? Well. . . because most TV shows wouldn't exist without the outline; that's why. The outline is the step in which you sometimes realize the episode is too long, the scenes aren't in the right order, a character disappears for two acts, or your lead isn't in the end of act one or the top of act two — that's a problem; maybe your act outs aren't as good as you thought on the board. In short, *as much as writers complain about outlining, it helps solve story problems before you go to script.*

The format and style of your outline will depend on the showrunner's preference. I've been tasked with writing a six-page outline and asked to write fifteen pages. I've heard of showrunners who want outlines that are thirty-plus pages in length and include dialogue pitches (most showrunners I know avoid dialogue here for the same reason they do in story areas, but it takes all kinds to make TV). So what you're asked to do will vary from show to show.

If you're on a first-year show, you'll probably write later in the order, so be sure that you read every document that comes out ahead of you, especially the outlines. This will help you short-hand the style of the show when you sit down to write yours. If you're joining an existing show, immediately ask the script coordinator if you can have outlines and scripts from past seasons and read, read, read. There's no better way to absorb the voice of a showrunner or the style of a show than from reading it on the page.

Some shows, especially more procedural ones, will group-write outlines. Once the break is finished, each available writer, and sometimes the support staff, will be assigned a few scenes in an act, whole acts, or if you're low on bodies, half an episode. This is another great chance to support the show and help make everyone's lives easier. Take it seriously, write the best version of your portion of the outline that you can, and then read the outline that gets published to see what changed in your sections. That will help you learn how to do better on your next go-round.

Typically in this situation, everyone sends their pieces of outline to the episode writer, who then compiles it, makes it cohesive, and submits it to the showrunner so that they can give notes or do their pass on the outline and get it off to the studio. So if it's your episode, you do get ownership over what goes to the showrunner — and you should make sure you believe in how every scene is described so that you can defend it, if need be. Does that mean you'll change or rewrite other writers? Yes. It's the process, and they should all understand that. Your name is going on that episode, and you need to understand everything that happens in it.

Except for when that's not how your showrunner does things. You may run into someone who says that your name on that episode is just your getting your turn at having a credit and you don't have ownership over the episode. Again, all you can do in that situation is write the hell out of what you are asked to write and hope for the best final product possible. Sometimes the hardest part of this job is the lack of control. But doing a good job in spite of that will only help your career and train you for those heady days when you're the showrunner and the studio or network is forcing you to take a note you hate (no, that part never ends).

Group-writing: What is it, and why does it happen?

I just mentioned that some shows group-write outlines. Some shows extend this practice to script writing. Full disclosure: I hate this method of TV writing. It is sometimes absolutely necessary, like when something goes wrong in prep, and you have to write out a character or change a bunch of scenes from one location to another. But I consider it a process for "break glass in case of emergency" situations only.

Why? Because none of us became writers to write four scenes in an episode. We did it to write scripts. And because there are some showrunners who utilize this style as their normal operating procedure on shows, you can finish a one-, two-, three-year run on a show without ever having written an entire episode yourself.

If you find yourself in this situation, again, the thing to do is to write the hell out of what you're assigned, get it done on time, and then read the published version to see what lived from your version and what didn't. Some adjustments will be lateral: You knew this was the perfect place for a joke and your showrunner changed your joke. That's a personal taste thing; take away from it that you were right that a joke was the correct impulse there and don't worry about the joke being rewritten. Some of the changes will be about a character or relationship idea your showrunner has and hasn't shared with the room and so he or she's decided to start setting that up. Some — a lot — will probably be about dialogue-writing style. All of this is stuff you can learn and accommodate if you put in the time to study your version vs. the showrunner's version.

If you find yourself on a show where group-writing is the norm, you should discuss the long-term effect of that with your reps. It's great to stay on the same show and get ongoing experience, but you also want to give yourself the best set of skills to someday run your own show. Obviously, you've written whole scripts before — that's how you got the job, by writing script samples. But if you've never written one on a five-day turnaround (or a three-day, which I have after an episode was rebroken to accommodate other storyline changes), then you'll still be terrified of having that expectation put on you. You need to know what it feels like to write whole scripts on a deadline while trying to manage your staff job. So think of that as you strategize the next move in your career.

Co-writing: How is it different, and why?

Co-writing is also a common thing you'll encounter while staffing. This is usually how it works: An upper-level writer is paired with a lower-level writer, each writes half the episode, and you both get credit for writing the episode.

That's not always the case — sometimes two upper levels who are friends and want to write together will ask to do that. Sometimes an experienced writer is paired with the writers' assistant or script coordinator to give them a shot at half a script.

So why would a showrunner like to do these pair-ups? Generally it gets drafts completed faster, and when you're on a broadcast TV schedule, where you're writing, shooting, editing, and airing within a month or so for every episode, fast is your friend. The other benefit is that showrunners who don't like to send lower-level writers to set can send the more senior writer to produce the episode, or that senior writer can supervise the lower levels and help them get some experience during production.

I had an unusual situation where I ended up on shows four seasons in a row that did co-writes, and to be honest, I got super tired of it. I made a point of asking showrunners in my next round of meetings if they did this and leaned toward jobs where they didn't. Not because I don't like sharing credit but because again, I didn't become a writer to write part of a script. I want to do the whole thing.

But if a team-up means a shot for a writer more junior than I am? I am happy to do it. A lot of shows will give you one solo script and one co-write to make sure everyone gets enough experience and credits and that you also get a chance to write one fully on your own. And I'll admit that I dislike it less now that I'm the senior writer on the script (and I try really hard to model the great upper-level collaborators I had so that the junior writers always feel involved and valued in the process, not run over and squeezed out).

Your first script: navigating the pitfalls

So, your outline's approved and you're ready to start writing your first draft of your first episode of TV. If abject terror sets in here, don't feel like you're alone. That's how it feels for just about everyone. It's a dream come true, but it's a lot of pressure. You are, in fact, writing for your screenwriter life because you want to do well on this first one to make sure you get a next one. But at the same time, you need to remember something: *No one expects a staff writer's first script to be perfect.*

Let me say that one more time: *No one expects a staff writer's first script to be perfect.*

So what do they expect? They expect you to respect the outline that was broken in the room and approved by the studio and network, doing your best to execute the scenes as conceived. They expect you to do your best to mimic the voice of your show and the script style established by prior drafts. And they expect you to remember that you have help — you may be doing all of the above and realize that a character story is still missing a beat to make it really work. It's fine to reach out to your Number Two or another upper-level writer and say, "Hey, I think this story needs one more thing. I had an idea to try X." They'll probably tell you to go for it — and if they don't, then they'll probably suggest taking that area back into the room for a quick chat so you have the full room to brainstorm a solution — or they'll tell you when a certain story is very particular to the showrunner and advise you to write it as is and see how he or she reacts to your version.

It's okay to ask for help. It's okay to do your best on a scene and say, "I'm still not quite sure this works, but I tried to get exactly what we broke," and then wait for feedback. It's all part of the process, which will look something like this.

You write your first draft. And when I say first draft, I mean this — say you have five days to write your script. I'd try to get a "vomit" draft done in two days. Then give yourself the rest of that time to make it better, better, and then better again. We all have our ways we like to accomplish the speedy first pass. Some of my writer friends import the outline, roughly format the lines of dialogue they know they'll need, and create a very basic script doing only that so they have a "draft" they can edit.

Most of us like rewriting better than writing from scratch. . . and that's why this method is super helpful.

My personal preference is to do all the actual typing — I can't import the outline because I like to type to get into my flow. But I have definitely literally written. . .

> CHARACTER A
> I need to talk about my relationship issues
> without giving too many details.
>
> CHARACTER B
> I need to refuse to let Character A off the hook.
>
> CHARACTER A
> Says snarky shit.
>
> CHARACTER B
> Says snarky shit back.
>
> CHARACTER A
> Pokes at something that pisses Character B off.
>
> CHARACTER B
> Reveals he already knows about Character A's drama
> because of their mutual friend Character C."

I do this to remind myself what the scene is about while I'm still trying to get my creative juices flowing — then I'll come back through and make it good later on. Whatever it takes to help you get into a good flow and bang out those pages is what you should do.

Typically after this, you'll get notes back on the draft, have a chance to implement them, and then your showrunner will take a full pass before turning it into the studio. When the studio gives their notes, hopefully your showrunner will let you take the first stab at implementing the changes, then he or she will take another pass, and the script is off to the network. Same deal after this. The network will have notes, the showrunner will hopefully let you try to address them, and then he or she goes through the script to get out the production draft.

That's not the end of the road, but that's the main immediate draft structure you'll be most involved in. Whether you take part in production draft changes will depend on how involved your showrunner allows you to be in prep and shooting. But more on that later.

There are situations where writers have turned in their first draft and then never see the script again because the showrunner "takes" it. This can mean the script wasn't up to snuff, but it can also mean that there's a scheduling issue and the showrunner simply doesn't have time to go back and forth with you. In either case, be sure to carefully study the next draft to see what changed and what you can learn from the work the showrunner did.

Who reads your drafts, and who gives you notes?

Once you finish your draft, you will hopefully have time to ask a fellow writer on staff to give it a read — the designated "mentor" upper level, if there is one, or the writer you feel most comfortable asking for help. This mentor can give you a set of notes to help you get closer to the showrunner's voice and style and help find any story problems you may have missed.

After that, it's off to the showrunner. Hopefully you will get notes and get to take another pass. (Remember what I said above: Sometimes that doesn't happen for a variety of reasons.)

You may be on a show where the showrunner likes the whole staff to read the script and chime in with any helpful thoughts or suggestions. Usually the showrunner will have the writers send thoughts to him or her to decide independently what works and what doesn't, passing on only the notes that should be further executed.

Some showrunners like to table notes, meaning you'll all gather in the writers' room, and everyone will discuss their thoughts on the script. This usually happens before you get the showrunner's notes, which are often incorporated into this process. Full disclosure — I hate this with the heat of a thousand suns. It feels unfair to make a writer listen to the room debate notes, often relitigating issues that were already discussed during the story break. But if you find yourself in this situation, remember that you can always go back to the showrunner later and say, "That note on act two — did you want me to try the thing Niceole suggested or keep it the way it is?" The goal is to be sure you're doing the notes the *showrunner* cares about and wants you to execute — even if that means you're ignoring a note from an upper-level writer who spoke up at the table. At the end of the day, that's the job.

It's very uncomfortable to have a showrunner say to you, "Why'd you change this?" and to say, "Well, X writer gave me notes and suggested this," but it's important that you speak up when the showrunner is questioning a change. Who made the suggestion may impact how it's considered. I've had this happen, and because the showrunner had a long relationship with the co-EP in question, he knew that writer's quirks and was able to say, "Yeah, he loves that stuff, but I don't. Can you change it back and then send it to the script coordinator for distribution?"

On some shows, my showrunner's methodology has been to say, "Everyone's responsible for reading the drafts as they come out, and if you have thoughts, please pass them on to the writer." If that's the situation you're in, you can decide if it's a note you want to try or not or bring it to the showrunner's attention if you aren't sure.

Notes: how to take them, even when you don't want to

The trick with notes is to remember that this is not your show. And frankly, even if it is, you'll still get notes you hate and have to address because that's just making TV.

I know. . . that's frustrating to hear (or read). But notes are an essential part of the process. Sometimes notes make your work better, sometimes they identify things you missed, and sometimes they help you find more creative ways to execute big ideas.

One of the most important lessons I can pass on to you about notes is: *Don't try to litigate them in the moment.* If you hate a note, if you don't get how in the world someone can be giving you this note when what they're asking is *right there* on the page, when you think it's the dumbest note you've ever heard, your best friend is this phrase *"I'll take a look at it."*

Some writers use this as a blow-off, but it's also true. Sometimes you need to sit and let your brain marinate on the note before you start to see what the issue is.

Sometimes a note is addressing a feeling that something is off in the scene. The exact note may be wrong, may sound dumb to you as articulated, but "this exchange felt juvenile" could be code for "we're not feeling their chemistry here," and so that's what you need time to figure out. This is a classic way in which the phrase "the note behind the note" comes into play. The reader is simply feeling something off in the scene — and maybe he or she can't clearly identify it. But the fact that something is wrong in the read is reason enough to look at it and see if you can figure out how to make the scene/story work better.

Engaging in debates over notes while you're hot or annoyed is always a bad idea. It's fine to come back later and say, "Hey, I got to this note and wasn't clear on the intention. Can we discuss it?" and have a conversation about it when you're calmer.

But when the notes come from your showrunner — the truth is, you have to take the note. You can say, "Hey, I wanted to try this version of the note," and put your spin on it, but you can *never* ignore a note from your showrunner.

Notes calls: Know what your showrunner expects of you.

Once your draft makes it to the studio and network, you will hopefully be included on notes calls. This is invaluable experience because you can see how your showrunner (and possibly your Number Two, if on the calls) handle these interactions with the execs who cover your show.

If you're included, ask someone ahead of time how to handle the calls — meaning, "Do you want me to say anything or am I supposed to sit here quietly?" Usually it's sit there quietly while you're a lower-level writer — but that doesn't mean you can't also be of help during the call. Say the studio isn't clear on a twist in the story and you remember that there was a line that would help that was cut from the draft. You can write a note that says, "We can add back the line about who made the reservation" and prompt your showrunner who probably doesn't remember that cut but can pitch it now and see how the studio or network responds thanks to your good memory.

Sometimes showrunners empower lower-level writers to speak on notes calls. But it's important to know if that's okay or not. The thing you never want to do is speak up when it's unwelcome. If you are empowered but the studio or network says something potentially controversial, try and hold your tongue until your showrunner reacts. This can give you direction on the best way to approach. For instance, if they react negatively to a race or gender element in a story, your showrunner may come back with something like, "Well, I completely get why that's a little jarring. What we were going for there was. . ." and explain the intention behind the choice. That's often all it takes. And then there are the times when your showrunner will say, "Sure, I'll take a look at that" while shooting you a "Can you friggin' believe this crap?" look across the room.

You may also have special circumstances on a call that are worth pointing out ahead of time. On one of my shows, two of my former network writing program mentors were going to be on the notes call. I made sure to tell my EPs ahead of time. When the execs were like, "Well, we love this script so much," my bosses said, "Well, Niceole is here listening to that, just so you know." It let the execs and me have a moment and then we dove into the notes and got the work done. If someone you know is on the call, it's okay to acknowledge that with your boss(es). That way if the relationship comes up on the call, it's not a surprise to anyone.

My script got taken away and given to an upper-level writer. What does that mean?

As I mentioned above, sometimes you won't get a chance to keep working on a script. Yes, that can mean that the showrunner had an issue with the draft you turned in — and hopefully you'll get clarity on that by way of the showrunner, the Number Two, or an upper level who will walk you through where you went wrong.

But please, please, please remember that the show is so much bigger than you and your draft. Directors fall out, necessitating episode shuffles, and now that script that wasn't scheduled to start prep for two weeks is needed in two days; a storyline that's particularly worrisome to the studio or network has the showrunner wanting more control over the pages they read; a budgetary issue means your episode with the big outdoor set piece needs to be a bottle episode. Any of these things can and will happen. . . and the best you can do in this situation is to read the drafts as they come out and learn from what changed.

If your script is taken away and no one talks to you about it, this is another great time to rely on your allies on the show. Ask them what they know about the situation. It's easy to jump to the worst-case scenario, which is "my draft was shit," but again — you don't know the truth until someone tells it to you. And if all else fails, it's okay to ask your Number Two why you didn't get a shot at addressing notes.

Jumping credits: the difference between "&" and "and"

You'll hear writers talk sometimes about jumping credits. What does that mean? It means that you wrote an episode, your showrunner did a heavy pass on it, and when the script is next distributed, your showrunner's name is on the cover as one of the writers.

There are some showrunners who are legendary in this business for jumping credits. And it is their prerogative. But most other showrunners will tell you it's a shitty thing to do.

Credits are about more than just whose name is on the script — it affects payment for the episode and residuals. So a showrunner who does this is taking money out of a writer's pocket when he or she does it.

But it's also the general principle of the thing. *Rewriting episodes and making sure they feel like the show is the job. . .* every showrunner does this on multiple episodes every season, sometimes doing several page-one (full) rewrites. But the showrunner knows that's the job, and those showrunners never put their names on the script.

When you see "written by X writer & Niceole R. Levy," it should mean that we were assigned to write the episode together, or that I as a showrunner co-wrote an episode with another writer to give them an opportunity. The ampersand can also signify an actual writing team that always writes together.

If you were to see "written by Niceole R. Levy and X writer," it would be an indication that I wrote a draft and then my showrunner/another writer did a rewrite and got credit on the script. How does that happen? The magic of arbitration.

Arbitration

So let's say that you turned in your writer's draft, the showrunner asked a co-EP to rewrite it or rewrote it themselves, and because it was what's considered a page-one rewrite, he or she now expects credit for writing the episode.

Welcome to WGA credit arbitration!

What does that mean? It means that you'll get notification from the WGA that it is evaluating the script to determine who deserves full or partial credit on the final draft and on screen.

This is a whole logistical process that involves writers turning in their drafts to the Guild so the arbitrators can determine who did what work in the final product. You'll be asked to submit proof of when you sent your drafts in and to whom you sent them, and to provide copies of any and all drafts submitted officially to the show.

The important things to know about this process are:

1. The WGA skews heavily in favor of the original writers on projects. Why? Because these writers are often lower-level or underrepresented writers — those most likely to be powerless to say anything when an episode is taken away and given to an upper level/showrunner to rewrite. And the truth is, it's often impossible to say that no ideas, themes, or moments from the original script are sustained in the rewrite — so it's nearly impossible to say the original writer is erased entirely from the final product. So what usually happens is that you and the upper level/showrunner will share credit — "written by Niceole R. Levy and X writer."

2. Everyone with a soul thinks this is a dick move. If you're an upper-level writer or a showrunner, rewriting is your job, and you get paid well to do it. You don't need to take a credit away from another writer. So when you're the upper level or showrunner, remember that and graciously allow that other writer the benefit of your experience and talent in making his or her episode better. And if you're really doing your job, go through your rewrite with that writer so he or she can actually learn how to do better if writing for you again.

True Tales of Life Inside a Writers' Room

Male BIPOC comedy writer on the real difference between comedies and dramas

I know folks will hate on this, but comedy is harder. Yep, I said it. Hate. Hate. Hate. There is a general agreement that we all have around drama. Losing loved ones. Broken hearts. Medical hardships. Missing kids. There isn't a person alive, or exec working who wouldn't agree, that's dramatic. Comedy changes daily. That original scenario or killer joke today may not play tomorrow. The scenario is suddenly contrived, and by the time you do the draft, those jokes are "familiar." No, it's not familiar to the audience, but to the team that has seen it one hundred times, yeah, it's familiar.

Female BIPOC upper-level writer on ways to make an impression

As I was one of several producers on a first season show, I took it as a personal challenge to get the voice of the showrunner down before the room went to script. Back in my days when I was trying to get my first break, I would pore over the showrunners' scripts and learn their syntax. I would study whatever they had written. But I hadn't done that in some time. I realized that maybe I needed to pick up that old drive. So I went to the Writers Guild library and pulled every episode the showrunner had ever written on his other shows and his movies. I studied his style and took notes on how he got in and out of a scene. I did this in the evenings when we broke early from the room or on a Saturday.

As the scripts from the other writers started coming in, I paid attention to how he noted their drafts. I actually learned a lot from his critiques, but most importantly, I discovered how to measure the taste of a showrunner. Some want big emotions; others want a sense of cool. But his questions always revolved around: Is this scene interesting? How can this scene be elevated?

When I went to script, I spent five days in a hotel room just ordering room service and writing. I wrote my ass off. I went over all the notes I'd taken about his writing and then that of the season scripts. I watched movies related to the genre of the show. I did a ton of research. I turned the draft in on a Friday and waited with bated breath for his call. He actually reached out first to the other EP Saturday morning to say that I had exceeded his expectations. The text that preceded his call was something I'll never forget. I was still unprepared for the praise I got when the call came. And then came the true writing process — I ended up rewriting over and over again, not just for his notes, as he was constantly asking to make it better, but for production needs and the post-table read and on and on. Luckily, the thrill of having solid bones on a first draft stayed with me through the very long process of going from script to screen. Whether you crush that first draft, or get there eventually, we all have to deal with notes — either from the studio or the showrunner, or well, everyone.

FEMALE COMEDY SHOWRUNNER
ON HOW COMEDY GETS WRITTEN

Drama and comedy are similar in that they both write to the act break. Make it big, make it emotional, make people come back after the commercial (when TV has/had commercials). In network, comedy acts have grown. We used to have just two acts, and that is where the big funny twist happened (oops, that was his purchase, not his wife's on the credit card bill that he has been making her feel guilty about, and now the tables are turned). Now, some shows still have two-act structure, but it is not uncommon to have three or even four acts. I worked on a multicam with four acts s — with roughly five to seven pages an act. Sometimes less. Single-camera comedy bloomed with a three-act structure, and once networks realized they could get more commercials in — well that three-act structure became a standard.

Multicam and single-cam scripts are different. Multi is double spaced and limited (in general) to the sets of a sound stage while single camera in general has more scenes and is not limited by location as much. In both, the first section of the script is considered a COLD OPEN or a TEASER. This can sometimes be an act in itself or a two-page joke that has nothing to do with the story. And lately, much like drama, those openings are being lumped into the first act.

In fact, with the popularity of streaming platforms, many shows now have no acts at all. Oftentimes, a room will still break the show like it has three acts (which as mentioned seems to have become standard practice). Then when the show is written, there are no acts put into the script. It all blends together, but you are still building to important jokes and moments in the script to keep the audience entertained.

The big difference between comedy and drama in acts is that in comedy you are telling the story in a way that leads the audience to a big "blow" at the end of each act. It needs to be a joke. It has to hit hard. And it has to have weight to it. It can be a belly laugh, it can be a character laugh, but it had better have a joke at the end of the act. Scenes within that act also end on a joke. Once or maybe twice a show there can be an "emotional out," which is where the characters don't end the scene having told a joke, but that depends on the show — and rarely is that the end of an act. Sometimes, whole acts are built around one joke or one concept that writers and producers know will be the big funny blow.

MALE DRAMA WRITER ON HOW A CONSULTANT CAN HELP SETTLE CONFLICT

When I was in my first job as a staff writer in a diversity position, I worried about the optics of constantly pushing back on storylines that made me uncomfortable. There wasn't always an ally in the room, so I asked other writers for advice and assistance *pushing back when things got too sticky. As my level increased, I found myself able to handle things in different ways, sometimes speaking directly to an issue, other times suggesting the room utilize a consultant. It's sometimes easier to identify what's wrong than it is to fix it, and a good consultant can bring new information to light that not only helps solve a representation issue, but also makes the story better.*

6

Writers' Schedules

The good, the bad, and the WTF, are you kidding me?

A GOOD SHOWRUNNER OR A FABULOUS NUMBER Two will create a writers' schedule, even if it's just for internal use, as soon as decisions are made on how many episodes are being ordered and how many staff members have been hired. (Sometimes showrunners don't like to pass these documents on to studio/network, hence the "internal use" bit.)

Why is this important? Because that schedule tells you when to panic. If you're working on a broadcast show, that schedule is the literal lifeline between "Hey, we have an idea for an episode," and "This episode starts shooting on X date," and the window between them is smaller than you'd imagine — sometimes a few months, sometimes a few weeks. In a dire emergency, it can be a few days.

How much time you get for each step depends on the style of the showrunner or the Number Two creating the schedule. As a broad guideline, here's a general idea of how things work after the room comes up with the story area and how much time you may get to work through the process.

1. *Room breaks the episode* — anywhere from five to ten days depending on the room, though long breaks are pretty rare in broadcast. On cable shows where they're

shooting everything after the writing, you can spend a little more time on the process.

2. *Writer writes the outline* — this is anywhere from two to five days depending on whether or not the outline is a group-write or a solo/team write.

3. *Once your outline is approved and you go off to script* — you have anywhere from five to eight days to write a script. Be prepared for five, and celebrate if you get more time. This is the writer's draft.

4. *Revised writer's draft* — you'll usually get anywhere from two to five days to turn around notes from your showrunner depending on the level of notes.

5. *Studio notes* (for network draft) — I've generally had these turned around in two days unless there was extensive rebreaking or rewriting needed.

6. *Network notes* (for production draft) — again, generally two days, though your showrunner may give you longer if there's a significant bit of work to do.

So what does that look like on a schedule? Let's use this as an example. It's not exact because the notes turnarounds can vary, but this is a general idea of how your time will be spent. And this is counting business days only (if you're writing on nights/weekends, that will be factored into your schedule).

Ep #	Writer	Outline Due	Writer's Draft Due	Studio Draft	Network Draft	Production Draft
105	Niceole	8/2	8/16	8/20	8/25	8/27

As you can see, that's not a ton of time between the start of the episode writing process and the start of prep (right after the production draft is sent out). That's why it's important to think about how to use your time wisely and to always try to stay current on the due dates.

Sometimes rooms don't have writers' schedules. It's not ideal, but then you just have to say, "When do you want this turned around" and get a firm due date.

But the most important thing to remember is: *Never assume you have extra time.* You may get it because your showrunner tells you, "I won't read it before Monday anyway, so you can hold it over the weekend," but never expect it.

Assignments: When do you get to find out what episode you're writing?

You may get a writers' schedule early on that has episode numbers and dates but no names of who is writing what beyond the showrunner, who is probably writing the premiere or pilot, episode two, and the finale, as an example.

Why? There is a belief among some showrunners that if you pre-assign episodes to writers, some of them will check out during the break of episodes they know they aren't writing. And much as I hate to say it, I've seen it happen. It's annoying and frustrating to the writers in the room working their butts off to make sure *every episode is good,* not just the ones with their name(s) on them. A showrunner I worked with asked if there was a name for these people who only "show up" when the showrunner is in the room, and I decided I liked the term "on/off switches" — they only turn on when the boss is around.

My feeling on dealing with these types of writers is that, as a showrunner, I'd make it clear on day one that if I see this happening in the room, you'll hear about it directly from me. I'm not conflict-averse and am willing to call people out when they aren't carrying their weight.

But some people want to avoid this altogether. They keep everyone invested (they hope) by withholding the script assignment. Then either partway through or at the end of a break, they'll assign writers to the episode. So that's when you'll get the heads-up that it's time to think about that episode with a sense of ownership.

Quality scripts on time: Learn it and believe it, even if your showrunner doesn't.

The Showrunner Training Program at the WGA uses a simple mantra: quality scripts on time. What does that mean? Well, according to John Wells, showrunner extraordinaire, it means that on the first day of prep you should have a shootable script ready for production.

"Shootable" doesn't mean perfect; it doesn't mean more changes won't be coming as you and the director and the crew prep the episode. But it means if push came to shove — you could shoot the episode as is.

Why? Because if you don't have that script ready, everyone from your director to your Art department to your costumers and construction team are waiting to find out what they need to do to accomplish that episode. . . and they can only do so much work off an outline. Stunts needs the general idea of how many set pieces there are to start planning for safety and scope. Picture cars needs to know how many vehicles they need to buy or double. Extras needs to know how many additional bodies they need for each scene. All of that information comes from a script. . . so everyone needs that guide to do their jobs.

What can you do about this if you're on staff? Well, the truth is, only what you're allowed to do. Because the showrunner is the one who has to approve every draft that gets distributed, he or she can become the obstacle keeping things from getting done on time. The studio, network, or another EP will do the wrangling there and try to get things back on track.

But from a staffed writer's POV, what you can do is always get your work done on time and keep track of the schedule so you know the due dates without needing to rely on anyone else to keep you in the loop. And you can always say to the show-runner, "Hey, is there anything I can take off your plate?" in the most helpful, team-player way you can manage. Sometimes what's costing your showrunner time is writing sides for casting or rewriting a story area or outline — and depending on who you are and what that person views as your strengths, the reply to your offer may be, "Actually, yes, can you take these sides?" and then the showrunner can get back to the job of getting drafts done and out the door.

If you have a showrunner who thrives on chaos and therefore doesn't care about deadlines, prep dates, and how stressed out the director, line producer, and cast are, just know that none of that reflects back on you. Everyone knows whose job it is to get those scripts out on time. Just keep your head down, try to help as much as you can with whatever is holding up the effort, and look out for your fellow writers as the stress builds because it will. Production may also be short on calls and frustrated, and if you're helping in prep, you'll have to deal with that. Just assure them you're trying to get them what they need, even if that means going to get specific answers to questions before the script is done. (More on this when we talk about production.)

There's no such thing as "I can't make my deadline."

I've said this already, and I will say it a few more times, because it bears repeating: *Deadlines are absolute.* You must always be ready to turn in a draft of whatever you're working on. . . story area, outline, script. . . on the day you were told it's due. The ramifications for being late could be anything from not getting another episode to not getting your option picked up — and so even if it means burning the midnight or weekend oil, get that draft done and turn it in.

I once wrote a script that everyone universally loved. . . and then we had to re-break the back half of the season and that meant rebreaking that episode. . . throwing more than half of it away.

But our schedule was our schedule. . . so the ask from my showrunner was "can you write a new version by the studio due date," which was three days away. So that's what I did. In that case, he sent me out of the room and I locked down until a new draft was ready. . . because the deadline is always the deadline.

Where to do your writing: Pro tip, the office is always the answer.

I mentioned earlier in the book that sometimes showrunners may say that people can write at home (when you're allowed to leave the room to work on your drafts). A lot of upper-level writers will take advantage of this because they prefer to work at home in their own environment. But my advice for any lower-level writer is to say thanks for the offer, but then to show up every day and write in your office.

Why?

Because you're trying to build a reputation, and being the person who is present, is always part of the team, and works hard is the foundation of that reputation. But you need to be around people for them to see it. If you're in the office and something comes up regarding your episode — a casting issue, a guest star change, a location idea — the showrunner or upper levels can find you immediately and have that conversation with you in person. That helps them save time, and it benefits you because you are getting face time with people who will be references and maybe future employers someday, and they're seeing you in your office, working hard, being accessible to them.

Which leads me to an important point: *Don't close your office door.*

Sure, your showrunner probably closes his or her door when working — that's because everyone wants to talk to the show-runner, and the closed door is a sure sign: I'm writing, and leave me alone until that door opens.

But you? You are, again, building a rep. And you'd be shocked how often someone might wander past your open door, pop in, and say, "Hey, did you use X pitch in your episode? If not, I might have a space for it." Or, "Hey, I know you're writing, but can I just run this logic by you? Everyone else is gone for the day."

Part of why I still write at the office, even as an upper-level writer, is that my showrunners are still going into the office while other writers are working at home. *You never want your showrunner to be the only writer in the office during business hours.* What if an idea arises and there's no one around to riff with? Or worse, what if there's an emergency on set and the show-runner needs help making script changes? So I tend to go in even if I have permission not to — and it has never failed that I end up getting a visit with a "Hey, what do you think about X?" while I'm in there typing away.

So even if you really want to shut that door. . . don't do it.

Learning your "working writer" process; it may not be the same as your "writing my own stuff" process.

We all have our perfect writing setup at home. Mine is on my couch, TV on, bulldog right beside me. I always write with the TV on. It's the latchkey kid in me, and I just can't be productive without it.

So how did I make that work when I had to write in an office?

Thankfully I came into the game after the birth of streaming. So Netflix and Hulu were already great options for me because they had some of the classic shows I write to over and over again. I keep that door open, as stated above, but I pop in my headphones and on a minimized screen, let *Friday Night Lights* or some other perfect writing show play in the background.

Writers who love to write with music can do the same thing.

Are you the type of writer who needs to take a break every hour? You can do that in the office, too. Set an alarm or get an hourglass for your desk. When it's time, head for the break room or the restroom or go outside for a quick walk. You can even pop in the room to see how things are going without you. You don't have to be tied to your desk for eight hours straight.

I've worked with writers who like a lit candle in their office while they're writing, or who need a blanket to be cozy; writers who bring their own little cache of snacks or beverages because it's what they'd usually have at home; and writers who requested couches in their offices so they could write lying down.

What I'm saying is, you can make it work. It won't be just like home, but you can make sure you're in your best writing headspace and still be present in the office.

Emergency re-writes: how to be part of the solution

Whether it's your episode or not, you may get an "all hands" request that brings everyone back into the writers' room. As I mentioned in my rant about group-writing, emergencies happen. Production may call saying Number One on the call sheet has a medical issue and can't film for two days or a location falls out and the room needs to brainstorm alts.

These types of emergencies are usually about surgical changes. For instance, if Number One is unavailable for two days of shooting, everyone will look at the scenes that have not been shot and brainstorm ways to trim that actor out of the story entirely, postpone the scenes if the schedule has some wiggle room, or reconstruct the story so that another character can carry the weight of important information.

Have a location drop out? That usually means something like that huge set piece we had carefully constructed in an abandoned mall now has to take place in a park. What can we still do that's cool and fun and gives us the spirit of what we started with?

Sometimes the goal is trimming pages out of an episode that's either going seriously over budget or running into production issues — like weather. Again, you'll start with the scenes that haven't been shot — figure out what's crucial to make the episode work — and then try to pitch changes that will help accomplish the goal.

When this happens, don't feel like you have to be the one to solve the problem, but if you have something constructive to offer, do speak up. It can be intimidating at first because you probably have a production schedule — a "one liner" — in front of you, and if you don't have much experience with them, it can be hard to know exactly what everyone's discussing when they say they need to "replace 4 3/8 pages." (For the record, scheduling is done by breaking every script page into eighths. That's what that number means.) But remember, no one necessarily expects you to know what all that means (though we'll discuss that later on). Listen, learn, and ask questions after the emergency has been solved so you are better prepared for the next time.

TRUE TALES OF LIFE INSIDE
A WRITERS' ROOM

FEMALE DRAMA WRITER ON MOVING UP
IN THE EPISODE ORDER

Our show shot out of state, so I was on the East Coast producing one episode when my Number Two — and co-writer of my next episode — called me from LA during lunch. We had just turned in our studio draft and weren't expecting to get network notes until the following week with a production draft still two weeks out. But during the day an issue had come up with the episode scheduled to shoot before ours, which meant we were moving up in the shooting order. That meant that even though I was on set and had been working for twelve hours, I had to make time to read through the notes, help figure out the adjustments we needed to make, and get the network draft in ASAP. So I went home, read the current version (my Number Two had already made several of the changes), adjusted the scenes I had taken responsibility for, and shipped the script back to

California. Then I went to bed, got up, and went back to shoot the episode I was on set to produce the next morning. A true "that's what the money's for" moment.

FEMALE DRAMA SHOWRUNNER
ON WHY SCHEDULES MATTER

One of the least sexy things about running a show is keeping everything on track and on schedule. Back when I was a Number Two, it was always my job to make the writers' schedule — building in healthy turnaround times for every draft of every document, from story area to production draft.

So on the first day of a new season one show, I went to my showrunner and asked if he wanted me to make a writers' schedule as I usually did. He said no. He hated schedules, didn't want one, because they made him feel like he was always behind. That a schedule "kills creative genius."

This is some bullshit. And yes, that showrunner was one of those "creative geniuses" who's also a toxic, abusive, "avoid unless you can't make the mortgage/college tuition for your kids" problem.

A good schedule keeps everyone on a staff accountable. It lets writers see their deadlines — and reminds the showrunner of when to expect documents or drafts and makes it possible to schedule time. On my shows, I circulate the schedule on day one, and I hang it on a whiteboard in the hall. Everyone gets the same time for documents, regardless of level. And I put script assignments on the board — no wondering when you're going to get a script, or if your script is going to land at the same time as your best friend's wedding, or when you can schedule that overdue but agonizingly necessary root canal.

Any showrunner who doesn't have a writers' schedule? Fasten your seatbelts; it's gonna be a bumpy ride.

WRITERS' SCHEDULES   115

7.

ROOM POLITICS

How to avoid taking sides, not become a pawn, and stay out of harm's way

I DON'T THINK IT'S A GREAT SURPRISE to anyone that when you have a group of people who work together five days a week on an intense creative project, sometimes people have bad days, lose their tempers, get snippy, or frankly just behave badly. We're all human beings. . . and we'll all have bad moments. Having a little grace for each other goes a long way toward keeping things calm and friendly.

Room politics, though, is more than just folks having a moment. It's when someone or multiple someones allow their insecurities or competitive natures to affect the room. It can start at any level. . . showrunner, staff writer, and anywhere in between. It can fall along gender lines, slip into obvious power dynamics, and be utterly destructive to the creative process.

For example, what if you have two EPs on a show who have wildly different views of what the show is, and they both have equal say in how the show moves forward? This is incredibly difficult to navigate. You're talking about two people who both have the showrunner's ear, but the showrunner has consciously or unconsciously created a dynamic in which two people who can't agree on much are both giving writers input on their room breaks and drafts.

This is definitely a tough one — because you have to respect both of these people and you need to make a real effort to accommodate their notes. But what happens when you think one is right about something and the other gave you a totally contradictory note? That's when you do the fix you feel is correct but send in your next draft with a note saying, "I tried it both ways, and this felt best to me, but obviously I can go the other route if you all think that's best." Or you ask to have a conversation with both parties and discuss it so they can talk it out with each other, and you get resolution on the direction they can agree upon. I'm not going to lie: No parts of this are comfortable to deal with. But to the extent you can take action to keep other people from becoming obstacles to your meeting your deadlines, do what you can. If it means an email to both EPs saying, "Hey, just wanted to clarify. Writer X, you said this, and writer Y, you said this. If I try this, does that address the note for both of you?" Or you can set up that call to discuss. Or you can just take a swing and add the "tried it both ways" note when you send it in. So take a deep breath, pick your approach, and do what you can to get a clear answer.

And what happens when you have a co-EP who is a natural-born shit stirrer? First of all, you need to realize this person is all about himself or herself. This person likes chaos and pissing people off, and often people get used to achieve that goal. What does this look like in practice? It looks like a toxic co-EP telling another writer to "stand up" to the EPs or showrunner about something in the process that isn't actually an issue — a note, an assignment. That is someone setting a writer up to get a scolding or to be looked at as a problem. Or the co-EP gets a great piece of gossip and spreads it around the room as quickly as possible so that whoever is the subject of said gossip will be ambushed by it when the room reconvenes. Or the co-EP likes to talk shit about other people on staff and wants to try and rope you in and get you involved.

The latter happened to me once, and I emailed a trusted friend who was already a co-EP to ask for advice as the conversation was happening because I was in my office, trapped by an upper-level writer, and I had no idea how to stay safe. My friend told me, "Don't agree to anything; don't disagree; just try to get out of it asap." So I nodded a lot, said a lot of "huh," in acknowledgment to statements that felt like traps, and found an excuse to leave my office when it felt safe to do so. I escaped without agreeing to anything that could come back to bite me later if this person wanted to go to my boss or someone else on staff and say, "Well, Niceole thinks. . ." about anything.

Some of what follows will definitely feel like common sense stuff — but the pressure you'll feel in the moment these issues arise is intense. You're usually managing the B.S. of people with more power than you — and it's uncomfortable and difficult. But you can do it and escape without doing damage to yourself or getting dragged into someone else's drama.

Never punch up. Never punch down. Basically, don't punch.

You'll hear this phrase a lot in this business: "Don't punch down." Generally what it means is, don't ever intentionally do harm to those with less power than you. Even as a staff writer, you have more power in the room and on staff than the PA, writers' assistant, and script coordinator. Don't be a jerk in your interactions with them. Respect the hard work they do and remember even if they want to help you asap, they may have requests ahead of yours. Basically, just never lose sight of the fact that people deserve to be treated like people, not robots there to run errands, get your lunch, or answer your questions.

For instance, if the PA messes up lunch, you can take him or her aside privately and point out the need to double-check the order before it comes back. You don't have to make a scene in front of the showrunner, humiliating that person. If the writers' assistant didn't get something in the notes, you can again speak one on one and ask if there's a reason that the thing we pitched yesterday didn't make it into the notes. You don't have to embarrass the person by calling the issue out in the room.

This can be much harder than it sounds. Because not every person on your support staff will be great at their job. While the overwhelming majority of assistants, PAs, and coordinators I've worked with have been fantastic, a few have not been up to the job. And I'm not going to sit here and tell you I've always handled that well. In one particular instance, my showrunner later teased me about trying to egg on a particular support staffer whose constant inattention in the room made me crazy. I had to actively bite my tongue to not snap at this person when I saw them not typing while we were pitching our hearts out. But being a bitch wasn't going to make me feel better in the end, so I fought that instinct to be one every single day.

Another time, a PA I worked with was convinced he should have been staffed and deserved to be in the room. So he would only order us lunch from places that delivered so he could try and spend more time with the writers. But let me tell you this: *Hungry writers are bastards,* and writers tired of eating at the same three or four places are hungry, angry writers. And that PA didn't last much longer after we figured out what was happening — not because we didn't understand the desire to move up, but because the only way to do that successfully is to be invested in the job you have at the moment. We all knew someone else would come in and be grateful for that gig instead of feeling resentful he or she had to take it.

Still. . . human beings make mistakes, and they don't deserve to be yelled at or belittled or "punched" by those above them.

Now I'll admit, I had never heard anyone discuss punching up until I saw it in action. To say I was stunned is the understatement of the millennium. . . because *who does that?!* And yet. . .

In one instance, a writer empowered by the showrunner to perform above their official rank threw a tantrum because they didn't like the story we were working on in the room. Said writer stormed out and didn't come back for quite a while. . . and the showrunner let the writer get away with it. Now some of that has to do with the fact that this showrunner had created an unrealistic power dynamic in the room. . . by treating this writer like an equal in rank, the showrunner had given this writer unspoken permission to assume more power than the writer really had. But still. . . you don't storm out of the room, ever. You *can* however excuse yourself to go get a snack or go to the restroom, and then cuss and grumble in the bathroom or out in the parking lot before you shake it off and come back inside.

In another instance, a writer a few levels below me decided a favorite pastime was going to be trying to pick a fight with me in the room. It was so obvious that at a certain point other upper-level writers in the room called it out and the behavior finally ended. But it undercut my natural desire to mentor and help writers below me in the hierarchy. I knew this was a writer who couldn't hear what I had to say because of whatever fueled this weird need to try and challenge me, so I focused my attention on the other writers and support staff who wanted my mentorship. . . and left that whole situation alone. But everyone in the room saw it, and none of them have forgotten it.

P.S., Every room has the person I affectionately call "the puppy." Trust me, that's not a derogatory term. This is the person in the room who is so universally beloved that the idea of any-one being short with or mean to them is unimaginable. *So you know who you never want to be? The person who kicks the puppy.* Your room will *never* forgive you for this. Whether it's an assistant or another writer, you can't lash out at the person everyone adores and unconditionally supports. It's the kind of thing that literally separates you from the rest of your room, probably forever. So don't do it. Don't treat anyone that way. . . obviously. . . *but definitely, positively, do not kick the puppy.*

Not everyone will like each other; the room can survive this.

Name me one group of people where every single person likes every other person.

I'll wait.

Right. . . that doesn't exist. Not in our families, not in our friend groups. There are always levels of love, friendship, and tolerance.

We've all heard stories about casts of our favorite show or movie who hated each other even though they were amazing together on screen, or teammates from championship-winning sports franchises who literally couldn't stand to be in the same room with each other when they weren't engaged on the court or field. It happens. . . sometimes because of insecurity, some-times because of jealousy, and sometimes because it's just bad chemistry.

This can happen in a room, too.

It is not fun, it can be hard to manage, and yes, it takes more energy to get through the room every day if there are one or two people who just make life harder. But the room can survive it.

Plenty of rooms aren't the kind of rooms who get together every Friday for a drink. Plenty of rooms are full of people who go to their offices and shut the doors as soon as possible to get away from people who drive them crazy.

But the work gets done.

It gets done because, hopefully everyone has a fundamental understanding of the fact that they are getting paid to do a job. . . and that they have an obligation to do that job to the best of their ability. They are not required to be friends with anyone. . . just to do the job.

Again, because we're all human, sometimes this will be hard. Some days you'll need to go into your writer buddy's office and just bitch for a few minutes about how that asshole can't even be bothered to contribute to the holiday bonuses the writers are putting together for the support staff, and seriously, what is his problem?

If you can have your rant, leave it behind you, and walk into the room to get the work done. . . everything is going to be fine.

And when all else fails, remind yourself that no job is forever. . . and you can put up with just about anyone for a finite period of time. So give yourself rewards for making milestones on your patience maintenance. Every week that passes with some small "I didn't lose my shit" pat on the back —a cookie, an extra drink, a treat from your favorite shop — is one week less you have to be around said person.

But the best way to deal with this is to build kinship with the writers and support staff you do enjoy. You can get together outside of the room, chat after hours, and be there for each other so that the hard moments in the room feel less hard because you know you're not in it alone.

I would also encourage you, though, to give everyone a chance and let them prove they don't deserve your consideration. I have a pretty firm policy in life, especially having grown up as a person of color, that I see how people treat me and react in kind. And I've been in situations in a writers' room where everyone — support staff through the Co-EP ranks — has one person on staff they just don't like. And they don't want you to like that person either. I will take the warnings about danger and bad attitude to heart, then I see how this person interacts with *me*. I don't let other people's takes on that person set the tone for my behavior.

In one particular example of this, I found the "nobody likes this person" target to be brusque and difficult. . . but generally respectful and eager to support my writing efforts. So I gave this writer a little brusque back (minus the difficult) — and it seemed to be exactly the thing that made us friends. No one could believe that I got along so well with this writer, but I firmly believe that it was about my giving this person a chance to show me who they were without letting other opinions cloud my judgment. Some people aren't easy; that doesn't mean they these folks can't be friendly and helpful. They just require more work to get to know. them. You can do the work or you can choose to save your time and energy. But definitely make the choice for yourself and never let the room tell you how to react to someone.

The big exception to this is if you are told "don't be alone with so and so" for whatever reason. . . she throws writers under the bus, he is handsy, he's a screamer. *If someone has the potential to be dangerous to you — physically or career-wise — don't let yourself get caught alone with that person.* Yes, I know. . . *why is that person still there?* But we're still trying to uncover some of the monsters in our business. . . and they are still working. You don't have to give the benefit of the doubt to someone who is a known abuser of writers — you just have to keep yourself safe. So if that writer wants to talk to you, make sure the office door stays open, or ask if the assistant can come in and take notes, or recruit an upper-level writer to ride shotgun.

If you can't avoid the situation, try and set up a plan to keep your safety paramount. Ask the assistant to interrupt at a specific time, ask that upper-level writer to come in with a question, and if all else fails, and you're in this alone, get up and say, "I'm sorry, but I have to go to the bathroom" and walk out. (We'll get into more of these strategies when we discuss toxic rooms. . . but I wanted to be sure to mention this here.)

Factions: why they happen, how to deal with them

The development of factions is a terrible thing for a show. . . but it does happen. This is the worst form of room politics. This is when, say, a co-showrunner is pushing for A and the other co-showrunner is pushing for B. Some people got hired because the A showrunner loved their work, and the B show-runner wasn't so sure. Some were the exact opposite. Some have been friends with one or both of these showrunners for years and have history that plays into their reactions to what's happening.

And then there's you. . . the staff writer, wondering what the hell is going on.

People will start to feel like they have to choose sides when factions develop. But I'm here to tell you: *Don't do it*. Because whether you're on the winning side or not, you'll create bad feelings with the writers on the other side, and that could translate into people shit-talking you to execs, to nonwriting producers, and later to other showrunners.

This will mean a concerted effort on your part not to get pulled into any closed-door conversations with either side. Because it only takes one for people to think you've made a choice about which team you're on. And it means thinking long game vs. immediate gratification. Sure, if you support that idea showrunner A loves, that person will think you're great, but if showrunner B has already voted firmly against going down that road, you aren't endearing yourself to that showrunner at all by chiming in.

Factions don't always have to exist at the showrunner level. Remember when I mentioned those EPs who have different visions of the show? Or when you have co-EPs competing to be the showrunner's favorite? Those situations are also prime fodder for factions to develop and for people to feel pressured to choose sides.

Another way this room division can happen is when you have talent that is also a producer on the project. If Number One on the call sheet also has the power of an EP credit, he or she can actively end up causing problems by recruiting writers to one side of a dispute with the showrunner.

All of these situations are fraught, but they are all survivable. The key is for you to remain true to yourself and to keep your best interests at heart. . . *meaning to keep your career in focus.* Is being part of a victory in this moment going to serve you long term? Is keeping your head down going to help you stay popular with the studio rather than making them think of you as a problem? Is it going to help you if one actor thinks you're on their team when the rest of the cast feels betrayed by your allegiance to said actor, especially when the majority support the showrunner?

If you find yourself in one of these situations, the best thing you can do for yourself is reach out to one of your mentors and talk it through. Get advice. And let that network that you've built help support you through a difficult show.

Silly stuff and room superstitions (a.k.a., why someone might freak out if you put up a poster in your office)

You've gotten your job, your ID, and your parking pass, and you've gotten your new office where you're going to write TV for a living. Now you want to make it feel like yours.

So what do you do if someone says, "Don't decorate"?

I've never had it happen to me, but I've heard stories of it happening. . . and while it may seem silly, there's a logic to it for the showrunners and writers who feel this way.

Most TV shows don't succeed. It sucks, but it's true. So imagine that someone says, "If you decorate your office, the show will get canceled," and you do it anyway and then the show gets canceled.

Your brain surely knows that your putting up your favorite TV or film poster didn't affect the success or failure of the show. But someone said it out loud. . . and it's hard to shake.

So yeah, you'll encounter this on first-year shows because frankly everyone is looking for a little good luck to keep you on the air to get to season two. No one is punking you. This is real TV show superstition, and you are just on a show that believes this wholeheartedly.

But let's say you do decorate and your showrunner hates something you put up? Do you take it down? For me, the answer is no. You just have to find a way to be you and deal with the shit you're going to have to take for whatever the item is.

For example, on one gig, I put up a poster for a show my showrunner hated. . . and he used to say things to me like, "I can't believe I hired you and you like that show." I'd just say, "Well, it's too late now" and joke right back to him. Another writer had a piece of Army memorabilia in his office because he was a West Point grad. One of the other writers, who had been in the Navy, gave him shit about it constantly. But he'd just say, "Hooah" and keep it light.

Sometimes decorating becomes an office game, and it can be a fun way to keep everyone's spirits up even when the ratings are falling. I worked with a die-hard Patriots fan. . . and if you know me, well, *no*. So we had a constant back and forth decorating each other's doors with anti- and pro-Patriot images. We had a lot of fun, and it let everyone in the office play along. One of my favorite exchanges was when this other writer put a photo of Tom Brady on my wall with a dialogue bubble where he declared his love for me and wondered why I didn't love him back. I added an image of The Rock and wrote a note saying, "Tom, she has me. Why in the world does she need you?"

I mean, fair question. Also. . . I still hate the Patriots. And Tom Brady. (I'm sure he cries about this a lot. . . /end sarcasm.)

True Tales of Life Inside a Writers' Room

Female drama writer on managing difficult personalities

Your first year on the job can take you many places. In my case, the most defining might've been: the cold, wet basement of one of my co-EPs. But context might help explain how I got there: Very early on in my first year on the job, I realized that my show offered very few "openings" for me. Openings as in: positions I could step into and shine. Our writers' assistant was brilliant taking notes and writing on the board, the other staff writer was internally promoted and pitched like he was Sorkin himself. (Of course, being a white man among white men, he was also listened to like he was Sorkin). So what's a girl gotta do to earn her keep? Enter: the crazy co-EP.

It very soon became obvious that one co-EP, whether by sheer personality trait or a psychotropic medication imbalance, was unable to focus, unable to produce, and on top of it: loud and purposefully disruptive to the process in the room. Said co-EP would hijack entire days unraveling story that needed no unraveling. Pitching into the Nirvana of utter nonsense with enough conviction to accept nothing less than to be heard. Crazy co-EP, it seemed, was determined to derail the entire production. And after crazy co-EP's episode lingered on the board for about six weeks and even the showrunner couldn't get it off, while the room looked on in Stockholm Syndrome-inducing terror, one thing became clear: Something needed to change. Crazy co-EP needed a babysitter. A babysitter who would be nonthreatening enough as not to kick political hornet's nests but also smooth enough to guide madness toward sense. That would become my opportunity to shine. So while it brought me to the brink of my sanity, I befriended my "new mentor" and with an angels' patience that I never knew I had, I began to serve as both an audience to crazy co-EP's antics as well as a barely noticeable ghost writer. And now that crazy co-EP finally had a friend, the room and showrunner soon proposed a "split": Send crazy co-EP and me away to work out of crazy co-EP's home, so the remaining staff could actually get some real work done. So there I was, managing crazy. Trapped in crazy Co-EP's basement.

My takeaways on managing crazy (or "difficult personalities," as some like to call them) are relatively simple and anything but easy: Know that it will be hard. Know that it will require a lot of patience and self-control. Know that you will have to parent *parents much older than you, but most importantly: Know that your sweet spot lies between a nonthreatening approach, slight flattery, and a perceived sense of admiration and collaboration, and the magic trick of making them believe that your ideas were theirs. In other words, story muscle was less of what I built during my first year on the job. And I certainly couldn't see the benefit of learning how to handle crazy while I was sitting there, trapped in that cold basement. I felt isolated, unappreciated, and forgotten until daily messages began to pour in from the rest of the staff: "We appreciate you taking this hit." "Hang in there." "Stay sane!" And that, I did.*

FEMALE DRAMA UPPER-LEVEL WRITER
ON ROOM CONFIDENTIALITY

On the first day of every room, the showrunner usually reminds the staff that what we say in the room stays in the room. We need that cone of silence because the writers' room can't function without trust and confidentiality, making it safe to share the personal experiences that enrich our stories with nuance and authenticity.

Sounds good. But it doesn't always happen that way. My second week as a staff writer, I told a story in the room. It was a true story about a situation I'd been a part of. But it wasn't just my story. As soon as I finished telling it, a co-EP said to the room, "I'm so writing that story as an episode." My heart hit the floor.

At the break, I told her it wasn't her story to tell — hell, it wasn't only mine. She laughed in my face. I begged her to understand. The other people in the story knew I was on the show; they'd recognize themselves in the story. And I couldn't do that to them. Someday I might tell that story — if they were ready, with their consent.

She was unmoved . . . and just tauntingly said, "Welcome to Hollywood. Everyone's story is up for grabs." She told me to get over it. She said if I complained, the showrunner would probably fire me for trying to spike a good episode.

I didn't know better, so I believed her. I cringed as the story got broken, written, and shot, and even garnered an Emmy nod. The whole time I felt awful, but I didn't think there was anything I could do. Decades later, I know better. What I should've done was go to other writers on the staff for help and guidance. I shouldn't have suffered in silence. There are always mentors and allies on every staff, but you have to take the first step and let folks know you need help.

And anyone who breaks the confidentiality of a room, dead to me.

8.

Oh, the Places You'll Go. . . Once Production Starts

Writing the script is one thing.
Now you get to talk about it. . . a lot.

Once you've survived all the notes and revisions to get to a production draft, it's time to expand the team from the writers' room out to production. That means a lot more people are going to ask you questions about what things mean, play word semantics, dig for more detail, or ask for changes.

Welcome to prep and production!

But before you dive in, here are a few things to be aware of.

Most importantly, being part of prep and going to set for production is not guaranteed. If you're getting the opportunity, make the most of it, don't be afraid to ask questions, *and be clear on what your showrunner expects from jump.* Some showrunners empower even staff writers to make line changes and decisions in prep and on set; some want everything cleared through them; most of them will want you to call them for major changes that are requested on the fly.

Being clear on what you can do and what you need approved is imperative. In prep, you'll have more time because you can always say, "Let me check with the showrunner on that," and get back to folks. But on set, time ticks by fast, and if you have permission to handle issues on set, then you'll want to make a decisive, informed choice as quickly as possible, even if that choice is to pull out the phone and say, "Let me get an answer on that" and call the boss.

Once you're clear on what you can handle yourself and what needs more direction, the next big piece to remember, even if no one tells you, is that lots of people will probably try to get you to talk about upcoming episodes they haven't read yet because those drafts are still in progress — especially your actors — but sometimes the crew as well. So the rule you never want to forget is: *What gets said in the room stays in the room.*

Now, I say "never forget," but the truth is, at some point you could slip up because you'll be friendly with people, and someone will ask a question framed innocently enough, and suddenly you'd find yourself saying something you know you shouldn't about a story that's been pitched or an idea that got shot down. The best way to prevent this is to think about it ahead of time, to remind yourself that everyone knows what's happening through X episode (whatever scripts have been distributed to cast and crew) and that's all you can discuss. Pre-plan an answer like, "Good stuff coming, but you know the men in black will come get me if I tell you," or think of some other fun way to brush the questions aside.

Part of why I'm giving you this warning is that it's happened to me. I was once in a situation with a difficult director who was fighting me on how a scene was supposed to be staged. I knew the director was trying to put more importance on the scene than was warranted because this wasn't the launch pad for a great romance. One of these characters was being killed off. And so exhausted and frustrated, I blurted that out to my director.

Yeah. . . *not good.*

I immediately did what I've told all of you to do in sticky situations. I called a trusted upper-level writer friend, told them what I had done, and asked for advice. The advice was simple and clear but something I couldn't think of myself in my panic. I sent the director a text basically saying, "Hey, obviously what I told you today is confidential. The cast isn't aware of that, so please keep it between us."

The director responded that of course this was understood, and nothing was ever said about it again, even though this director and I got along worse and worse as the shoot went on.

But that wasn't the end of it for me. I was worried sick that actor would hear the news before my showrunner was ready to share it. It wasn't until that episode with his death was filmed, honestly, that I stopped worrying about my slip-up and was able to let the mistake go with a promise to myself that it would never happen again.

In retrospect, I think if the same type of thing happened to me now, I probably would have made a call so that my showrunner was aware there was a small risk there. Not because I'm brave and noble, but because the stress of living with the worry was overwhelming. I'd rather risk getting yelled at and get it over with than worry about the other shoe dropping at any time. So learn from my mistake and try not to say the thing in the first place, but if you do, minimize the damage as quickly as possible. . . to the show and to yourself!

On another show, someone else dropped the bomb on an actor that the character was going to be killed off before my boss and the actor had that conversation, and my showrunner got to deal with the fallout of that. We were lucky because this actor was incredibly gracious and really just wanted to tell us why, hopefully, the character was not "dead dead," and it was because of how much this performer loved working on the show, but it was a stressful walk up to set that day — let me tell you!

In another situation, a scene that had been cut from the production draft was added back in on a shoot day when we were trying to fill time due to a late actor. When I was asked why the scene had been cut in the first place by the actor featured in the scene, I honestly said, "we were worried about time" because it was clear that the episode was going to run long. But I didn't want the actor to think we didn't consider the scene valuable. We obviously had wanted it, but we were trimming pages for the shooting schedule. So it was important to me that the actor, who was pivoting very quickly to accommodate our request, knew we thought the words were important to the episode.

If your show is on the bubble, everyone may be asking you what you've heard about the chances of a back-nine pick-up (if you're on broadcast and starting with an episode order under twenty-two) or if you're getting picked up for the next season. Even if you have heard something, this is where you say, "We're all really hopeful," and leave it at that. The last thing you want to do is be on set prognosticating about the chances of your show's survival, because if you call it wrong or reveal information that your boss discussed with the writers in confidence, you're going to feel like a total jackass.

Okay, now that we've talked about what you shouldn't say, let's talk about all the talking you're going to have to do, because prep is a lot of talking about every single detail in your script.

First things first: Print and prep your script. Keep it with you at all times!

Yes, I said "print." That's a thing some of us dinosaurs still do. If you're a person who doesn't like paper drafts and works off a tablet or computer, also fine — *but you'll need to be sure you're always on the most current version of the script* and that you have a way of moving/adding notes to your current draft as things evolve in prep. You'll also want to be able to add notes from your Tone meeting, where your showrunner lays out specific desires to the director about the emotional content or beats in a scene (more on this later).

By "prep your script," I mean, get it ready for all the notes and changes to come. If you're old school, put the script in a binder and you can add other important documents to this as you go (schedules, call sheets, etc.). Make sure you have pens on hand and tabs or sticky notes for quick reference items. For instance, if you know you're going to have to discuss a scene on set that comes up later in the shoot, have it flagged so you can flip right to it once your director has time to chat. If you're using an electronic version, be sure you know how to add notes to the PDF or script file so you can deal with them later.

Some important terminology

These are names or phrases you'll hear a lot in prep or on set, so for quick reference:

One liner. the shooting schedule for the episode, broken down into the work for each day, the page count, and the estimated time each scene will take to complete

Day out of days. a chart of which cast members are needed on each shoot day

Shooting schedule. a day-to-day listing of scenes, locations, and vital elements: picture cars, extras, costumes, graphics, props, etc.

Prep schedule. the daily list of meetings needed to prep each episode. These change frequently depending on everyone's schedule, so always be sure you have the most current version.

Scripty. your script supervisor. Be friends with this person, who will help you get every shot you need for your episode.

Comteks/cans. Comteks refer to the sound packs provided to you, Scripty, the director, and others so you can hear the dialogue delivery during shooting. "Cans" refer to the headphones. You can definitely bring your own headphones if you have specific needs — for instance, I can't wear over-the-ear headphones, so I bring my ear buds to all my shoots.

Call sheet. the detailed list of who's needed on set each day and when. You should receive one daily for your episode. Be sure to check for crew call time — that's usually when your first rehearsal is up, and you want to be sure you're on set at least fifteen minutes before that. Also check with the 1st or 2nd assistant director (AD) to see if any pre-call director's rehearsals are scheduled and if you can attend. (Pro tip: You're the writer; you should always be welcome to attend.)

Five-dollar Fridays. On Fridays, everyone writes their name on a $5 bill (or more) and tosses it in a bin. At the end of the day, a winner is chosen. If you win, donate your winnings to the PA department. Writers should never keep the Friday fun money! (Sometimes this is also done by writing names on playing cards — same basic idea.)

Abby. the penultimate shot setup of the day

Martini. the last shot setup of the day

Meeting your director

Hopefully this is step one of official prep for you — either before your Concept meeting or at the meeting itself. Try to set up time to chat with the director separately so you can find out how to handle the process. Does the director want to save up script notes from a few meetings and then come to you with ideas/changes or does he or she want to send you stuff after each meeting? Find a way to establish good communication right away — exchange emails and phone numbers so you can text easily and forward each other documents and photos from departments during prep if one of you doesn't get them.

Good vs. bad directors = good creative partners vs. bad creative partners

When it comes to directors, an important thing to remember is that, unless you're working with the producing director of your show or someone from your cast/crew directing, this person is coming into your show as a guest — but a welcome one. The hope is the director is a good partner and someone the crew and cast enjoy working with.

So what makes someone a good director vs. a bad director? A big part of it is being a team player. Someone who understands that you're the expert on the show but that you respect the creative vision and input of your team. The director will ask you, the 1st AD, or the line producer questions about how the show functions — how rehearsals are handled, whether there is a table read, which actors like to have sidebars about the script. . . and they'll come in with pitches on locations or design that enhance what's already on the page. They will probably also have story notes — which is part of the gig. Your showrunner usually has final say over whether those story changes make it into the script, but always pass them on because you want your director to feel heard.

What makes a bad director? Someone who thinks rewriting the episode is part of the job is a big one. You end up needing to point out the obvious: This script has been vetted by the producers, studio, network, and showrunner — so while you're open to thoughts, there isn't going to be any major rewriting happening here. If the director is not listening to you when you say those things, that's a problem because it means he or she won't listen to you on set when you raise issues that go counter to your showrunner's wishes. You also want someone who is respectful of the crew and department heads — directors who don't learn people's names or who treat the crew in a servant-like manner make professionals care a little less. . . and that's never good for on-set morale. You also want someone who understands that while a director is needed and welcome, the goal here is to follow the model of the show. No one is coming in to reinvent the wheel after the style of the show has been established.

What you can do if there's conflict

If you find that you and your director have gotten off on the wrong foot, the first thing I'd recommend is asking if you can jump on a call or sidebar in person, just the two of you. You can frame the conversation like, "Hey, I just feel like we're butting heads a lot, and I want to feel like I'm supporting you on this episode. So can we talk about the process a little?" and see if you can reach a resolution. Directors coming into TV from features bump up against the level of involvement TV writers have in prep and on set, so you may also need to say something to this type of director like, "I know this is different in features, but here the showrunner has final say, and I'm the showrunner's proxy, so we need to make sure we're communicating well with each other so our episode can be really successful."

If you have a good, supportive line producer or unit production manager, you can also ask these people for advice. They may have worked with the director before or know people who have and be able to give you some insight into how to build a better relationship with the director.

And you can always, always talk to the 1st AD, communicate that the showrunner is going to have issues with X, and ask them for help steering the conversation on that point with the director.

What you can't do if there's conflict

You will very badly want to say to your showrunner, "So and so isn't listening to me," when conflicts arise. But you want to avoid that. That isn't to say you can't express some frustrations to your showrunner — you may need them to be part of the conversation. But you need to always frame the conversation in terms of your trying to solve a problem, not your throwing the director under the bus. (Trust me, they usually do that themselves.)

For example, I had a situation where a director wanted to cut a scene. I ran it by the showrunner, and the response was, "No, I like that scene. I want it shot as is." I relayed that to the director. The next day, the director had gotten the actors up in arms about the scene and came to me with, "Well, the actors don't want to do it now." Yeah, that wasn't fun. So I called my showrunner, explained the situation, and asked him how he wanted me to handle it. He decided he needed to step in and have that conversation directly because it was also about our relationship as writers to our cast. After that, we agreed that we could do things as scripted and then try them the way this director wanted — but it remained a struggle for me to keep the director on script and to stop the attempts to rewrite the episode to a different idea of what the show was.

On a different show, another writer was on set to produce an episode I had co-written. They called to inform the other writer and me that the director wanted to change the choreography of a big action set piece, but the choreography change didn't make sense storywise. The writer stressed to us that the director didn't much care what we as writers had to say. So we did the only thing we could: We went to the showrunner and pointed out what the director wanted to do and why it didn't work and asked the showrunner to step in. Unfortunately, that showrunner thought we were being "hysterical" and didn't make the call. When the dailies (the selected takes the director likes from the previous shoot day) of that set piece came in and they were disastrous, the showrunner came and asked us what happened. And I clearly and calmly said, "We tried to warn you there was going to be a problem." The showrunner knew we had and went off to try to fix it in post without further comment.

Let me stress here that most of my directors have been great. They have been people who love directing episodic TV and like having fun and want the environment to be one where the cast and crew feel set up to succeed. But if you run across the other kind, you'll have to be strategic in how you handle things.

As an addendum, I'll say that if you have a bad director, do what you can to help support your crew at all costs. If that means eventually you have to pick up the phone and call the showrunner and say, "Director X wants to do this and it's not safe for actor A or crewmember B," then you do it. *Safety is number one, always.* . . and you should never let a director move forward with something that feels unsafe to you until you have sign-off on the people above you because if something goes wrong, the showrunner, studio, and network are going to want to hear what you thought and why you didn't say anything if you were worried.

But it's also about emotionally supporting your crew. If they need answers the director isn't giving them, try to get the answers for them. If the cast is frustrated over an issue, see if you can help the director smooth it over. In production, the crew is an extension of that family unit you have in the writers' room, and anything you can do to be appreciative, supportive, and encouraging is going to help you get through hard days with more smiles and better results. A bad director can cause a downward turn in morale. So if you can arrange an extra-special food truck treat or plan a fun giveaway on set, do it. They will know you're invested in them, even if they feel discounted by the director. (Food trucks or special giveaways near the end of shooting are commonplace. You'll never go wrong with a quality coffee or dessert truck — or a giveaway for something like Apple Store gift card. The cost for this is usually split between the director and on-set writer [you!]. If you're director balks, do it yourself. Trust me! Someone in the production office will help you set it up. . . and everyone will love you.)

Prep: What are all these meetings? Why do they matter?

This segment will include a breakdown of key prep meetings and what happens in them. Keep in mind that for some of these, the writer is mostly there to answer a question if it comes up. The 1st AD and director should be driving the meetings, and while you can definitely ask for clarification on issues or offer opinions, if you're in conflict with something the director mentions, it's probably best to sidebar it, talk one on one after, and then communicate the resolution to the people who need to know the final answer on the issue.

Concept. This is where the 1st AD will run through the script scene by scene highlighting props, cars, makeup requirements, locations we may need to find, sets we're using, sets we need to build — basically calling out the headlines of the story/episode. This allows the director to make specific requests early *(for example, can we try and make sure the cars in the parking lot are high-end, not beaters?)* and lets the department heads get to work on what they need to acquire/create for the episode.

Location Scouts. Your Locations department will start brainstorming locations to accommodate the episode the second they get the script (or even earlier, at outline). With input from the director, they'll select spots you'll go see in person. Depending on the show, the director can get final approval on locations — but in some cases, photos/videos get sent to the showrunner to say, "This is what the director picked" and the boss will approve or tell you to keep looking. Ultimately most of these choices will be made above your pay grade, but it's okay to say things like "this looks like what I imagined" or "I'm not sure the action will work as written because of x, y, and z" just to make it clear what will and won't need to change if the director goes with that spot.

Location scouting usually involves a whole day (or several days) of driving around in a van where you will probably also have time to talk about script concerns or other issues the director wants to discuss. So take advantage of that time if you can.

This will probably also include a tour of your standing sets if your director hasn't worked on the show before. And if it's your first episode, be sure to ask your 1st AD if you can get a walk around so your first time on the show's stages isn't the day you start shooting there. You may see things on the tour that will help when someone's like "Hey, can we shoot this somewhere other than the hallway?" because now you'll be familiar with the geography and be able to pitch an alternate spot for the scene.

Table read. A lot of shows don't do table reads anymore, which is a bummer, because it's a great chance to get feedback from the director and actors *before* you're on set with the clock running on your shoot day. If you do have them, hopefully your showrunner has stressed to the cast that they have a window after the table reads to bring up any script issues they have. This will also help cut down on day-of conversations. If you are on a show that doesn't have time in the schedule for table reads, be sure to try and get intel from other writers who have been to set on who in the cast is well-prepared, who may come to set without knowing their lines, and who's likely to make a stink over dialogue or scene content at a rehearsal. This will help you strategize with your director on ways to head-off problems.

It depends on the show if Stunts, Picture Cars, Special Effects, and Visual Effects departments are grouped together or in separate meetings, but in general, they are:

Stunts. self-explanatory; your stunt team asks questions about any stunts written into the script so they can start planning to handle the scene. They may also pitch you alts if something feels too dangerous for the location or conditions. Large stunt sequences have separate rehearsal meetings. Be sure to ask if you can attend.

Picture Cars. Every car that appears on screen falls into this category. Some are "series regulars" — like the cars your main characters always drive or the police/fire/ambulance vehicles in procedurals. Some are determined by what's written in the script. If you write "luxurious Rolls Royce SUV," they're going to try to find one — but the show may not be able to afford that, so expect to get some pitches on what's more budget-friendly. And P.S., This is where word semantics can come into play. I wrote "metallic blue sedan" into a script and Picture Cars delivered exactly that — but the technical definition in the auto industry of a "metallic blue" paint was different than what my producers imagined, so they were shocked by the car color. It all worked out fine, but if someone's really particular about those details, you can always double-check with the director or an upper-level writer that the color/model is okay. (*In some cities, picture cars are handled by the Prop department and will be part of the props meeting.*)

Special Effects (SPFX). What effects are we doing practically in the episode? Smoke? A broken water pipe? An explosion? Are we setting squibs to create "gunfire" on set? These are the types of things that your special effects peeps will take care of. You are entitled to (and should) ask any questions you have about safety as SPFX are discussed.

Visual Effects (VFX). Depending on your show, VFX can be a long meeting. Every show uses visual effects, even cop shows. Enhanced fires, explosions, car crashes, gunshots, inserting the LA skyline when you shot a scene in Valencia instead of downtown. . .VFX will fix all of it for you. If you're on a VFX-heavy show, these conversations will usually involve your bringing in information from the showrunner and taking it back. For example, when I was on *Fate: The Winx Saga*, I took in specifics of what we wanted in certain scenes, the VFX team would get examples, and then I would relay to my showrunner what options we were trying and why.

Extras. Extras is the strange land of bringing in large groups of strangers to populate your scenes. You will think at first that you don't need to pay much attention to this, but it's a great place to really put your producer cap on and think about the full visual. The director will obviously also be keyed into this, but you can help point out potential problems that may not have come to mind yet for other people in the meeting.

For example, on one show, it was a story point that one of our lead characters was one of the few Black students at a private school. So we had to be sure our extras in the background supported that narrative. While working on location in a foreign country, you may need to tell Extras casting early on that they need to find diversity because that country is predominately white, but your show takes place in a city like New York or Los Angeles, and you want the background to feel like those cities.

And if you are counting on an extra to help sell a moment — to deliver a cutting look to a main character or play a visual cue — if your director doesn't suggest it, you can ask if they want to "cast" that person, meaning extras will ask for video of people doing the look or action you need them to do. All extras are not created equal, and if you need that snide "screw you" look as a button on the scene, you want to be sure the person you choose knows how to deliver.

Costumes. Your involvement in costumes, and even the director's, is dictated largely by what the process of the show's hierarchy is. I've been on shows where showrunners literally never want to hear about "approving a costume" and ones where they want to sign off on the looks. I've worked on shows where the studio and network or EPs weighed in heavily on looks for main cast and featured guest stars.

Mainly here, your purpose is to help communicate the vision if it's not clear in script: "I was thinking of urban sex appeal, like something H.E.R. would wear," and to confer with the director as costume choices come in to make sure everything looks the way it needs to for the episode. Keep a keen eye on having too many people in the scene in the same colors — you'd be amazed how easy it is to have everyone in a shade of blue because you like the individual looks but didn't imagine them all together. As your costume designer sends you looks, be sure to confer with the director (once shooting starts, it's easier for you to walk up and say, "Hey, did you see the costumes for our senator?" and show them the photos so you can both make a choice).

If there's an issue regarding what an actor wants to wear in a scene, that's a conversation for you, the director, and the costume designer to have together. Some actors may want to wear something less revealing when you have them in sexy attire or they'll have strong opinions on how their character would dress in a specific situation. And sometimes, if your talent has a producer credit on the show, they pick their own wardrobe and it's very tricky to push back on that unless you can get the EPs to support a choice because it's absolutely necessary.

Graphics. Graphics is everything that will appear on screens in your episode. . . text messages, cell phone caller IDs, computer screens, website text, ID photos, etc. And it can take a lot of effort to prepare all of this depending on the show you're on. (Imagine filling all the screens in S.W.A.T. HQ with info!) As with all these meetings, the director will provide leadership here, but it will be on you as the producing writer to make certain the graphics people get all the information they need.

In this meeting, your graphics designer will go through the pieces indicated in the script — "A text message from Niceole reads: Get out! Now!" and ask about what device it appears on, how you want it to look, etc. They'll also bring up things you may not have thought about. Oh, right. . . there's an online obituary in this scene. Someone needs to write that obit for the screen. Or if you have a scene where characters are in an "ops"-type center with lots of screens, you and the director will be asked what you want on all those screens during the scene.

This is where you do that reach-out to your support staff and see if they have time to help create all the additional text you need for screens. And remember, always give them a shout-out to the showrunner!

Graphics will also include photos you need for the episode — sometimes this involves a photographer (usually coordinated with the Art department) to take photos; sometimes it's your 2nd AD grabbing images as they can. I once was asked unexpectedly to supervise a photo shoot for an episode because the director had arranged a special rehearsal that day and couldn't do it. Legit thrown in the deep end, I made choices on the fly, asked questions when I wasn't sure, and ultimately in one situation did text my boss to get clarity on what an image really needed to convey. We got most of it, thank goodness. . . but I hope I never have to do that again!

Hair and Makeup. Hair and Makeup is something that, for regular cast, gets set pretty quickly in the life of the show, and like wardrobe, the actors, the showrunner, the EPs, and the studio/ network may have opinions on these things. But when it comes to your role here, it's helping the director identify any special makeup needed so the department heads can get to work on options. Does a character have a tattoo? That's makeup. Is there an accident and now someone's head and face are cut and bloodied? The hair and makeup people will be needed there, too.

You and the director will also be asked for input on important guest stars. Do you want them clean shaven, to have stubble, short hair, long hair, etc. This is an important reason you should have an image in your mind of what the character on the page looks like so you can communicate that vision and then be open to other ideas from the director and your team, who will often have the best solution to a hair or makeup issue.

Art department and Set Dec. The Art department and Set Dec peeps are going to create your entire environment for the shoot. They fabricate or find all the signage in that store you're making up. They make sure the teacher's house you wrote in act two looks like a teacher's house, not the house of a movie star pretending to be a teacher (i.e., too fancy). And when you need to make a backlot in LA look like an NYC street, they are the team that will pull it all together for you.

Try, if you can, to walk the sets before it's actually time to shoot so that you and the director can find any issues beforehand. Miscommunication happens even when you've had two meetings about the décor of a room. You go in expecting minimalist design, and it's a little too "Pottery Barn threw up in here." You can ask your production designer to have someone make adjustments before it's crunch time and you need cameras to roll.

Props. Props is exactly what you think it is. . . a list of everything someone touches, sees, or uses in an episode. Cell phones, computers, dishes, weapons, wallets. . . but there can be bits that get confusing here. The watch that a character specifically utilizes for a story point is probably a prop, but the one they wear because it's cool and looks good on the character is probably from Costumes. Things that are routine for characters like badges, wedding rings, sunglasses, etc. are the province of the Prop department. If you're ever not sure who handles something, it's okay to ask.

In this meeting, you'll run through details of the props: caliber, size, and color of guns; types of knives; a motorcycle helmet with a full visor or with no visor; a coffee cup with a logo that represents a story point — can we have options? Be prepared to answer questions and be a team player with your director. They'll be making most of these choices, but if you know something isn't quite right, you can bring it up and push a discussion.

On one episode I did, I was on set the day before I was actually taking over — so it was really the last day of the prior episode. Options for a prop that ran through both episodes were brought to set and the director picked the one he liked and off we went. But later I realized that in my episode a line of dialogue had changed, and the coffee mug didn't actually fit the line. Only we'd shot the line and the coffee mug already. It became one of those "oops" moments that happen on shows. . . though thankfully it was noticed by far fewer people than when a certain paper coffee cup ended up on a certain period fantasy show.

There is also often a follow-up Show-and-Tell meeting where prop options are shown so that selections can be made. This is another great chance to spot issues ahead of shoot day or to ask for additional options if the exact right prop hasn't been found.

Tech advisor (depending on the show). If you're on a show that requires a Tech advisor, you and the director will probably meet with him or her to work out specifics before you're on set with the actors. This helps present a united front on set when actors want to do things a certain way, but you've already had the discussion and there's a plan in place. On procedurals, this is usually a former police officer, on medical shows a former doctor or nurse, etc., etc.

Tech Scout. If you thought you spent a lot of time on Location Scouts, welcome to Tech Scout! Tech Scout is a day when you load up in the vans again and head for all the places you're actually shooting the episode. . . and this is where a final check is done on logistics for those shoot days. Where is crew parking? Where will all the trucks park? What rigging needs to be done for stunts? When do the Art department and Set Dec come in to set up?

This day is a lot of you being there to confirm elements that have already been discussed. . . yes, you did move that scene that used to be on the roof to the sidewalk, and the new pages are coming out today. That kind of thing. And it's a good chance to double-check any details you remain unclear on. How exactly is that one special shot in the scene where we see the bomber's hand going to be achieved? It's good for everyone to hear it again, so go ahead and ask the question.

Production meeting. The Production meeting is the final conversation with you, the director, the line producer, all the department heads, and the 1st AD. It's one last triple-check of all the details.

Tone meeting. The Tone meeting happens when the showrunner prefers it to happen. Some do it a day or two before shooting starts; some prefer earlier in the prep week. But this is essentially a meeting with you, the showrunner, the director, the EPs, and the line producer where the showrunner walks through the specifics of the most current draft of the script. He or she may highlight emotional notes they want to be sure the director is thinking of, ask questions about how something is going to be shot, talk about the pace and style of the show, and talk about on-set issues the director may not be aware of. Is there a rivalry between two actors that can slow production? Is there a set that's difficult to light? Is there a stressful situation going on with an actor that may make this episode more difficult than others?

It's important to make notes of these points for yourself because when you're on set, the director may have forgotten that it was really important to see character A fight back her emotions before she turns to bravely face another character. But if it's in your notes, you can say, "Hey, I think showrunner wanted to be sure we got this," and remind them. *This is also a really good reason that your script — printed or electronic — should never leave your hands and go to anyone else.* You don't want an actor to see a note that says, "Be sure her hands are busy, or she flails and it's distracting." That note is for you, so if you see it happening you can remind the director to put something in that actor's hands.

Casting: What's your role?

In most cases, casting for your episode will involve receiving audition videos for all the roles, watching them, and giving your top one to three choices. The director will do the same. Usually the showrunner gets the final select. If you have really strong, specific reasons for wanting to cast something a certain way, it's fine to say in an email to the director and showrunner, "I thought all three candidates were good, but I think it would be really fresh to have a female here, so X is my top choice." That doesn't mean it will go your way, but it's fine to make the case and see if you get the win.

Speaking up gets really important, though, when you see things you feel obligated to address. If you're casting a Black female guest star and you know that so far every Black woman cast on your show has been light-skinned, there may be some inadvertent colorism at work. So you can say, "Hey, I feel like we've been in a rut with our female casting, I think this actress has a fresh look, and her performance is great." If you need to be more overt with it, find the most helpful way to say, "I think the women we've cast have been great, but there's definitely sensitivity to this in the Black community, and I think it would be good for us to change up our dynamics a little." And of course, that advice works for all underrepresented communities. Speaking up to break harmful stereotypes is important, but when you're a lower-level writer, it takes a little political savvy. You can also always ask an upper level to help you fight the fight until you get a little more experience doing it yourself.

And you may lose the fight. . . but you'll know you tried, and you'll be less afraid the next time you have to speak up.

I once worked with a Black director who didn't even realize that everyone they picked to be a criminal was Black. They just wanted to cast Black actors they liked, which was great — but it was potentially about to send a message we didn't want to send. So we switched up our bad guy cast so they came from a mix of racial groups.

Sometimes people at the studio/network level also don't realize the patterns they've fallen into. They want to believe they're being inclusive and leaving all the old "isms" behind, but often the behavior is unconscious. That's why you still see older men cast with women who aren't age appropriate even though many of us now want to see the forty-something guy with the forty-something woman. You should choose your battles here wisely, and usually the best strategy is to express your concern to the showrunner and let them push back on the studio or network if they agree with you. Remember, it's not your show, so ultimately the decision is out of your hands.

A quick note for any showrunners or execs who might be reading this book, though. Sometimes we'll include things in our character descriptions like "he uses a wheelchair" or "she's deaf," because we want to include a disabled character and we want to cast a disabled actor. But then we get asked questions like, "But why is he in a wheelchair?" This is another place we're trying to be more inclusive as writers. Sometimes people are just disabled, so sometimes characters are, too. It's not part of their story. It doesn't define them. They were born that way or they had an illness and don't talk about it. It doesn't always need to be a story point, just as gender and race do not always need to be story points. So before you ask the question of "why do they need to be disabled/Black/female/etc.," think about why you're asking the question. *Does it make you more comfortable* to have a "why," or is it really important to the story?

Being on set

Once you get to set, there are some important details to remember to position yourself for success. If you have someone there to supervise you — a co-EP for example, be sure you have talked ahead of time so there's clarity on any conversations with the showrunner about what you should and shouldn't do (remember that thing about what does he or she wants you doing on set?). This ensures you are both on the same page.

I stress this because once, I did not have that conversation, and my showrunner and co-EP had different ideas about what I should be doing on set. Eventually, I made a mistake that pissed off my showrunner, but my co-EP told the showrunner he had asked me to handle the issue and hadn't been clear enough on how. A stand-up human. But it was still terrifying to have misstepped for even a moment in front of the boss. It all worked out fine — the showrunner knew I was there to learn, and I learned that lesson quickly: Ask what you're supposed to be doing!

Okay, here's the definite "do not" list.

Don't jump the director!

One of the biggest no-nos you can commit on set is jumping the director. What does that mean? It means don't step in to solve an actor problem without the director. On a TV set, while you are there as the showrunner proxy, *the director is in charge of the set.* . . and that means the director is the primary communicator with the actors. In fact, your giving notes to the actors is technically a Directors Guild rule violation. So even if Number One on the call sheet, whom you adore and who adores you, tries to wave you over to ask a question, say, "One second," grab your director, and then go over and have the conversation with both of them.

Your actors won't be trying to get you into trouble, but some of them prefer talking to the writers they know. That's fine — but it's on you to remind them the director is part of the team right now, too. Now, you may work with a director who says, "Actually, I don't care. If they want to talk to you, go for it, and just let me know if I need to know anything." If that happens, then fine, you and the actor(s) can talk amongst yourselves.

That doesn't mean you can't have friendly chats with your actors — but if they start talking about the scene or the episode, it's time to say, "Oh, let me grab director X, and we can all talk about that."

I said this earlier, but it bears repeating: Don't let the actors pump you for information. They may be wondering if their new love interest is sticking around or if there are any big cliff-hangers in the finale about their characters. Again, there's no intent to get you in trouble. . . but talking about that stuff isn't cool. Loose lips and all that. . . so have your canned "Oh, lots of exciting stuff, but you know I can't talk about it" response ready to go.

P.S., Sometimes, you'll have to write on set, either making changes to a scene in the current episode or because you're already writing your next episode and the deadline is fast approaching. People will look over your shoulder at what you're typing; they can't help themselves. So if you're working on something sensitive or confidential and your actors or other folks are hanging around to chat, close your computer for now and work on it later.

Whom to know (the keys to your survival)

Your 1st AD is the person who is running everything — the set, the actors, the director, the cameras — you name it. This is, to me, the hardest job in Hollywood, and I don't know why anyone does it except that they want to be directors, and this gets them there. But your 1st AD is invaluable. Be good to this person, and get to know the 2nd AD, who will usually be the person managing minutiae with you (photos for the criminal profiles you need, stock images for the computers, etc.)

The on-set PAs are your lifelines. They know where the bathroom is, how to get to Crafty (food!), where you can duck out to take an emergency call with the boss, and if you need something, they are the folks who will get it for you. Again, be good to them, treat them like the working pros they are, and if they want to ask you questions about how you got where you are, answer them. These are folks trying to get to the next rung of the ladder.

Your script supervisor is the amazing human who is somehow logging every line change and misspeak and shot for every take of every scene into a program that communicates that info back to post. They are usually your buddy at Video Village (the monitor station where you, the director, and Scripty watch the takes), and this is the person you can talk to about something before you take a note to the director. "Was it just me or did she mispronounce that name?" Scripty will also run in your notes to the actors on lines/dialogue/pronunciation stuff that isn't about the emotional content of the scene. Any emotional notes you have should go to the director to pass them on.

Your Sound team is also key to your success on the set. They not only make sure you can hear what happens all day, they need to be notified either by you or Scripty any time a line change occurs so they can be certain they got the corrected version clearly.

When to call for help

I've discussed this a bit in the director section, but the truth is this: You should call when your gut tells you to call. If an actor is trying to force a line change and the director is like, "Either way is fine with me," but you worry it's changing the meaning in the scene, call an upper-level writer or the show-runner, depending on the protocol for your show. If a prop looks ridiculous at the last minute and you're afraid it will ruin the seriousness of a scene, you can phone-a-friend and ask for an opinion.

Phone calls are always appropriate for things that threaten the integrity of the scene or story, may lead to conflict with a series regular, or may endanger the safety of the cast or crew.

Yes, you do have to memorize the names of *everyone* on the crew.

This is no easy task I'm giving you, but if it takes a cheat sheet, a memorization trick, or your handy dandy cell phone camera — you need to be able to call people on the crew by their names. And it's a lot of names. I get that. But the respect this conveys to everyone who is busting their tail all day for days making your episode is immeasurable. This is your team. They want the show to be great. If you make that effort to be able to say, "Thanks for the chair, Mike" to props, who, yes, has to wrangle your chair, it acknowledges your on-set prop person *as a person.*

I was about to tell you this is so important I can't even say it strongly enough, but the truth is, I can. One of those difficult directors I had? When my boss was unhappy with the episode and wondered what had gone wrong, the crew and production team had my back and made sure the showrunner knew that I had done all I could to keep things from going off the rails. I earned that support by being respectful and kind to people working hard to do their jobs when circumstances were trying to make their jobs very difficult.

Don't be an asshole is really the best advice on set. Please. Thank you. Using someone's name. Asking what people are doing on their days off. It all matters.

Set reports

Every show I've been on requires some form of set report, but they've ranged from the totally brief and informal to the incredibly detailed. Sometimes the showrunner just wants to know if we're on time at lunch and if it looks like we'll make our day. They assume you'll reach out with other issues as needed. Sometimes the set report is a quick email at the end of the day — "made the day, Number One was in good spirits despite some hair/makeup difficulties this morning, but we may have bad weather tomorrow for location, so keep your fingers crossed."

Some showrunners like more detailed reports — they want to know scene by scene how things went, what takes you liked, any issues that came up with the actors, or production issues that may affect that day or the episode in general.

Whatever your showrunner wants, be sure you complete this in a timely manner every day. It's part of your producing responsibilities to keep the showrunner tied to the set and what's happening there.

Post: how to handle invitations to post, how to ask to be included, and why post is important

Post is that part of the offices, as a lower-level writer, you may never go near. Why? Because some showrunners simply don't include lower-level writers in post. They don't believe you have the skills at this point to contribute to the conversation and thus don't invite you in.

Some showrunners make certain that all writers at every level get the cuts of the episodes to watch (director's cut, producer's cut, studio, network, and so on). Usually if they make these cuts available and you see something and have an idea, you can email the showrunner directly saying, "Hey, in scene twenty-three, I remember we had a shot in the dailies that holds on actor A's face longer and it was really powerful. Just wanted to mention it." Stuff like that. (Also this is why it's great to take your own notes on set, even if you aren't required to send a written set report. You always have a record of your favorite shots/takes.)

Some showrunners consider it part of their mentorship of the next generation to give them a chance to experience post. If you have that showrunner, you are beyond lucky and please make the most of it.

If you get invited into the process, know that your notes are going to be vetted by the showrunner or other EPs so they'll decide what they pass on and what they don't. But it's very helpful to be in this process because it teaches you how to make clear, strategic notes that help improve the episode.

These are the things I try to focus on early in the process: Are there moments that feel too long? Too short? Is there a shot missing that you loved from dailies? Are there rough transitions?

Do you think there was a better take of that big kiss than the one in the cut? Now that you see the cut, do you think the story makes more sense if you re-order a few scenes? Can you hear all the dialogue clearly? Do you think an added line (additional dialogue recording, or ADR) would make something clearer? Do you remember that on set we said we'd VFX something to make it cleaner/better? If there's no VFX note on the cut (a superimposed note saying "VFX fix hairline" or some such), you can note that it needs to be added. Is there a soundtrack song when you wish it was score or vice versa? Go ahead and mention it.

One of the things you'll see if you get copied on the notes sent in by your showrunner and other EPs is that no one catches everything. Every producer/writer has things they're more in tune with, so don't feel like you have to catch literally everything that needs work in the cut. That's why multiple people watch it and give feedback.

Watching dailies, reading drafts, and how to make the most of your time outside of the room to build your skill set

Even before you go to set, you can be building your post and production savvy by taking advantage of the materials from episodes that come before you to learn. Be sure you read every revision that comes out so you see what's changing in the episodes and why. Get a feel for the kinds of adjustments that seem to come up routinely. For example, does one character always require dialogue trims? Try to remember that when you write your script so maybe you can make the dialogue for that actor tighter from jump.

Once shooting starts, if you have access to dailies, watch them. And I'm not telling you that you have to watch every last take, because sometimes there are five takes of one scene plus coverage (angles on the individual actors). But watch a few shots from each scene so you can get a feel for how the actors are before "action" through "cut." See what you can learn about the actors and their skills from watching these raw scenes. And once you see a cut of the episode, as I mentioned above, if you watched the dailies, you'll remember if there was a take of something you loved that you want to call out to the showrunner.

Once you start production, watching dailies can be difficult because you're on set twelve-plus hours and you have to prep for the next day and sleep and. . . yeah, it's a lot. But if you really loved a scene and want to do your director a solid, you can find the best take and shoot your boss an email that says, "Hey, just wanted to call your attention to this scene. It came out great!" That could lead to a happy showrunner calling to bolster the spirits of your director, which usually means production has a great day because everyone feels good about the work.

Conversely, if there's a problem on set and you think the dailies communicate it, you can also use them to call out a problem. "We've been having real problems with X actor knowing the lines. If you look at the dailies of scene five, you'll see what I mean." That lets the showrunner see the issue and decide whether to take action.

I'm looking at the page count on this chapter, and yeah, I know. . . that's a ton of information. But you can come back here again. You don't have to memorize every detail.

But you still have to learn all the names!

TRUE TALES OF LIFE INSIDE A WRITERS' ROOM

MALE UPPER-LEVEL BIPOC DRAMA WRITER
ON HANDLING CONFLICT ON SET OR IN THE ROOM

Conflict in a writers' room and on set is inevitable. It's a matter of when, not if it will happen. First, determine whether or not the matter is serious enough to require your time and attention. Part of effective conflict resolution is recognizing when your involvement will help or hurt (unnecessarily wasting time and possibly escalating) the situation. Most conflicts will work themselves out if you facilitate and allow people the opportunity to effectively communicate with each other.

If the conflict requires your attention, ascertain how urgent the matter is. For instance, conflicts on set may threaten the progress of production, which makes resolution vital for the progress of the show. Resolution is often a matter of accurately diagnosing the problem. Listen closely and determine what the core issue is. Every person feels that he or she is the good guy in the story. Why does each party feel that he or she is correct in the matter? Is this a matter of miscommunication? A personal gripe? A sincere disagreement? A lack of respect? Or factors that are unrelated to the issue?

Accurately diagnosing the cause of the conflict is often the most important factor of determining whether or not it can be resolved, and if it can be resolved, what the best form of resolution might be.

FEMALE DRAMA WRITER ON WHAT IT'S LIKE TO BE ON SET
AS A WRITER FOR THE FIRST TIME

After co-writing my first episode of TV with our show's Number Two, I went to set on-location (with the Number Two) for the episode. As nervous as I was about being on set in this capacity for the first time in my life, I was able to keep my cool because I could tell myself that I knew the script and the story better than anyone else. It was a confidence crutch that I needed to let myself take up space as a writer.

During one scene, my co-writer stepped away to take a call. Right before rolling, the director suddenly had an idea about action for background actors, but the AD and director were debating if it made sense within the scene. Realizing that my counterpart had stepped away, I moved forward to try to join the conversation. Unfortunately the director thought of me as a glorified PA and wanted to wait for my co-writer to be found or to just move forward with the suggested action. But I approached with my script and calmly made my case: The action proposed did not make sense in the scene. The day's sides didn't include the following scene that would have been contradicted by their suggestion. But with my full script and confidence that I was there to protect the story, I could show and tell them.

FEMALE MID-LEVEL DRAMA WRITER
ON CONFLICT-AVERSE WRITERS

Some showrunners and upper-level writers are just conflict-averse, and it can be really frustrating. Actors get away with what they're allowed to get away with on set, and if the tone has been set by the boss, then you, as the on-set writer, aren't going to fix it.

Same in the room. If the Number Two doesn't like to rock the boat and there's a problem in the room, you either have to decide to let it run its course or approach the showrunner on your own. But that can cause tension between you and the Number Two.

NOTE FROM A SHOWRUNNER ON GOING TO SET

When I send a writer to set, I tell them they are there to represent a few things:

1. The hundreds (if not thousands) of hours of work done in the writers' room. You were there for all the ideas that seemed great, but upon further exploration, did not work for the character's

journey. Some of these ideas will naturally come back in production, and the director (or sometimes the director and an actor as a pair) will want to go down those roads. You need to be informed there's a question and explain why the road leads to a place the show doesn't want to be.

Tied to this, the thing I find myself doing most on set is understanding what scene (for the character) comes right before and what comes right after in terms of context. Sometimes the actors, or even the director, don't have a strong grasp on it, and a reminder puts everyone on the same page. Even wardrobe or set dressing can get some things out of order on occasion.

2. The continuity of the show from hour to hour. The director, by definition, has to lock in on making this hour great but may not know what you know about what's coming up. You are there to make sure their hour is not only brilliant, but a piece of the puzzle that works with the one before and after that, and with the season as a whole.

3. The vision/taste of the showrunner. Many of my staff have a good sense of the things I would love or hate, and I give them permission to use me as a cudgel to make sure we get what is on the page, in the can, at least once. This isn't often a problem, but when it is, it tends to be a slippery slope that could lead to a muddled vision, which is the only thing worse than a bad one. This is not to say the taste of the showrunner is better than anyone's on set, but he or she is the person who will have to live with it in the editing bay.

4. An understanding that you are a manager. Your name is on the first page of the production document, and there is some responsibility behind that. If you see harassment, neglect, or any safety issues you need to make sure the showrunner knows about it.

NOTE FROM A PRODUCING DIRECTOR
ON WHAT NEW WRITERS SHOULD KNOW ABOUT SET

New writers haven't really had a chance to see something that they have created on the page get transformed up onto the screen. They've gone through their script over and over countless times, so it's inevitable that they have an engrained vision in their mind of what it would look like on the screen. But more often than not, what's shot is going to be different than what they'd imagined. A scene written at night at an inner-city bus stop becomes a scene at a suburban bus stop in the daytime. There are so many factors that can contribute to needing to move this scene to the suburbs and make it day instead of night, and they have nothing to do with the quality of the writing.

So to the new writers, I say: Don't get frustrated. Respect the system that has been hard at work long before you came to the set. Try to have an open mind and heart when you start collaborating with production. Yes, what's captured on film may not look like what you had in your mind, but here's what matters: Is the story still being told? That's the goal of production, to get the story up onto the screen in the best way possible. But the "best way" also depends on budget, location limitations, actor availability, and a hundred other things. The director and the crew will rally to achieve the best version possible of what you wrote, so sit back and enjoy the experience of producing on set.

When it comes to notes, only give your director corrections if the tone of a scene is absolutely wrong or if the story isn't being told. Nitpicking the small stuff will only cause friction between you and a director, whereas really knowing when to step in (as the last line of defense for the script) can be very helpful and help form an alliance with the director that will make him or her want to serve your story even more.

9

Moving on Up

**What those titles mean as you move up
the writer/producer ladder**

T HE HOPE FOR ALL OF US is that, if we work our butts off
season after season, we'll be asked back to our shows and
promoted to the next level of the writing hierarchy. This is
usually all negotiated in your deal and of course, hinges on
whether or not the show gets renewed.

A big part of why we're all excited to get past staff writer
level is because staff writers don't get paid for their episodic
scripts. Because staff writer is essentially considered an entry-
level/training position, script fees are considered part of your
WGA minimum salary. But because script fees can earn you
upwards of $40,000 for a script — depending upon the length
of the show, the outlet, and whether you get solo or co-credit
— getting that promotion means a significant increase in pay,
especially if you get to write more than one episode per season.

But there is not a guarantee that each season means forward
movement in pay and title because there's this thing that happens where writers are asked to repeat levels. This is wrapped
up in tricky stipulations in contracts at lower levels, like spec-
ifying that your promotion from staff writer to story editor
depends on completing twenty-two episodes (or whatever the
full order of your particular show is). Sometimes it's about
moving from show to show, due to cancellation or because

you're interested in moving on to a different opportunity, but having studio business affairs say something like, "Well, she only did nine episodes at story editor, so she has to do at least thirteen more for us before she can have the bump to ESE."

But the most common hold point is staff writer. So what happens when your staff writer year becomes more than a year? And why does it happen? What plays into the decision for a studio to make this ask beyond what I mentioned above?

Business semantics is part of it. Studios are always looking to get the best product for the least amount of money — and putting off pay increases for writers is a way to do that.

The first series I worked on was canceled after nine episodes. So when I was told that the same studio wanted me to do staff writer again on my second show, I wasn't completely shocked. It was for thirteen episodes, then I'd get my promotion to story editor in season two.

But there was no season two. My second show was canceled as we were finishing up the season finale. Which meant I had to move on to another show.

I fully expected, though, that now that I'd done twenty-two episodes of TV as a staff writer, I would get my next offer at story editor. My reps were pretty sure, too. Until I got that offer from a different studio and the line I got was, "Well, because you've only done twenty-two episodes of TV, they are only willing to do staff writer again. . . but this time with script fees and with a ten percent raise." That meant I'd get paid above staff writer minimum and that I'd get paid for my scripts, but it also meant I was subject to a contractually required *additional* twenty-two episodes in order to make story editor.

Then they reduced our order to sixteen episodes. So guess who wasn't getting to twenty-two episodes that year? Yeah. . . this kid.

Had that show been renewed, it was entirely possible the studio would have tried to say I owed them six more episodes at staff writer level before my promotion — in my fourth year as a TV writer.

Instead, I moved to another show at a studio I'd worked at before. My reps were able to argue that I had done all the work required to be at the ESE level — even if it meant jumping me past story editor from third-year staff writer. And the studio did it — so I was back on track in terms of my levels.

While I can't say definitively whether my three-peat as a staff writer was affected by the fact that I was also a diversity writer out of the network writing programs, this type of title repetition strikes underrepresented and female writers harder than overrepresented writers. In the 2021 *Behind the Scenes* survey conducted by the Think Tank for Inclusion & Equity, results showed that 35.8% of underrepresented writers had to repeat the staff writer level vs. 24.2% of overrepresented writers. So it's something to be keenly aware of as you enter the staffing pool. Have conversations about this with your reps — make sure they know the statistics so they can try to push back on business affairs in your negotiations if title repetition comes up.

If all else fails and your choices are to repeat a level or pass up on the job, only you can make that decision. I've passed on offers that meant repeating the level because I knew the work environments were toxic and no way in hell was I taking staff-writer money to deal with a room bully. But I accepted others because the shows provided good learning opportunities even if they didn't come with a title bump. As with all things in this business, talk to people you know, ask their opinions, get the best advice you can and then make the decision you believe best suits you.

It's also worth mentioning that requests for title repetition don't necessarily go away once you reach the upper levels. I was a supervising producer on a short-order show where I ran several room breaks, helped do script rewrites, and produced two episodes of the series. Then I was told at my next job that because I hadn't had the title for twenty-two episodes, I couldn't come in at co-EP. The job and the opportunities it presented to me were worth waiting sixteen episodes to get my title bump (the minimum they required), but again — you'll have to decide for yourself if the same decision would be right for you.

Once you land at co-EP, you'll pretty much be living at that title until you get an EP credit — on a show where you're that needed or on a show you create. Whichever comes first.

But let's hope none of that applies to you and you are moving up the writer/producer ranks at a steady pace. What the heck does it mean when you do get that promotion?

How your role shifts as your title increases: responsibilities, management, mentoring, and showrunner support

In general, you should look at every title bump as a chance for you to become more helpful to the show and your fellow writers. If you're already mentoring support staff as a staff writer, then do the same for the new staff writer(s) who come in after you. And so on and so on.

And as you grow and get more experience, it means that your upper-level writers, showrunners, and EPs will lean on you more for support. So don't be surprised if the showrunner calls and says, "Hey, I want to do a story in this area. Can you do some research to kick us off?" They're asking because they know they can count on you — and that's amazing.

Story editor. Once you make story editor, you are generally guaranteed at least one script per season. Since staff writers are rarely guaranteed a script, this is a huge win. Depending on the needs of your show, it's also likely you may come up earlier in the writing rotation than in your staff writer year because you've already proven yourself to the showrunner or you're coming into a new show with that prior experience. You may also be called on to write more often or get a designated show duty that's yours to cover because you've proven you're good at it, like writing story areas or formatting group outlines. This is also usually the first time you'll get a credit on the show outside of your "written by" credits on episodes. Story editor credits usually run in the end credits. (Staff writers rarely get these, though some networks do include them in the end credit runs as well.)

ESE (or the executive story editor, introduced on p. 12) is more of the same. If you haven't gotten a chance to participate in post, this is a good level to at least ask your showrunner about observing. This is also when you typically begin to be paid episodically vs. weekly. That doesn't mean you no longer get a check every week. The WGA requires minimum payments per week at every level of staffing. But now you're committed to the show for a specific period of time depending on the episode order.

This is where something called "span protection," negotiated by the WGA, will kick in for you if you work on a show that's 12 episodes or less. When you get paid episodically, essentially each episode payment covers 2.4 weeks of work for that episode. So say you earn $15,000 per episode, and you're working on a show that's 10 episodes. That means that after 24 weeks (2.4

weeks x 10 episodes), if you have made less than the current cap ($400,000 or $375,000, depending on broadcast, streaming, basic cable designations), then the studio has to pay you additional money beyond the $150,000 you negotiated for 24 weeks if they want you to keep working on the show. That rate is 2.4 x your episodic rate, or $15,000 divided by 2.4, which would equal $6,250 for each additional week of work. An example of how this can play out — when I was on a series for Netflix, they wanted me to work three additional months, so my new weekly rate was calculated after my initial contract was fulfilled, and I received that amount per week for the 3 months of extra work. *I know, that's a lot of math. Don't stress over it too much. Your rep(s) and the WGA will make sure you get paid correctly.*

Why is span protection important? Because writers were being kept on shows for months beyond that 2.4-weeks-per-episode period of time and making only scale, which basically meant they were losing money compared to what they would have been making on another show. So the WGA put this protection in place to make certain that writers were able to get the extra compensation they deserved for extended periods of work. *Your script fees do not count against the span protection cap, just your episodic fees.*

Co-producer. Welcome to being a mid-level writer! *You did it!* In terms of what this means, it's your move to the top of show credits — now your parents can find your name easier with your fancy new co-producer title! This is also usually the first year in your deal that the studio will allow you to develop projects of your own.

In the room, you can start to take a little more initiative with interpersonal issues and see if there are ways you can head off problems before your Number Two or showrunner has to deal with them. Is there a writer that could use some coaching up on their room pitching? Take them for a walk, ask what's going on, see if you can help them out. Mini-conflict brewing in the room? See if you can talk to the writers involved and get it handled before it becomes a thing. You may also be asked to cover prep meetings or answer questions for production as you become more integrated into the overall production picture.

Producer. If no one on your show is in charge of helping the staff writers out, this is a level where you can say, "Hey, I think it might benefit us to have someone be the point person for the lower levels. I'm happy to do it if that's cool." You'll probably get a resounding yes — and this means potentially reading drafts for them or helping them come up with story areas if your show is one where people come in with individual ideas for their episodes rather than one where those ideas are generated by the room. In production prep, this will also mean you probably carry more of the load with less supervision from your upper levels and your showrunner.

Supervising producer. Congratulations on making it to the upper-level writer ranks! What does that mean? Probably that your showrunner will ask you to take passes on drafts from lower-level writers or on other documents. Definitely that you'll be the backup to run the room if the co-EP isn't available or, if your co-EP is more geared toward production or post, you may be the person running the room.

Co-EP. Co-executive producers are essentially the backstops for the showrunner. You may do rewrites on scripts, you may take casting sessions, you may run the room, you may help with hiring the writers coming on for a new season, and you'll likely be involved or at least updated on any big meetings regarding studio and network issues.

EP. There are two ways to get to the rank of executive producer: selling your own show or becoming so senior and so invaluable that you get hired in at this level. What does it mean? You're more than the backstop for the showrunner; you are a linchpin. You're in all the big meetings about budget and casting and safety and production. You're often the conduit of that info back to the writers' room because you'll go in to work on the episode that's being broken while the showrunner wrangles a giant to-do list. You may handle cast issues before they get to the showrunner — unhappy actors, actors with script requests, conflicts between actors — or at least get the low-down to inform the showrunner before he or she has to step in. You may also be called on to produce more episodes if it's a show where lower-level writers don't produce.

There's also a position called *consulting producer* (CP). This is usually a writer with an overall deal at the studio who is also developing projects but who has some skills that the showrunner finds invaluable. Some CPs work daily in the room; some are there as they're available. It really depends on the situation and the show.

All of these moves come with increases in pay as well. There's an element in negotiations called "overscale pay." This means there's a base pay rate negotiated by the WGA, or a scale rate. But in contract negotiations with the studio, your reps can push for additional pay — overscale — that is commensurate with your experience and the value-adds you bring to the show.

In past years, what we all got paid was something of a secret. In recent years, writers have realized there is power in knowledge and begun disclosing their rates to one another in order to make sure compensation is fair and not affected by gender or racial bias. It's infuriating for a woman co-EP to find out a male co-EP with less experience than she has is getting paid more than she is. . . and it's usually a result of women not knowing they can push for more because the men have. So the more we help each other, even within our own networks, and make certain we're all being paid fairly, the more we keep our industry honest about these biases.

But it's important to remember that the money isn't just coming to you because of what you've done in the past to earn it — it's about what they know they can count on you to do when the going gets tough in the present. A co-EP or supervising producer who can do a page-one rewrite on a script and save the showrunner days' worth of work is invaluable; a producer the bosses know can run the room if they have to duck out for an urgent meeting is someone every room loves to have; and a mid-level writer who is taking care of the room emotionally and prevents some of that stress from reaching the showrunner's door? That's a person every showrunner wants to have around.

You don't have to be all those things — your job as you move up the ladder is to find your strengths and hone them; your weaknesses will also diminish. But the things you shine at — fast first drafts, great rewrites, running the room, mentoring — whatever they are, they are what will make you the person every showrunner wants to hire.

It's about becoming the best writer/producer that you can be — that's the goal.

True Tales of Life Inside a Writers' Room

Female Upper-Level Writer on Knowing When to Help and When to Walk Away

One of the tricks to moving up the ladder is knowing when your stepping in will make a situation worse. I once had a lower-level writer who was a total distraction in the room, but this writer had already made it clear he had zero respect for me. So I went to my Number Two and said, "Hey, I know there's a problem here, but I don't feel like I can step in. Is there any other way I can be of help?" My Number Two understood why I couldn't step in and encouraged me to just stay aware of how it was affecting other people in the room until such time as the showrunner decided to address the issue. Had I just gone at that writer, I have no doubt it would have blown up in the room and potentially cost us days of work while the dust settled.

Female BIPOC Drama Writer
on Knowing Your Worth

At the beginning of my career, I assumed that my reps were always getting me the best deal they could. But once all the information on rates and averages came out during the WGA Agency Action (the WGA's fight to end packaging by agencies), it became clear that some of us were being told by the studios that we could only get X amount of dollars when writers (see: men) who were less experienced than we were were making more money. It's important to pay attention to info on salaries, to have friends you can openly discuss rates with, and to make sure that you are really getting the best deals you can as you move up the ladder. Sometimes a low pay increase is worth a credit bump. Other times, not so much. Only you should get to make that decision.

10.

MENTORING

How to accept it and ways to pay it forward

THE IDEA OF MENTORING HAS COME up a lot in this book, and that's no accident. It's also not my just loving to use the word. It's a crucial part of a successful career. . . both to build your own skill set and to train and prepare a group of writers to support you as you become a showrunner, create a production company (POD), and start producing multiple shows.

When I thought the writing thing might not work out before I finally started to make some headway, I decided to pursue a baking business. And I reached out to several local bakeries who all did very different things from what I was doing, and I requested to sit down with the owners and ask them a few questions. No one was willing to speak with me. And so I had to struggle and figure it all out on my own.

My experience as a writer couldn't be more different. People have been willing to have coffee and let me reach out to them on social media or via email to ask questions, and a select group became my touchstones in this crazy business. And now I'm that person for several of the writers I've supported and mentored along the way.

Mentorship isn't a given, though. Some people feel entitled to it and will ask people they just met to mentor them, but it's not that simple. You have to make the right connection with people. . . intellectually, emotionally. . . and you have to approach it the right way. Even if you meet a writer you really admire, you can't immediately ask them to be a mentor. That's like asking someone to marry you on the first date. Recently I heard about people direct messaging writers on social media asking them to read scripts and mentor them — y'all. . . *just don't do it*. That's never going to work.

So what *do* you do? If the writer you met is willing to stay in touch, do that. Write them when you see their names in the trades or when you have legit questions or when you have news to share like doing well in a competition or getting to the interview rounds for a fellowship. In other words, keep the relationship going in a back and forth that isn't all about you. A mentor should be someone you genuinely respect and care about. Otherwise, the relationship won't be the kind that lasts.

Once you've shown your investment in that person and your relationship has continued to build, that's when you can ask for assistance. I met a particular writer/director during my time in the ViacomCBS Writers Mentoring Program. We kept up a back and forth and stayed in touch, and it was two years later that I was stuck on a pilot and asked him for a read. His notes confirmed my feelings about what was not working in the script, and I was able to push through and finish the sample that got me my first two jobs.

The same idea of real chemistry and connection should be in play when you start mentoring. You'll meet a lot of up-and-coming writers, either in the room, at mixers, when you speak on panels, if you guest-speak in screenwriting classes, or just on social media when people seek you out. And a lot of people will be hoping that you'll be interested in mentoring them. Hopefully you'll have that desire. But you also need to remember that you can't help everyone. You should look for those genuine feelings of kinship that your mentors had with you. . . and those are the writers you should consider giving up your precious free time for.

But let's look at a few more specifics on this topic, because it's such a crucial part of building and sustaining a career.

How to make the most of the mentors you meet on your show

Finding mentors on your shows can be a process, or it can be the easiest thing you've ever done. On one of my shows, the Number Two immediately made it clear that she was there to answer our questions, read our drafts, and just generally help the lower levels get set up for success. But that offer was only half the job of forming our relationship. I had to do my part to be someone she wanted to keep investing in. . . so on top of doing an amazing job, I also made sure to chat in the mornings about normal human things — kids, weekends activities, etc. — so that she could get to know me as a person beyond just my work. This is my standard MO in all my rooms. In this one, it turned out I not only found a mentor but a friend who's never getting rid of me. And in all of my rooms, I've found people who continue to be mentors and allies because I took the time to build real relationships with them.

If your show doesn't have a designated mentor figure, then pay attention to how the mid- and upper-level writers function in the room. Is there a producer who's more likely to walk someone through a pitch they didn't understand? A co-EP who is willing to read pages for you when you ask? That's your potential new guiding light.

It is possible that one of your showrunners may also be a mentor. My first showrunner will still tell you he's terrible at it, but he taught me so much about what it means to support your lower-level writers once you hire them. So he can say that all he wants. . . he is a rockstar mentor. Just remember that your showrunner is essentially the CEO of a major corporation, so he/she may not be as available to you as a writer at the mid- or upper level. . . so always consider if you have somewhere else to go with a question before you head to the boss's office.

How to survive if no one on your show will mentor you

But let's say you have the bad luck of being on a show where no one is interested in providing guidance or helping you succeed. What do you do? This is when you utilize that network outside of your show for help.

Obviously, that's less than ideal because when you can talk to the people on your show, they are in the same stew as you. They know the personalities, the attitudes, and the details of the work. And you want to respect the sanctity of the room. But you also can't flail around without someone to talk to about hard or confusing things happening, be it in the room, with your fellow writers, or on the page. So having the network, people you've built real relationships with and trust, is crucial.

You can also call upon your reps here. If you need to ask questions about tricky room politics and you don't know someone who may have the answer, you can ask your reps if they can connect you with someone who might be able to help. Or your reps may be able to give you some advice because they've had other clients who worked with this showrunner or they may have insider knowledge that you, as a newer writer, aren't privy to.

Another thing you can do is to lean on the support staff. . . not for mentorship but to have allies. Support staff is also dealing with the issues going on, and if you trust them and have gotten to know them as people, you can take a walk with your writers' assistant and say, "Was it just me or was that thing in the room today kind of weird?" so that you have a gut check on your feelings about what's going on. Be careful, though, not to put them in the middle of anything — your support staff members have even less power than you, and they need to avoid factions and politics even more than you do. But that doesn't mean they aren't frustrated and needing someone to talk to as well. Sometimes just being able to vent about things is all you'll need to get through. And speaking of the show's support staff. . .

The support staff on your show want to be you; be their friend and ally.

Even as a staff writer, you should make yourself available to the support staff on your show. Get to know them, what they write, what their strengths are. . . and offer to read their work. This is the first way you can pay forward the mentorship you've received. . . and if you weren't lucky enough to have mentors coming up, then this is your chance to break the cycle and make a difference to the next generation.

This will benefit them by giving them guidance. . . even as a staff writer, you've probably written more pilots than they have, so your notes will matter; you've likely done a ton of executive and/or showrunner meetings, so help them learn how to prep for theirs; and invest in them as human beings — take them to drinks or to a movie or something to say thank you for how hard they work. As stated above, they may be the only people you can talk to if you're in an unsupportive environment, so make friends where you can.

This will also benefit the show, because you'll have a good understanding of who is great at what, then if you have those moments I discussed in Chapter 8, you'll know who can write a great news article for that computer-screen text you need, and who lives on social media and can come up with twenty-five quick tweets to put on someone's phone for that scene in the third act.

And once you leave the show, if you genuinely like these folks, stay in touch with them. Offer to keep being a resource and connection for them. You never know when you may be hiring and need someone you can trust absolutely who you know is great at research. . . and guess what, you may already know that person because they used to be the PA on a show you worked on — and now they're ready to staff.

You can also be a reference for them as they go out into the world to start trying to land early gigs. If they're up for a show and you happen to know an upper level or the showrunner involved in hiring, you can definitely reach out with a quick email or phone call and say, "I heard you're meeting with X writer. . . he/she is AMAZING! And here's why. . ." That kind of endorsement helps so much when people are trying to get their first gig and don't have a showrunner who can speak to their abilities in the room yet.

There may be support staff along the way, just like other writers, that you don't connect with or who you think just aren't good at their jobs. You aren't required to mentor everyone, and you can always politely say that your mentorship schedule is full at the moment if you just don't think you're the right fit for someone. But that doesn't mean you should throw in the towel completely. I once worked with an assistant who didn't know how to create a beat sheet for an episode once we were finished with the room break. I got a great sample from another assistant I had worked with to try and help. It did not solve our problem, but I at least made the attempt and could honestly say I'd tried to help this person succeed. And yes, I did that for the show more than I did it for this person because at the end of the day, the show running more smoothly is the goal. So sometimes you have to help people even if they frustrate you or you don't like them. Teamwork can be a pain in the ass, for sure.

If you came through the network writing programs, *stay in touch.*

I can't tell you how many times my mentors from ViacomCBS and NBC have reached out to ask if I'm working, whether I need to be submitted for anything, or to just check in and see how I'm doing. Their support has been constant, but part of that has also come from my willingness to stay in touch with the executives who run those writing programs. And go back and be a mentor to their ongoing cohorts of writers. Don't forget, people did it for you!

You're a part of a writing community. Be active, be committed, and fight for the people coming up behind you.

It sounds clichéd, but it's true that writers take care of writers. In the most literal sense, that involves our union, the WGA, and the fact that writers come together and elect officials to go into negotiations to hammer out our contracts with the Association of Motion Picture and Television Producers (AMPTP). Our ability to grow financially and to maintain the importance of the writer in the creative process depends upon these negotiations. So first and foremost, I'd encourage you to be a person who pays attention to what's going on at the Guild. Vote in elections, attend membership meetings with information on priorities for contract negotiations, and find the committee(s) that you're most interested in and join into efforts to build education and equity for your fellow members.

But how else can you be an active part of your community? That will vary from person to person. You can accept invitations to speak on panels about career development; give podcast interviews about the process of making a TV show, or write articles or blogs if that's your preferred method of communication. Offer to guest-speak for people who teach screenwriting courses. Volunteer to mentor in the various writing programs that the major networks participate in. Offer to do Q&As on social media. Whatever fits you and your personality best.

The important thing is to find your way to be in the world of your fellow writers. Because we are responsible for making sure we keep pushing forward, making the business better for the writers in it now and the ones who come next.

Some of you right now are thinking, "Yeah, that all sounds great, but I really am *not* a mentor. So what about me?"

That's fair. We're not all natural-born teachers or mentors. So maybe you're never going to be as fully engaged as someone like me. But that doesn't mean you aren't part of the solution in our business. The one that makes it more humane and open. What I'm asking of everyone who reads this book and launches a career in TV is: *Don't forget what it was like when you were hoping to get your shot.* Remember how much hard work it is, how hard it was to get by on assistant wages (or a survival day job) while trying to write and take meetings. Be a person who reaches back and helps someone else come forward. . . and who doesn't inflict the mistreatment you may have endured onto others.

That doesn't just benefit you as a human, which. . . we could all use the good karma. . . it also makes good business sense. How? Some of the showrunners I know who are most successful are people who brought writers up in their rooms and then were able to hand over room running, post, or production duties to those writers in later seasons. You do, in a way, want to train people to take your job because you may not want to run one show forever. You may want to get it off the ground and then go create something new in season three. But you can only do that if you have good people to trust with your firstborn. And if you train them, if you help them become the Number Twos and showrunners you want to see in the world, then you will know your baby is in good hands.

True Tales of Life Inside a Writers' Room

Male upper-level BIPOC drama writer on how to mentor

Mentoring writers is something that every writer on staff does, whether he or she realizes it or not. Lower-level writers help set the tone for assistants below them and peers around them. The question is, what type of example do you want to provide? For better and for worse, lower-level writers often take cues from the behavior, attitudes, and work ethic of the writers above them and develop their management style well before they become bosses with power and authority.

Male drama writer on looking out for support staff

I read and gave notes on a researcher's personal script. Her job was thankless and time-consuming on this particular show. So when, six months later, she came back to me with tears (of joy) and told me that script got her into one of the network writing programs, it was worth every minute of my time. It's important to give back and remember that, for most of us, someone did something for you along the way.

Female drama writer on how relationships come back around

My first time in LA was for a summer internship after my freshman year of college. I was working for a young producer. I got coffee, rolled calls, and wrote coverage. Did my job and did it well. Fast forward fifteen years, and I had a friend who is a showrunner, and she said she was up for a piece of development that was dream IP for me. . . and it turned out that project was in the hands of that same producer from my long-ago summer internship. With my friend's blessing, I emailed the producer and told him how much I wanted to pitch on the project, and it worked! I got hired to write the adaptation. That's why it's important to make a good impression on people. . . you never know when you'll run into them again in this business.

Male drama writer on making the most of mentoring and room opportunities

I'd been an assistant in film and television via music for about five years. Worked for some of the biggest companies in the industry. Supported high-profile bosses. The track I was on could've easily landed me upward mobility as a lawyer or a producer or an executive, but not as a writer. I'd hit a dead end. So I decided to take a new approach: I'd leave and sort things out from the outside in. I worked lucrative survival gigs in restaurants, music, and theater venues. Offered my services as a freelance writer. But always in proximity to entertainment. Still, I wasn't really getting anywhere. Until a close friend returned from Malaysia as the key director's assistant for the first season of Netflix's Marco Polo. *Her stories of shooting in the jungle were unbelievable. She came back changed and finally on her path. She was getting promoted to a producer-level role — did I want to take her job next season?*

I didn't say yes right away. Working as an assistant again felt like a step backward. I'd tried that already and I'd be starting over. Besides, wouldn't working with directors just be another dead-end track? Not to mention, I had zero production experience. I'd never stepped foot on a set, let alone in the jungle. The whole thing seemed daunting. I walked away from that conversation thinking that maybe a TV writing career just wasn't in the cards for me. Thankfully, I also have a little-big voice inside me that processes fear as a compulsion to take the leap. In other words: Do the thing that scares you. So I did. I went into the interview honest about my limitations. I'd never read a production schedule in my life. But I was fully committed to learning. I got the gig. It was the best move backward that I could've ever taken. I learned so much on production for season two. My hard work and grace-under-fire attitude in other jobs really paid off. I was asked to come on as script coordinator for the third season. And from there, I worked my way up in various writers' rooms and on production. I established close ties with my bosses and colleagues. I adapted and grew to love the guerilla nature of breaking and producing episodes. I learned the language of filmmaking and storytelling. And all the while, I wrote, and I wrote, and I wrote. And then I got staffed.

11

RACE, GENDER, SEXUAL ORIENTATION, AND DISABILITY IN THE ROOM

Let's have the conversation here in case you have to have the conversation there.

I N THE WRITERS' ROOM, JUST LIKE in life, "othering" can happen. Sometimes it's malicious, targeted, and clearly intentional. Sometimes even people who are generally allies are the culprits, having stumbled into their own blind spots. And sometimes even writers from the same community will have different experiences and backgrounds that make them disagree on key points of how X character would react to something, leading to room conflict that can feel acutely personal.

As ever, with so many of the things that happen in the room, always remember that we're just a group of regular human beings trying to get along when, as writers, what we really want to do is go home and sit in our favorite spot in our pajamas and write alone all day. It is forever a work in progress. . . and we will *all* make mistakes. We'll say things that seem insensitive. We'll misgender someone because we're adjusting to new pronouns or someone's new identity. We'll tell a joke without realizing how triggering the language feels to someone else in the room. Even conversations about which words are okay to use and which ones are harmful can get difficult quickly. . .

so we all need to grant each other a little grace. A conversation about this book and whether to identify writers as male/female or man/woman threw me for a loop. First of all, did I need the identifiers? I felt I did, because the experiences of men and women can be very different in writers' rooms, as can those of overrepresented writers vs. underrepresented writers. So knowing the context of the writers' background when it comes to the anecdotes in the chapters felt necessary. But I really respect the person who brought this up to me, so I had to take in the argument, think about why I felt the way I felt, and make a decision based on the best information I have right now. I decided that it was easier to read "female drama writer" or "male comedy showrunner" than "drama writer (man)," etc. But the conversation about words that indicate sex vs. gender and whether we actually need to include them at all will continue, and we'll all have to pivot as it does.

But if you step in it instead of pivoting, the important thing is to *recognize your misstep, own it, apologize, and correct it.* You never tell that joke again; you write a note on your notebook that says "they/them" so you can look down at it and remind yourself about someone's pronouns. *You do the work.* And hopefully the other writers in your room will do the work, too, and no one will feel isolated by bad behavior.

But that's a more perfect world. The way it ought to be. The reality of how our differences can be weaponized against us in the room can be very different. So we're going to talk about it. But I think the easiest way to make this topic digestible is to break it down into bite-sized chunks. So let's move through it bit by bit.

Being the "only" anything in the room

It wasn't until my seventh season of TV that I experienced being the "only" in a room. I was the only writer of color in a small room, though not the only woman. But the difference between many of my friends who had previously had this experience and me was that I was an upper-level writer. I had the seniority to stand up for story issues and myself in a way I wouldn't have as a new writer.

So what happens when you're the only anything in the room and you're new to the game or in your lower-level writing years?

First of all, you employ some of the earlier advice in this book. Read the room, get a feel for what the general tone is. . . inclusive and open-minded or exclusive and closed-minded. Look for allies and talk to your fellow writers outside of the show to get advice on how to navigate it.

But the biggest challenge of being the "only" usually comes up in the story breaks. This is when the only writer of color or a specific gender or sexual orientation or disability can be put on the spot to be *the spokesperson* for that group. The problem with this, of course, is that no group is monolithic. My experience as a Black woman who grew up in small-town California will be very different from that of a Black woman who grew up in New York or the South or another country. Yet I'm expected to be an authority on Black women, as if there's an easy way to classify and describe us.

So how do you combat this? One of your best replies to an awkward situation is to say, "That's a very different experience than mine, but I can do some research and bring information back to the room." This may solve your problem, or it may get you attitude from people who think you should just be able to answer the question. *But it is okay, no matter what anyone tells you, to say, "I don't know."* It's okay to consult resources like the Think Tank for Inclusion & Equity fact sheets, which you can bring in to say, "Hey, I was reading this and saw that the angle we were taking on this female character falls into their stereotypical portrayals for this community, but I spoke to someone and they were saying a fresh take on this might be X." Pro tip: Even if you didn't "talk to someone," you can say you spoke to someone. It's a great cover to share information and preserve someone's ego.

Another common issue is that the "only" writer of color is expected to somehow magically be an expert on *all* communities of color. This, again, is a place to say, "I know some people I can ask. . ." and go ask your friends from that community or do some research. . . and if you need to, you can say something to push back on the notion that you are the room minority expert. This might be uncomfortable, but it may also need to be said. You can approach it humorously to try and soften the blow. Something like "The thing is, I was absent on 'be an expert in everyone's diversity' day at school, so I may need to do some research on that." Or, you know, whatever works for you.

And of course there are people who are just outright jackasses when it comes to this sort of thing. Someone who can't quite pronounce a writer's "ethnic" name correctly or one who just decides to nickname a writer because "their name is too hard" (This needs to be corrected immediately, fyi — *only you* get to decide what people call you). Someone who makes comments about the food someone eats when it's cultural. Someone who makes cracks about religious or cultural holidays if a writer takes time off to observe them. It happens. Hopefully this is the kind of thing that someone in your room at the upper levels will handle, if they aren't the perpetrator. But this type of behavior is real harassment and should never be allowed to continue. . . so this is a time to reach out for help and advice on how to move forward.

It can become exhausting being the "only" in a room situation, so another smart move you can make is to team up with another "only." Are you a Black, Indigenous, and People of Color (BIPOC) writer or an Asian American and Pacific Islander (AAPI) writer and there's also one lesbian, gay, bi, trans, or queer (LGBTQ+) writer in the room? Make a deal with that person. "I'll be the person to fight some of your fights if you fight some of mine." That way you know you've got an automatic ally when you decide to step into the fray.

But a key piece of advice I would give is: Look out for yourself. You will want to bend over backward to fit in and make yourself a vital piece of this room. *But if that effort comes at the expense of your mental, emotional, or physical health. . . it is not okay.* So it's fine. . . absolutely fine. . . to step back for a bit. You don't have to fight every battle for your group or every other underrepresented group. You should stand up for what you truly can't ignore, but know that other people have a responsibility to fight, too. It doesn't mean anyone else will. . . and that will be hard to see. *But you are not solely responsible for the integrity of your room when it comes to accurate presentations of underrepresented groups.* If you need to, write that on a sticky note and put it inside your notebook for a reminder — or save it as a note on your cell phone so you can look at it when you know you could take up a fight, but also *don't* have the energy.

Diversity writer backlash

I wish I could tell you that this was no longer a thing in writers' rooms. But the truth is, diversity writer backlash may be at an all-time high in our business as I write this.

Why? Because as initiatives and mandates are put in place by more studios and networks to increase the diversity of story-telling and the people telling those stories, a narrative has come into play that is untrue and infuriating.

Diversity writers are taking all the jobs.

It would be laughable if it weren't so damn rage-inducing.

Statistics on staffing in Hollywood will tell you that the major-ity of showrunners and upper-level writers remain white males. According to the UCLA *Hollywood Diversity Report* from 2020, show creators on broadcast TV were 89.3% white vs. 10.7% diverse. In cable, it was 85.5% vs. 14.5%. When it came to gender, in broadcast the numbers were 71.9% male vs. 28.1% female, and in cable, it was 77.6% male vs. 22.4%. In stream-ing, creators were 89.7% white vs. 10.3% minority and 71.4% male vs. 28.6% female.

When it comes to staffing, the same report indicates that writ-ers of color in broadcast totaled 23.3% of writers, in cable 25.8%, and in streaming writers of color accounted for 22.7% of all credited writers. (By the way, when it comes to disabled writers, they make up about 0.6% of the WGA membership, but 20% of the overall population, and about 1% of on-screen depictions. We'll discuss how to fight this battle more a little later when we get to accessibility.)

So the numbers will tell you, by no means are underrepre-sented writers "taking all the jobs."

So where does that come from?

First of all, it comes from misinformation. I can't tell you how many people I know who have said that executives, agents, and managers are the ones saying to their white (overwhelmingly male) clients, "You didn't get the job because they had to hire a diversity writer." It's an irresponsible, easy way out of having difficult conversations with writers who may not be as talented, have inferior samples, or who didn't have a meeting with the showrunner(s) as good as that of the writer who was hired.

And to be clear, *that's not all reps and execs.* It's just the ones who are clearly perpetuating this myth without giving it any context.

And what's that context? *The reality of staffing.*

Showrunners staff top down, meaning they want to find their Number Two and other upper-level writers before they fill in the rest of the room. Part of that is sometimes wanting input from your Number Two in forming the room. *A bigger part is a business reality: budget.* The more a showrunner spends on those upper levels, whom they are hiring for their experience and the ability to rely on them to take on large amounts of work, the less money there is for mid- and lower-level writers.

So how does that play into the diversity conversation?

Again, the majority of showrunners and upper-level writers are white men.

While that's getting better, it's still reality, which means that oftentimes diversity, equity, and inclusion have not been a factor in filling in those top spots in the writers' room. That means the only spots left are mid- and lower-level positions. And the most common thing we see in rooms that haven't made inclusion a priority is that it's left truly until the end of hiring and only implemented at the lower levels.

So yes, if you're a white male trying to get a staff writer job, you may not get it because the show wanted to hire a diversity writer. . . but only because they didn't look to hire inclusively throughout staffing and isolated that staff writer position to make sure they had a diverse writer on staff for the least amount of money (or for free if the network supports funding diversity hires).

To be clear: *That's not the fault of diversity writers.* That's the systemic part of staffing that needs to change. It means that showrunners have to make it a priority to hire inclusively at every level so that staff writer positions aren't isolated and held for diversity, making the system fairer to everyone.

And if you are the diversity writer on your staff now or in the future, please remember this: *You earned your spot.* You were chosen out of a giant pile of scripts and dozens of meetings as the writer your showrunner wanted to hire — that matters! Don't ever let anyone make you think your start in this crazy business is somehow "less than" because they have a bad attitude about creating real equity in entertainment.

How to be an ally

If you're an overrepresented writer and you want to make a real difference in this effort to be more inclusive, then the best thing you can do until you're in the position to hire is to be a true ally in the room and on staff. When I say that, it sounds simple, but truly, it's a complicated ask.

Being a true ally is more than just not being racist or sexist or homophobic or ableist. *It's being willing to step in when you see that bad behavior in action.* It's not abandoning those writers to stand up alone when they are trying to push back against harmful or stereotypical storylines and characterizations. It's not laughing at the joke you know is inappropriate. It's saying in the moment, "Do we really think that's room appropriate" instead of just waiting until later to tell the offended party that you didn't think the off-color joke was funny either. It's pushing for more inclusive casting as you climb the writing hierarchy, and pitching female and diverse directors when you get asked for input on directors for the season.

It's doing the work rather than just having good intentions.

Some showrunners truly believe they pay attention to all these things, and they want to be more inclusive, but we all have blind spots. I once worked in a room where we were discussing whether or not a female character wanted to have children. My showrunner said that he worried if she didn't want kids, it made her unlikeable. My entire room looked at me, a notoriously "no kids wanted" female who loves kids but has zero desire to parent (even though I am the world's greatest aunt). I was on the spot, but in a way I was comfortable with. I explained that I didn't want to have kids because I'd been a grown-up basically my whole life, responsible for holding my family together, and I didn't want to do that anymore. . . yet I still felt pretty likeable. It allowed other people to jump in and express their support for why this character wouldn't be eager to have children. We ended up not doing the story at all, but I hope that if it ever comes up in a room for this boss again, he'll remember that a writer he likes a lot once called this out and he'll have a different POV the next time.

Know your line in the sand when it comes to bad behavior and what you'll tolerate.

I know this has come up in other chapters, but this is just too important not to reiterate: *Only you know what's too much for you.* So only you know when someone's stepped over a line in a way that you can't let go of. Once that happens, you can reference the steps I discuss in Chapter 12 about documenting incidents and recruiting support, and if you decide to report, how to move forward.

But I say this again to remind us all that what offends me might not offend someone else in the room. Sometimes when people say, "It wasn't that bad," they aren't approving of the behavior so much as their tolerance for the comment or behavior is different than yours. *But that doesn't invalidate how it made you feel.*

I think one of the biggest problems we run into is people second-guessing their gut feeling that something that happened was wrong because they're being told it wasn't a big deal or that they're overreacting. I spent my whole life around military men and cops. . . it takes *a lot* to offend me, and blue jokes barely faze me. But I understand that other people feel differently than I do. . . and when I see someone react to one of these comments, I try to redirect the conversation or say something like, "Y'all, we're gonna end up in an HR meeting, so let's talk about football instead," or something to make it clear I see that other person's discomfort and am trying to address it. And even if you don't see it firsthand, if someone tells you, "That thing X said made me feel belittled or teased or diminished in some way," listen. It may be worth it to go to an upper level you trust or to the showrunner if you have a good relationship and say, "Hey, you know I'm not overly sensitive, but that comment the other day might have crossed a line. Can we look out for that kind of thing?" You can be an ally without throwing the offended writer under the bus and you can help point out a blind spot to people who often don't mean to behave badly.

Breaking the cycle of abusive room behaviors

This is the simplest yet hardest thing we all need to do as we grow in this industry. We need to not pass on the bad to the new people we work with.

For those of you who haven't been in your first rooms yet, I hope that you never see that bad behavior. But if you do, the best thing you can do is not internalize it. So many of the worst people you'll meet in rooms are miserable humans who want other people to be miserable. So live to disappoint them. Keep your shine on and refuse to be like them.

For those of you who have already been through the toxic treadmill a few times, pay attention to how you react in times of stress or in the ways you relate to the writers in the room and be sure you haven't brought any of those bad habits with you. Even when we know someone's behaving poorly, we may internalize it. So we need to fight our lesser angels when they rear their heads. When you feel yourself wanting to snap at someone in the room, remember how it felt when it happened to you and try to either calmly say what you need to say or wait and have the conversation later when you're less heated. When you say something unfeeling or unkind, own it, apologize, and move on. Remember that you needed sleep and time with family when you were coming up, and make sure your current writers have that now. Find moments for fun. Encourage group activities outside of the room so people can relax and build relationships and not just talk story.

Basically just never lose sight of the humanity of the people you work with. That alone puts you far ahead of the bullies and monsters that are out there in our business. If you can only remember one rule in a tense situation in the room, remember that.

It's not all bad: positive stories about diversity and inclusivity in the writers' room

You'd think from all the above that being an underrepresented writer kind of sucks. But I am living proof that people who are truly invested in building those voices make a difference. Yes, I got my first job because I was a diversity program writer (from NBC's Writers on the Verge program), but I also got it because I had lived experience that my boss believed would be valuable to the show. And because he walked the walk, he encouraged the staff's investment in me and my fellow staff writer to help us build our skill set. I was able to take that early experience and keep pushing forward to this point in my career.

And I've been fortunate to see underrepresented writers who started before me in the business become upper-level writers and showrunners, and to sign overall deals, proving that we can get past those barriers that get set up for us along the way. The staffing repetition and roadblocks to upper-level titles are real, but seeing people succeed in a way that you hope to just fuels the fire to keep pushing past all the crap trying to make you give up and go away.

And there are all the people I know from underrepresented communities who are thriving in this business. . . people I came up with who also are now upper levels, showrunners, and signing overall deals. We are the people proving it can be done, and we are the people who keep banging the drum for even more inclusivity when we meet with executives at PODs, studios, and networks. . . and we make it pretty hard to deny that those of us who were held out of those jobs for far too long are proving we can do them and do them well.

Accessibility

Something I want to be sure to specifically talk about here, because it's something only recently brought to my attention in the past few years, *is what it means to include writers with disabilities into the room.* I'm going to tackle this in two ways — first, speaking to disabled writers about accommodations they should feel empowered to ask for, and second, to showrunners who have the power to make those accommodations.

So, Disabled writers, know that we able-bodied writers routinely get asked if we need anything special for our offices once we're hired. . . ergonomic keyboards, standing desks, all kinds of things. So if you're a writer who uses a wheelchair, it's okay to point out that you need accessibility in the writers' room (elevator access, the ability to actually roll up to the table so you can be part of the group, office space that is easy for the wheelchair to navigate, consideration for safely navigating set and locations, and so on).

For writers who have disabilities that don't require a wheelchair but who do have mobility issues, it's okay to point out that you can't climb three flights of stairs and to say you need a solution for how to get to and from your office if an elevator isn't available.

I think there are other perfectly reasonable things writers with disabilities should feel empowered to request in order to do their jobs. Hearing-impaired writers, you may need/have an interpreter who works with you or need a specific seat in the room so you can easily read lips of the person(s) speaking. And someone can definitely provide closed captions on cuts of the episode or provide assistance on set as needed.

Visually impaired writer? These are all reasonable requests to make of your workplace: understanding that you may have a difficult time seeing the board and reading people's facial expressions in the room. You may do better by sharing a large monitor screen with the writers' assistant so you can better see the notes as ideas flow in the room. . . and you can request that each day's notes are sent to you in a way that makes them easier to review: large print, extra spacing, etc. Another idea. . . now that we've mostly all worked with virtual boards, maybe a PA can type the cards/boards into a virtual system every day so you can review them just like the rest of the team, who usually just look at the photos the assistant takes at the end of the day if we have questions.

Showrunners, this is on us, too. . . because the culture of this business will mean some of our disabled writers won't feel like they can ask for the things I've listed above. So we need to be aware and ask what accommodations need to be made. And if you love this person's work on the page, giving them a real opportunity to be a TV writer will mean more than just hiring them to write; it's about truly including them in the TV-making process like you would any other writer. That means thinking ahead and giving them every chance for success, just like you would for the rest of your writers. . . I hope. And it also means listening to these writers when they tell you what they need. Some will not want the accommodations I've mentioned above; some will need different ones. Ask, then listen.

Also consider that for a disabled writer, just like a diversity writer, they not only don't want to be identified constantly by their disability, they don't want only to write characters defined by their disability. When you hire this voice for your room, expect them to advocate for a doctor or lawyer who is married, has kids, and happens to be disabled. . . but it's not part of their story. Why? Because that's life. . . there are disabled people living rich, full lives in the world (just like with our BIPOC, Latinx, and AAPI communities, etc.), and your disabled writer is going to push you to do better than a cliché, to be truly inclusive. That means stories with disabled people that aren't about their disability. Stories where disabled characters are allowed to get angry and fail and even be villains. . . not victims or heroes overcoming their obstacle. Just people. *Everyone just wants to be seen as people.*

And for all writers, especially the working parents in your room, please, please, please remember that an employee's health and well-being is more important than anything, and now technology has given us an amazing way to stay connected when someone is sick or has to travel for a family emergency or needs to stay home with a sick kid: Zoom. Every writers' room can come up with an extra laptop pointed at the board to allow a writer who can't be in the room but wants to participate to be there. It keeps a needed voice present in the room, and it keeps the writer working without worrying about being in trouble or missing out on important conversations.

Gender/sexual orientation

As more and more of our trans and nonbinary writers make their way into writers' rooms, this is an area people are doing some hard work on right now. I still know people who sometimes misgender trans writers — and it's not always accidental. I still know people who don't understand the concept of nonbinary or who struggle with pronouns they didn't grow up using in the present-day context.

Here's the thing. . . I get it. A child I love is nonbinary, and trying to remember their "they/them" pronouns is a constant work in progress for me. But I do the work because it's what they need from me to feel whole in the world.

But in the same way that it would never be okay to constantly mispronounce a writer's name that may be challenging for you based on your unfamiliarity with the ethnicity/pronunciation, it's not okay to ignore someone's stated gender or pronouns. Period, full stop. That's basic respect that we all deserve.

Which is not to say that some of the old-school bigotry in this realm we're all used to isn't a problem anymore. We just have new problems to add to the menu. Sexism is still real.

Homophobia is still real. I still hear people talking about how bisexuality can't really be a thing.

So what do you do when you come up against this type of thinking in the room? More of the work I've already asked you to do. It's not laughing at the bad gay joke. It's reminding people that most procedurals have typically portrayed trans women as crime victims who get brutally murdered, and maybe let's not do that because it's gross and old-fashioned. It's pointing out that every romance in the show so far has been heterosexual in nature, and don't we have room to do something different? It's not letting the sexist lines of dialogue go unchallenged. It's paying attention to costume choices so we don't send unwanted messages onto the screen in the way our characters are dressed. And on. . . and on. . . and yeah, this one's going to probably be never-ending. . . I'll admit it. But that doesn't mean we don't fight. We just know we're probably going to be fighting these things for most of our careers.

Also I promise. . . TV writing is super fun. But it comes with social responsibility. . . that's just part of the gig none of us can choose to ignore anymore. In the room, on the page, and in casting, staffing, hiring. . . we all must keep our awareness level on high to be sure we're making the effort to include everyone.

And we have to be willing to admit what we don't know. I hosted a panel at the WGA and one of the Native American and Indigenous (NAI) writers who spoke opened my eyes to how NAI characters are portrayed on the whole on TV. . . and now I'm committed to creating characters from this community who are not casino owners or chronic alcoholics who live on reservations. I watched *Disclosure* on Netflix and realized how harmful the imagery around trans representation on TV had been until very recently and swore that I would do my best to try to avoid storylines that continued negative narratives around living a trans life.

We're all still learning, still evolving. . . and we won't always get it right. But the effort counts. Doing the work matters. That's how we will, hopefully, get past the point where we need to constantly have these conversations.

True Tales of Life Inside a Writers' Room

Female BIPOC drama writer
on diversity hire backlash

I was staffed out of one of the network writing programs. I joined the room as the only lower level on the show. I came in feeling very ready to staff. Weeks into the room, I made people laugh. My pitches were always praised, and many were used. . .and many made it to air! Great. So things were going well. And then a curious thing happened.

We went into production, and I was left off all production emails. I didn't have access to dailies — I had to beg for access! I kept offering to do things that upper levels didn't want to do (as Niceole suggests constantly here), and the answer was always no. "No, we don't need help on first passes on things. Thanks for offering to do X but no, we don't need you to do anything."

If you're trying to prove you can do the job, but no one wants to give you anything to do, how can you prove yourself?

The only person who tried to help me was the Number Two on the show, but ultimately he could not convince the showrunners to give me anything to do. They kept asking me, "How is your room study coming along?" and saying, "Are you learning everything you need to learn?" But I was extended past my initial twenty weeks. So I assumed that meant they didn't think I was useless?

And then, on my last day in the room, at the end of a thirty-one-week run, the showrunners said (in front of the whole room) — "We hope you learned a lot from this experience and take that with you when you become a writer."

And that's when I understood — they didn't think I was a writer on their show. They thought I was an intern. They did not understand what taking a writer from a fellowship meant. They thought I was there to shadow, that because the fellowship was paying for a good chunk of my salary, that I was someone who was not really staffed in full capacity.

Afterward I learned that these showrunners have done similar things twice before to network writing fellows. And of course they never had any intention of bringing me back for season two. And because I never got a script and they didn't give me a staff writer credit on the series, it looks like I've never had a job if you check my IMDB. It's beyond frustrating and obviously making it harder for me to get my next gig.

FEMALE BIPOC COMEDY WRITER
ON GOOD AND BAD ROOM DYNAMICS

Working in TV comedy rooms, you see and hear some things, for sure. And there's plenty of opportunity for the toxicity we find too often in this and, frankly, many workplaces. But there are times when we see what a healthy room dynamic can look like. I was a story editor writing on a new adult-animated comedy. To maximize our story development, the show creators split the writers into two groups. The room I spent many of the first weeks in was generating story paths for the creators to consider. Our group was run by one of the co-EPs. Every path, or even kernel of an idea, that I pitched that the creators sparked to, the co-EP went out of her way to make sure the creators knew it came from me. It seems so small and should be expected, yet it doesn't always happen. It was a joyous glimpse of a great writers' room dynamic.

Male mid-level drama writer
on choosing your battles

Our show had a cis het abled-bodied white "everyman" as a lead, and there were pushes for him to be "more active." For some reason, the Band-Aid solution to these story concerns became violent action. As in: Whenever he had conflict, even if it was emotional, if he punched the other guy, that solved the story bump. But I was concerned that it felt like the only times scripts had this character resort to on-screen violence was when it was aimed at BIPOC men. When I brought it up and suggested we try a different story solution, I was met with incredulity. People felt like I was telling them they couldn't tell the story they wanted to tell. While I've often found ways around problematic story points and representation concerns, that time, I failed. And eventually, the character got physical with other people, too, so at least it turned into equal opportunity toxic masculinity? My takeaway was— you can't win 'em all. Handling your losses tactfully can preserve your ability to keep working toward better representation over the following days, weeks, months, or years. That said, rooms are always full of choices. Every writer has to figure out for himself or herself which hills are worth dying on and which aren't.

12

MONSTERS

They can't all be slayed, but they can be survived.

S O HERE WE ARE, AT THE point where we have to talk about the open dirty secret of our business — abusive bosses. I wish more than anything that I didn't have to write this chapter because we lived in a world where all the tyrants have been driven out. But we all know that's not true. Light is starting to shine in the dark corners, but there's still a lot of work to be done.

First of all, let's be clear. . . tyrannical showrunners come in all forms; no gender or race is excluded from the history of bad bosses in this town unless they've been excluded from the opportunities to be bosses at all thanks to the roadblocks created by gender and race. But I've heard nightmarish stories about female showrunners and BIPOC showrunners, along with the more common and well-known white male showrunner tales that filter through Hollywood.

One of the worst elements of this is that many people who become toxic bosses had toxic bosses coming up the food chain. Instead of choosing to do better, they embraced the bad behavior they once suffered under and now perpetuate that work environment with the philosophy of, "Well, I had to endure it and I survived it, so just toughen up."

This is a business where a thick skin and an ability to pivot and let go of your ego is important. That doesn't mean that you need to endure truly toxic and abusive behavior.

This is also a business that still, unfortunately, ascribes to the genius auteur myth — one where genius is equated with difficulty. So people will write off bad behavior because someone is a brilliant writer and hypersuccessful creator. . . even though there are plenty of brilliant writers and hypersuccessful creators who don't trample on people — and therefore, this "genius" myth is bullshit, and we all know it. So just to say it out loud: *Being a genius doesn't mean you get to treat people like shit.* You're an adult and you need to act like one. . . and you need to treat the people around you with respect.

Whew. Okay, now that I got that out of the way. . .

What do I mean when I say, "truly toxic and abusive behavior"?

I mean a room where a showrunner thinks they have the right to put their hands on you without permission. I've been in a room with a showrunner who did this *the right way* — they wanted to demonstrate how someone was grabbed in a scene and said, "Niceole, can I use you for this?" and it was all good. But I've known other writers who have been subjected to "back rubs" that were not asked for or wanted, yet they felt paralyzed, unable to push the boss's hand away or say anything because. . . *boss*. I know female writers who have had male bosses drop a hand on their leg as if that's appropriate behavior with an employee. And I've known female writers who were constantly subjected to sexual innuendo or derogatory gender-based harassment from bosses who think it's still okay to talk to women like that in their workplace.

I mean a room where the showrunner considers it his or her personal mission to try to break the spirits of new and lower-level writers. Bosses who scream things like, "Are you an idiot? Why would you write this shit?" to someone who turned in their first draft of their script. Bosses who willfully ignore their underrepresented writers or talk over the women in the room to put them in their place. It can be both outright hostility and gaslighting. . . and it's horrible.

I mean a room where underrepresented writers are made to feel their "otherness" constantly. Where you're clearly "the Black writer" or "the Asian writer" to them and they barely know your name. I once had a friend get an email for an Asian writer on another show the boss ran because this person legit couldn't keep them straight. He had two Asian female writers, and he couldn't remember which one worked on which show.

But this otherness also comes into play in the room. Having a white male showrunner "Blacksplain" Black behavior to you (substitute whatever ethnicity or gender you represent) will make you want to scream bloody murder. You were likely hired because you have this specific experience, but now this person is going to denigrate your actual life experience by telling you how it would really happen. A friend of mine once had to explain to his showrunner that a Black man couldn't just run up and bang on a stranger's door. That comes with a whole host of dangerous connotations for Black men in this country, and it's just not something they'd do unless it was a life-and-death situation. This concern was dismissed because the showrunner didn't want to deal in that reality. Another friend worked in a room on a procedural show where every time someone tried to pitch a bad guy that wasn't Black or brown because, "Hey, let's not play to stereotypes," the showrunner didn't understand how that could be possible and therefore, literally every bad guy on the show was Black or brown.

I mean a room where a toxic situation is created by showrunners who establish factions on their own shows. This is perhaps the most insidious and pervasive form of toxicity you'll see in writers' rooms. A showrunner has his or her one or two favored writers he or she really likes, has worked with before, and relies on, and, usually to the detriment of the show, he or she empowers these people to run roughshod over the rest of the staff. I've seen writers with one or two years of TV experience blow off suggestions from seasoned co-EPs because they were the showrunner's "chosen one" and didn't think they needed to listen. This also damages morale because as writers turn in their episodes, this small elite group goes off to do the rewrite leaving the rest of the writers completely cut off from the process, breaking new episodes without any guidance from the main brain trust of the show. That usually leads to episode blow-ups and more alienation of the "nonchosen" writers, whom the showrunner then views as failing even though he or she has basically set them up for failure by not mentoring them or truly communicating what he or she wants the show to be.

I mean a room where showrunners treat their writers as if their salaries mean they have surrendered their entire lives to the show. People who hold writers for twelve- or fourteen-hour days in the room, call weekend meetings, and generally disrespect the personal lives of the people who work for them. Look. . . we all get paid *really* well to do our jobs. But that doesn't mean we shouldn't have the right to still see our family and friends and, you know, sleep. This type of boss will legit run the staff into the ground. . . it leads to a room where people get sick a lot, where stress may lead to more infighting, and it definitely leads to lots of turnover in the room, meaning for the folks who can't afford to leave and move to another show, every year is trying to get new people up to speed on the show and the culture. This is also the type of room where people are terrified to be sick, even when they have legitimate medical emergencies to tend to, and where women feel the need to hide it if they get pregnant because they fear they'll be fired if the showrunner thinks they may need time off to give birth.

I mean a room where the person is an outright bully. He or she just treats people badly, regardless of gender, race, or seniority. These people get off on power tripping. This person will verbally belittle people, punish people for pushing back on problematic story ideas, and institute weird paradigms that aim to separate the writers in the room and turn them against each other. I think of these people as the mean girls and boys from high school. They probably know better, but they don't care. Life has taught them that they get to be awful to people and prosper, so they haven't changed as bosses. I once heard a story about a showrunner who required everyone to dress up for a holiday, and people who didn't participate were punished by being asked to perform some demeaning task in the room. What is the point of that except to make it crystal clear to a human being that you have the power to make them do virtually anything?

There have, of course, been some very well-known examples of this toxic behavior — showrunners who have been publicly called out for being verbally, physically, and psychologically abusive to their rooms, crews, and casts. But the frustrating truth remains that showrunners who produce success and make the studios money are harder to topple than they should be. Because we're not talking about people who had a bad day and yelled at someone, then apologized. We're talking about people who treat those around them badly as a matter of practice and who truly believe they will never suffer any consequences for their actions.

So what do you do if you find yourself working for one of these monsters?

I've spoken a lot in this book about finding your allies in the room, but in a toxic room, you may have few to no options for allies. If that's the case, this is when you use your network. Go to writers outside your show to vent, to ask for advice, and to get strategies on how to survive or when to report the behavior.

You should also absolutely be certain to tell your reps what is happening. Make sure they know whom you're having problems with and what exactly is going on. Because you may choose to just try to survive the season and then eject. . . but they need 1. to know you do not want to go back and 2. to start looking for a new gig for you.

But it may be so bad that you have to report. If the behavior is harming you or others and you know it's crossing a line, it may be the only way to try and protect yourself until you can get yourself out of that room.

And yes, I know — we're all still afraid to do that. So it's easy for me to type that here when this business still makes you afraid of standing up for yourself against the monsters.

So here's how you can help yourself if you're thinking about filing a report:

1. *Write everything down.* Keep a log of every incident that worries you once you start to recognize the abusive behavior. Note the day and date of that offensive statement in the room or the inappropriate touching and who else was present. Be sure to describe the circumstances of that time he or she caught you alone and made you feel intimidated and uncomfortable. You can do this as simply as sending yourself or a trusted

friend emails documenting it. Then if you do end up reporting, you can go to HR with real records of the incidents, and they can't just say you're giving them vague details.

2. *Tell your reps.* You don't want your reps to be surprised by this. You should let them know that you're going to contact HR. *But you're not doing this to ask their permission.* You're doing it to keep them in the loop so if the studio calls them, they know what's going on.

3. *Make it a group effort.* If you have found allies on the show who are experiencing the same behavior or are willing to say they've witnessed it, report together. It's going to be harder for HR to ignore two or more people making the same claims.

4. *Contact the WGA.* The Guild can advise you on how to handle reporting and on whether or not your claims meet the legal standard of bullying, discrimination, or harassment, and provide support through the reporting process.

5. *Document any potential retaliation.* If you believe that you've been subjected to retaliation because you made a report of inappropriate behavior, document this as well. Were you suddenly denied a script? Were you barred from set even though you'd been allowed there prior? Are you being excluded from discussions that other writers are being included in? Have you heard that the showrunner has told other people you are difficult to work with? Try to keep track of anything you feel amounts to retaliation, then contact the WGA, get advice from fellow writers, and if all else fails — contact a labor attorney. Retaliation is against state and federal law.

Because the people we have to report to are still the studio HR departments, I won't lie and tell you this process is going to be easy or particularly friendly to you. Every time you start a show or join a new studio, you'll likely have to sit through that studio's version of the "don't harass people" seminar. Every one of the shows run by those notorious showrunners had these same seminars. . . yet the behavior went on for years because people were afraid to report, or because they did report and HR determined that slaps on the wrist would solve the problems. But until we can get an independent reporting body established, it is the system we have. So try to do as much as you can to protect yourself if you feel like reporting the abuse is something you need to do. And don't let anyone tell you not to trust your gut. *If your instincts are saying "report it," then report it.*

Once you are free of this toxic environment, whether you reported or not, whether you stayed for multiple seasons or left at the first opportunity, you have one obligation that I hope you take seriously. *Tell the truth when people ask.* And I'm not talking about the studio or network. . . I'm talking about other writers who come to you and say, "I got an offer on X show. How was the work environment?"

Allow the writers who ask that question to make an informed choice. Because here's the truth. . . they may have to take a job on a shitty show because they need a job. But prepare them for what they're walking into. Let them know this is a show where they might not be heard, where the hours are terrible, where the showrunner yells a lot, where every female writer quits in one year. You're not telling tales out of school. . . you're protecting your fellow writers, so they don't get blindsided the way you did.

Because our responsibility is to break the cycle of abuse. We do that in two ways: by not keeping secrets for the monsters and by not becoming monsters ourselves.

You aren't the bad guy in the story if you know someone's abusive and didn't choose to report because you were afraid of retaliation. But you are the bad guy if you let another writer walk into that situation without warning them what they're walking into.

And writers. . . when people do you this solid of absolute honesty — *it's confidential.* You don't go out saying, "Well, Niceole told me this guy is a screamer and so I don't want to work there." You say, "I did my due diligence, and it sounds like a work environment I don't want to be part of," or "I know it's not a great place to work but I need a gig, so let's sign on for this season and then look for other options for next year."

And then, when you become the boss. . . *never duplicate this bad behavior.* That doesn't mean you'll be the perfect showrunner. We're still all human beings and like I said early on, great show-runners have bad days. But it does mean that you have to fight the tendencies you've learned from these people. You don't throw out scripts after only reading ten pages. You read the whole damn script and see what can be salvaged and give notes to fix the rest or give guidance on what needs to be rebroken to fix the episode. You don't deal with people when you're hot — you walk away and then call the staff writer in later to explain why that thing they did in the room annoyed you or why you need them to up their game a bit. And you remember that the people who work for you will work as hard as you need them to, and your gratitude for that is best expressed in respecting their nonwork lives. Try not to keep people late, try not to steal weekends unless unavoidable, and try to be the kind of boss who lets people see a kid's first baseball game or recital because you know you wish someone had let you do that back in the dark ages when you worked for a fire-breathing monster.

I hope that someday no one needs this chapter of the book. I hope that all the current movements to make our business more inclusive to people with disabilities and people of color and women mean that it becomes more humane on the whole and the monsters get driven back into dark caves where they belong.

But until then, please remember, you are not alone. Even if all your fellow writers can do is listen and tell you how much it sucks to be in that situation, let us. And if you want and need to report, then do it and don't let anyone stop you. Lean on your friends and family for support and know that you're fighting a fight bigger than you. Every time a writer steps up and calls this bad behavior out, he or she is saving other people from enduring it.

And if you don't want to report, don't beat yourself up for it. It's hard to take on fire-breathing monsters. Focus your energy on taking care of yourself, find a way to get yourself to the finish line of the gig. . . and then get the hell out!

And then warn people to beware the monsters.

True Tales of Life Inside a Writers' Room

Female drama writer on sounding the alarm on toxic hires

As our show was beginning to prep for production, our showrunner arrived one day with the news that we had received a list of directors from the studio. But as I looked at the list, one name stood out to me. The name of a man who had sexually harassed a close friend on set. As a department head, she had to spend weeks working closely with him, and she had shared with me how bad the situation was. But for her own reasons she had chosen not to share it with the studio or higher-ups. I felt physically unwell at the idea of putting more people in the position of working with this monster. I had a very good relationship with our showrunner, and I requested to talk with him about another matter. Behind closed doors, I shared my concerns about the director without revealing the person to whom this experience happened. Our showrunner thanked me for sharing this info and assured me that this person would never work on our show. The idea that this person is out there, working and existing, still makes me shake with rage. But I could feel a little better stepping forward to say something and knowing that I had been able to protect our crew.

Male drama writer on surviving a monster showrunner

I was on a series for a showrunner who has since been correctly disgraced for various forms of misconduct. But when I worked for them (and a similarly problematic Number Two), there was always the question of how to stand out in a less-than-conducive work environment. My three biggest takeaways: 1. You can only control what you can control. Make sure your work product (story docs, outlines, scripts, etc.) are tip-top despite the circumstances. Even if your bosses don't notice, someone else will, and that will pay dividends down the road. 2. Even if the room isn't where the real decisions are made, never stop pitching. There's always the chance that you come up with something too good for bad bosses to ignore. 3. When a writers' room is dealing with poor leadership, always have your fellow writers' backs. If you know you're in a bad work environment, likely so do the other lower/mid-level writers around you. Stand together, encourage one another, and get through a bad situation the best you can as a unified team.

FEMALE DIVERSE DRAMA WRITER ON BEING FIRED FROM A TOXIC SHOW

On one of my shows, my last script was co-written with the staff writer (who was awesome). The afternoon after we turned it in, I got called into the showrunner's office. He told me that he had to let me go because even though I was good in the room, the drafts I turned in weren't the right tone of the show. I found that fascinating because all my scripts went through the co-EP for a pass before they went to the showrunner. So after that, I went to that co-EP and asked why I was really fired. This co-EP said it was not because of my writing; it was because I wasn't great in the room — the total opposite thing the showrunner had said. They couldn't even get their stories straight. But this was the type of show where everyone, especially women of color, didn't last very long. So it was no surprise that I was one-season-and-done on this series.

13.

BEING YOURSELF, SAFELY AND CONFIDENTLY

a.k.a., carving out space to be you, no matter the room

I'VE TALKED A LOT HERE ABOUT the things you need to do and should do to succeed in the room. And all of that is real and true, and while most people can't or won't do all of the things, doing a good chunk of them will give you a decent shot at success.

But none of that need to prove yourself and succeed should undercut you. And what I mean by that is, you don't have to sacrifice your whole being to succeed as a TV writer.

Now that's going to fly in the face of some advice you'll hear from other people. . . folks who believe that staff writers — and diversity writers especially — should flay themselves open and work twenty-four hours a day to prove themselves.

One thing I learned as a BIPOC female in the writers' room, though, is that boundaries are essential to your well-being. That goes for what you share and how much you work.

For example, even if you were hired on a show because you have a specific experience — you come from a community featured in the show, you worked in law enforcement or another career that's front and center in the storytelling, it's a family drama and you talked about your nontraditional upbringing in your meeting — *well, that experience is part of why you're there. That's an undeniable fact.* But that doesn't mean you have to share things you aren't ready to share. And that may seem like common sense. But you'll be shocked how, in the moment, you're thinking to yourself, oh, I have a personal story that might really help here, and you'll want to share it, but then your gut clenches up and says, "No, please don't share that," and then you're left trying to make a choice.

You don't owe anyone the worst moments of your life. Or the best ones. Not in a full-disclosure, brutal honesty kind of way. Not in any way that will do you emotional harm. *But there are ways to share those stories that give you a safe distance from them* and protect the tender spots in your heart.

"A friend of mine went through an experience where. . ."

"I read a story about another cop who. . ."

"I saw a news magazine story where a family went through. . ."

You frame it in a way that removes it from *your* experience and share the details you think can be helpful to the story.

But you can also choose not to share. I'm going to say that again. *You can choose not to share.*

Because your life is yours. *Yours.* And people only get access to it when you choose to give it. That means when someone puts you on the spot because of your life experience, you can say you don't have anything to share that fits the story or that you need time to think about it. You get to take a breath and think about how you can tell that story of your parents' divorce or your sibling's death or your awful experience surviving a crime without hurting *yourself.* And if you can't do it, then you don't tell the story.

Being yourself in the room isn't just about these story specific moments, though. I've known writers who will watch shows and movies they don't even like or never wanted to watch just to fit in with the room because everyone else is watching it. There are writers who undertake homework of a list of movies the showrunner keeps referencing so that they can know all of the films, or writers who get shamed for the TV shows they haven't seen, so they give in and watch them. And that may seem like it's not a big deal. Sure, I can watch [X hot show everyone loves]. . . how bad can it be? Well, sure, you *can* watch it, but do you *want* to? I decided a long time ago that I don't watch shows I know are not shows for me. . . things that are too violent or depressing or cynical. Just not my bag.

But it can be uncomfortable to be the outlier in the room. . . so if you don't want to watch, here's how you respond when it comes up in the room.

"I haven't had time to check it out yet. . ."

"Yeah, I tried. It's not for me. . ." (and hold firm when people try to talk you into going back for more.)

"I'm trying to finish up X show right now, but once I'm done. . ." (then never watch it.)

Now if you're a sassy pain in the ass like I am, you can also respond by saying something like. . . "Yeah, no. I'm never watching that. But y'all have fun."

My nickname in the writers' room has become "the unpredictable contrarian" because people claim it's hard to guess what I'll like and what I don't. I disagree. . . I think I'm pretty easy to track. But you only get that nickname if you're willing to speak your mind on what you like and what you don't. So you can imagine I'm not shy about these types of things. But that's not everyone, and I get it. The important thing is to find a way that you can be you and keep things fun and friendly in the room.

Like, what happens when the people in the room want to make fun of what you *do* watch? Well, you can stay quiet and not admit that you love that soapy drama they all mock or that reality show they can't stop slagging on. . . or when they're like "I can't believe anyone watches that," you can say something like, "Well, as someone who does, I watch it because. . ." and speak your mind. I take so much crap about the shows I love that I have come up with a standard reply when someone comes at me with, "I can't believe you like that."

Me: "It's not my fault you don't know what's good."

You'd be amazed how my earnest tone disarms people and makes them really have to stop before they say something else to me. And then usually I'll add on something like, "It's great that you love what you love, but it's not cool to shit on the stuff I love just because it doesn't appeal to you."

It's fine if it's easier for you to just hold your tongue and stay silent about this type of stuff. *There's nothing wrong with choosing the path of least resistance.* But it's also fine if you don't like having to hide who you are behind silence. You get to be who you are. . . you get to hate Mendocino Farms for lunch and say so when people want to order from there (so long as you also go get your own lunch so the PA doesn't have to run ragged over *you*). You get to say, "Yes, you guys talk about the finale of [insert X hot show here]. I'm going to go check my email," and let the room have their fun without feeling like a dream killer or without forcing yourself into a conversation you don't care about.

And what about limiting those work hours? That's not permission to not work hard. *It's permission to live your life while you're working hard.* Full disclosure: We get paid *really well* to work in crazy circumstances and to handle crises with quick turnarounds. I just heard about friends of mine who had to jump into a new episode with two days of prep because of a health issue on set. I've had to rewrite whole acts in hours and whole scripts in three days because that's what's required. *But* if you have plans for the weekend with your family and your boss says, "Hey, can you write those story areas this weekend," you should say yes, but you should also realize that you don't have to cancel all your plans so you can sit slumped over a laptop agonizing over every word you write.

Writers who sacrifice everything to work life not only burn out faster, frankly, they run out of stuff to write about. *Your life is what makes you interesting.* Funny family stories, that terrible blind date, the happy hour that turned into karaoke, the beautiful wedding of your two best friends. . . all of those things are important to who you are, and you can't start skipping them because you're afraid you can't get the work done.

You can get the work done. You work until you have to get ready for the event, you go to the event, you work when you get home, or you sleep and then get up and hit it hard the next day. And you get the work done.

I preach this to you because I am *terrible* at work-life balance. Carole Kirschner, my mentor and Jewish mother, recognized this about me early in the ViacomCBS Writers Mentoring program, and she started working on me immediately. And once I started backing off the work and started spending more time with my friends and family in ways that weren't laced with the underlying stress of "I should be working," everything in my life got better, including my writing. I needed someone to tell me it was okay not to work 24/7. So I'm telling you. . .

It's okay not to work 24/7.

Yes, sometimes you will have to cancel drinks after work because you got asked to rewrite an act by midnight so the showrunner can read it first thing in the morning and distribute it the next day. That happens. Our business is full of emergency moments that require a quick, fast dig-in to get the work done. But make that the exception. . . the times when the clock is truly ticking, and you only have hours to get something finished. You'll feel like that in other situations, but it won't be real. If you have five days to write your script, that doesn't mean you can't leave the computer for five days. It just means you have to manage your time so that when you go take a walk or grab breakfast with friends, you know that when you get home, you need to work X hours to feel like you've done enough for the day. (Only you will know what that X is because we're all varying levels of workaholic.)

This also goes for not carrying your cell phone in your hand 24/7. You get to take a shower or work out or go to church or be in a movie with the phone on silent, slipped into a pocket or purse. . . and if the showrunner called while you were doing one of those things, you don't need to panic and think you're about to get fired. You just call back right away and say, "Hey, sorry I missed you. What did you need?"

It will kill you that you missed the call. But you cannot live your life as if you're legit on call all day every day. Even showrunners miss calls. Because we're all human beings living our life.

So just take a deep breath and return the call when you can.

And finally, I'd say this. . . don't lose the *you* that you've always been to the drama that can take over some writers' rooms. If you're a naturally kind person, be that person. If you like to caretake, do what feels right to help your fellow writers and support staff. If you like to crack jokes, read the room, find your moments, and crack jokes. And if you know you have a tendency to get pulled into drama, watch out and create boundaries to protect you from getting dragged into someone else's problems.

Because that person you are. . . that person should have been who the showrunner met in your meeting. That's who they hired. *So it's okay to be that person now that you have the job.* That doesn't mean you don't have to get a feel for the overall chemistry of the room and do your part to make it work. Maybe you work with a bunch of writers who don't like sports, but three of you are huge football nerds. So be you — talk about football — but just know you can't take over the room with that; you get your moments, then you all move on and talk about something else.

This manifests in so many little ways. I got told early on I shouldn't wear dresses to work because they were too girly, but after forcing myself to wear jeans for a few days, I was like, no one here cares what I wear. . . and I wore a dress. And no one cared. So now I wear dresses to work all the time. . . *and no one cares.* You need closed toe shoes for set and you hate them? Buy closed toe shoes that you love, not what everyone tells you to buy. Get some Chucks or a cool pair of designer tennis shoes. What matters is that your toes are safe from heavy equipment, not that you follow some rule about what shoes to wear. Because I can't say it enough: *You get to be you.*

When I first started out, a writer I respect who had been doing this for years was talking to me about my absolute love of TV and said, "That will fade fast once you do this for a living." But I made a promise to myself that my inner fangirl who loves to talk about TV and movies with my friends would never lose her joy because of the shit I encountered while doing the job I spent my whole adult life dreaming of doing. And you know what? Ten seasons in, my fangirl is still so overjoyed to watch TV, talk about TV, and make TV. That's who I am, and I refuse to let anyone, anything, or any job change that.

So be you. . . while being considerate of the people around you. That's not pretending to be anyone you aren't. . . that part is just being an adult.

True Tales of Life Inside a Writers' Room

Female drama writer on how to properly utilize your network

While networking with other writers at my same level, I met up with someone from another show at our studio. Before our meet-up he asked me if I would read a new script he was working on and give him my thoughts. It was a fairly generic story about a father-daughter. He had chosen to make the main character a Black LGBTQ+ woman, but these qualities had no bearing on the story. When I asked him what inspired him to tell this story, he said that this is what he thought people wanted to read — LGBTQ+, female, and Black stories — but it was based on his own relationship with his dad. I pointed out that his own life experiences as an AAPI man with an immigrant family would come across as more authentic, but that wasn't the feedback he was looking for. His cultural identity was the first five words in his bio, but it wasn't the perspective he wanted to write from. . . the only notes I could give him suggested writing from a more authentic place — a note I do not think he ever heard me out on.

A Niceole story on identifying yourself

I learned early on that my mixed-race heritage meant people had a hard time placing my ethnicity. Since I was raised to identify as Black and have always only identified as Black, I was used to this confusion, because I get a lot of Hispanic or Hawaiian or Native American hot takes. So I came up with my own strategy. In my rooms now, when I introduce myself, I always include some line like, "and I tell a lot of stories about my crazy Black mama, so get ready!" — That doesn't tell the full scope of my heritage, but it does give people an easy, quick answer to "what I am," and it lets me roll out the rest of the story as I see fit.

14

EVERY ROOM IS ABOUT YOUR FUTURE

**The writers' room is where you learn how hard
the job of showrunner is, then choose to do it anyway.**

T HE EBB AND FLOW OF EVERY writer's career takes its own shape. I know people who spent their whole staffing career on one show, then jumped right into the creator/show-runner role. I know people who've had a few years at one show, then moved to another for a few more seasons. And then there's me. . . who ran season to season for the bulk of my career, mostly due to show cancellations.

Whether you're with roughly the same group for your rise from staff writer to co-EP/EP or you move around a lot, *the best long-term advice I can give you is to view every season as an opportunity.* What can you learn about how to improve your craft? Recognize how you're growing as a storyteller. Are you faster in the room, able to solve problems in minutes instead of hours, a faster draft writer? Pay attention to how you're developing and where you can keep working to push yourself. If you're returning to a show, is now the chance to ask if you can be involved in post?

Each season is also a chance to watch the room's relationship with the showrunner and upper levels and see how they share the workload (or do they?). If you're given access to notes calls, you can also observe the relationship between the show, the studio, and the network and try to absorb the dynamic. And hopefully, more often than not, there are production opportunities. The variety of experiences on set are as varied as shows and showrunners, so every one is a chance to improve and to learn.

But what does that all mean specifically? Well, here it is broken down a bit more.

Absorb things that work.

What do you like about how your room breaks story? What do you hate? Do you prefer that writers run their own episode boards, or does it all make more sense to you when one person runs the board for all the breaks and pitches the showrunner? Note cards or whiteboards? What script rules are you obsessed with; which ones do you hate? How are the staff writers integrated into the room? Who does the mentoring, if anyone? Are the assistants encouraged to pitch or clearly told to be seen and not heard?

All of those questions (and dozens more I'm sure I'm not thinking of right now) are things you'll want to ask yourself at every job. Because the integration of those answers will help you figure out how you want to do things when you are asked to cover the room because the upper levels are in meetings or when you're the Number Two. . . or when you become the boss.

For example, my preferred breaking style is an amalgamation of two rooms I was in. My process goes something like this:

To start the room at the top of the season, I like having tentpoles. "We're building toward turn one in episode three, turn two in episode seven or eight, and then in our finale (episode ten, for example), we want to get here. . . this is the loose idea of how the season ends." Then the room brainstorms what needs to slot into the episodes to make those big ideas work.

Once we get into episode breaks, I prefer to start by asking questions. What do we owe from the prior episode? What did we leave dangling that needs to be answered or moved forward? Did we have to drop anything that we need to integrate into our next episode(s)? Discuss and write those things down.

What do we need to set up for the next episode? Write those things down.

What batshit-crazy ideas has anyone had for what we could do in this episode? This could be breaking format — telling a story in reverse or doing a full flashback story or doing one act per character. This could be something we never considered like, "I know we haven't built it, but I really think X and Y need to sleep together in this episode." Maybe "You know, it feels like when that bullet hits so-and-so, we don't really have anything else for that character to do. Should we just kill the character off?" Stuff like that. Let people say it. Write it down. Talk about them. Erase anything that doesn't feel right.

Talk about your main characters with all those things in mind. . . what's that character's emotional story for the episode?

Talk about your B stories. Which characters need one, and what are cool ideas we have for emotional stuff for our secondary characters to play?

Once you have all that, you can start to loosely see the episode. You know that if X and Y are going to sleep together, that's probably the act four out so we can deal with the aftermath in act five (in a teaser/four- or five-act structure).

I had no idea that's how I liked to break episodes before I was introduced to elements like that in my writers' rooms because that's how my showrunners/Number Twos liked to do it. . . and that's how I found my style, by paying attention.

So what else have I learned?

If I'm shooting a show in a different city than I live in, I will almost certainly have a producing director. The consistency week to week helps so much and gives you someone who's boots-on-the-ground and knows the crew well, and who can problem solve at a high level when things go wrong that isn't your on-set writer, who is often just getting to know the whole crew.

I want an upper-level writer invested in mentoring the mid- and lower-level writers. It cuts down on the work showrunners have to do because someone who gets the tone of the show does some of the rewriting before it lands on your desk, and it helps your writers get better and learn the show faster when they receive one-on-one feedback.

I want all my writers to participate in the post process as much as possible. It's an important learning tool, and it helps you start mentally streamlining your scripts before you shoot when you see how much even a tight script may have to cut to make runtime.

I want to create real opportunities for my support staff to get partial or full episodes. And I will not treat them like career assistants. I will do my best to mentor them to the staff level.

I will always make sure a writer gets notes from me and has a shot at rewriting the script on his or her own. It's a crucial learning tool and even in a time crunch, there's still a way to get the work done and help the writer learn from your rewrite.

I will make sure that all my writers know that I hired them because I want to hear what they have to say. . . and if anyone tries to keep them from talking, I want to know about it.

I will always strive to maintain a safe workspace for my writers, my cast, and my crew.

Reject things that don't work.

This isn't just about bad behavior you observe in the room, but by all means — reject that! This is about the stuff that works for some people, but not for you. I hate group-writing — legit hate it, as I mentioned in an earlier chapter. Some people love it. You will not see that happen on a show I run unless we are in a "our hair is on fire" emergency. And when it does have to happen, for goodness' sake, give people whole acts to write, not storylines or scenes scattered through the episode. It's harder for writers to find a flow when they don't know what their scenes connect to, and it's kinder to whoever unifies the script for a cohesion pass if they don't have to copy and paste together a piecemeal set of pages.

What else will I not do?

I won't silence my assistants, even though I have been bitten on the ass by having an assistant who thought they should talk as much as the writers in the room. Sometimes the support staff have great ideas they're just sitting on because they don't feel empowered to speak. So give them permission to speak, and if there's a problem with them getting too chatty, deal with it. Which leads me to. . .

I won't be conflict-averse. If there's a problem on staff, ignoring it only makes it worse and damages morale. If you know someone in the room is misbehaving and you don't want to take it on, that's what you have upper-level writers for, or nonwriting

EPs. *Have someone have the conversation.* . . because you're also not doing that writer or support staffer any favors by letting that person think the behavior is okay. This is part of that mentoring thing. It's a shitty part no one likes. . . but you must be willing to tell people when they've made mistakes and then give them a chance to fix it.

I will never read a few pages of a script and throw it out. This is such a disheartening thing for a staff, and I know it made me want to throw up when it happened to me. It's fine to say, "this isn't working," *but you need to be able to clearly articulate why it's not working.* . . you're the showrunner, that's your job. And you can't do that if you don't finish the read. Because there may be scenes in there that work just fine. . . even if the structure of the episode needs help. But you'll never know that if you tossed the work aside without finishing the pages.

I will not come into a room and blow up the board at the end of the day. Again. . . a morale killer for your room. If you can see that a pitch is going to a bad place and you know that you're going to have to tell the room to rebreak it, be a human being and say something like, "You know what? My brain isn't in this. Let's start up again in the morning." Let everyone go home. Then in the morning when you've got a fresh room, you can say, "You know, I think some of this isn't working for me, so before we keep pushing forward, let's talk about the pacing in act two" or whatever the problem was. You're going to get real solutions if you start fresh the next day, instead of keeping people for hours longer after a full day in the room when their brains are fried.

I will not allow our room to fall behind to the point that we do not have producible scripts on the first day of prep. *It upends the creative integrity of your whole show. Don't do it.* Even if it means you take the script and stay up all night fixing it and then explain to the writer(s) why you did what you did later, you make sure production has what they need to do their job.

I will not allow actors to treat my writers like a problem. The tone set by the showrunner that says, "Writer A is my proxy. Treat them with the same respect" is key on set, and when that doesn't happen, high-level talent will try to run over the writers, especially newer ones. That can also happen with A-list directors, especially ones coming in from features, who aren't used to having to listen to writers. Be the person who says up front what the expectation is, then holds people accountable when they don't meet your standard. As long as you set the bar and maintain it yourself, no one has an excuse to do otherwise.

I will not be afraid to say I made a mistake, that I failed in one of these goals and need to do better. I've seen people drown because they can't admit they messed up. I don't want to be that person. Good leaders learn and do better the next time.

Scout talent.

That awesome writers' assistant who does killer research? The script coordinator who writes great copy for your graphics? The PA who is always early and who looks for ways to be helpful when they aren't busy (which is rare, but still)? These are people you want to remember. . . because they all want to be writers. Read them. Get to know them. Because when you're looking to hire, these will be some of the names you'll reach for so that you can have a lower-level hire (or better if they've already moved up the ladder) that you know you can count on because they've proven themselves to you before.

Keep track of the directors you work with that you love, or ones who did episodes you didn't write but thought came out fantastic. When you need to hire directors, those should be some of the first names that come up.

Remember crew members who really stood out to you. . . the boom operator who had the best spirit, the makeup person who somehow cut an hour out of Number One's makeup time when you really needed it, the costumer who just got what you were after. Again. . . when you're crewing up, these are people who, if they aren't available, can help you find people they like and respect, which puts you that much further ahead of the game.

This goes for the writers above you in the room as well. I've talked to at least four of the EPs I worked with previously about supervising projects for development when I still needed a supervisor to get things off the ground. That was about the relationship we'd built back on staff, the trust we'd created, and the fun we had working together.

One more thing — never be afraid to say, "Hey, I don't think I'm the right fit for this, but I know X, who'd be perfect" and make the introduction. Sometimes that exec who loved you and wants to develop brings you horror intellectual property (IP) that isn't up your alley, but you may know someone who loves horror — even if that's not you — so offer to introduce them to that writer. If a director you adore wants to develop something and you can't take on another project but think you know a great writer for it, make the intro. An opportunity that isn't right for you could be miraculous for someone else. . . so pass it on and be proud when your people succeed. Which brings me to. . .

Relationships, relationships, relationships

It's a cliché because it's true: The entertainment business is about who you know. But it's so much bigger than that simple statement. Agents and managers you work with go on to run PODs for some of your favorite creators; assistants become executives and then move from studio/network to studio/network, and they've always wanted to develop with <u>you</u>. That camera operator you worked with for ten episodes five years ago who made every shoot fun no matter how hard it was, they're now a great director and you want them for your show. That nice guest actor from your third episode of TV whom you hit it off with, they're perfect for this role in your pilot and you've kept in touch.

Yes, you can sell, staff, and shoot a show and not hire or involve a single solitary soul you've met in your career. *But why would you want to do that?* Working with people you enjoy and trust and know are talented takes such a burden off your severely overtaxed TV-show-creator shoulders. . . so find your tribe and utilize them.

Trust me, it will come back to you. When that exec you met with three years ago moves to a new studio and is looking for someone just like you for a new project, if you hit it off with them and stayed on their radar, you're going to get that call. . . and you're going to hopefully end up in a position where you can then reach out to some of the folks you love and say, "Hey, are you busy? Because I've got a thing."

One show at a time. One room at a time. One relationship at a time. That's how careers are made.

True Tales of Life Inside a Writers' Room

Male drama writer on finding inspiration on a less than inspiring show

One lesson I learned the hard way is that you need to respect or enjoy SOMETHING about the show you're joining. You don't have to love every aspect of a series to write on it. But also try to find your thing that you legitimately respond to - maybe that's a character, a subculture in the series, or even a style of storytelling that's unique to the show. If you take a job on a series that you just fundamentally don't respect or enjoy any aspect of creatively, that's going to inherently shine through and harm your work product. You won't deliver material that's up to your own personal standards, and it has the potential to set you back in your career as a result. Sometimes it's better to pass than to take on a show that you know in your heart is a bad fit from the jump, even though that can be hard.

Female comedy and drama writer on moving from comedy to drama

Switching genres used to be a big no-no in the world of writing TV, but nowadays it is not that uncommon. Going from half hour to hour is generally accepted (comedy to drama). It is much harder to go from hour to half hour (drama to comedy). Hour-long shows still need comedy. They still have funny characters and fun bits. The biggest change is that a comedy show requires the writer to work on a story that feeds jokes over and over. Once in an hour-long, the writer is no longer expected to end every scene with a joke, or every line. It's a lot more about the story. Which means more acts, sometimes deeper stories, darker stories, and no undercutting the emotional moments (making a joke after so viewers don't sit in the sadness).

It also means the meat of the script is not in the "blows" of scenes and acts, but rather how the emotional or mystery beats unfold. It is a real skill to impart information to an audience over time, especially in the more procedural shows. Sometimes in comedy, the story and facts are almost second to the jokes. A lot of half-hour showrunners say —fix the story with laughs. But in hour-long, that's not an option. And luckily for many half-hour writers, that is not an option anymore either. Which lead to deeper stories in the comedy world.

In general, the room hours in hour-longs tend to be better. This is not always the case. But there are still half-hour comedy rooms that run rooms late into the next morning, if not keep staff in the room multiple days at a time. They are often chasing the jokes that will make the scene or act blow sing. On the other hand, some dramas might work late hours on set. And writers might be flown out to other states or countries to supervise their episodes. This is less likely in half-hour comedy.

In half hour, a room sometimes writes all the scripts together, which is more rare in an hour-long. And by "write the episodes together," I mean the whole room sits down and says line by line, joke by joke the script and it is written on a giant screen by the assistants. Over the years, more comedy and half-hour rooms hand out scripts to individuals to write (like in an hour-long), but there is an older generation of writers in half-hour rooms who do not know how to type in the current programs and have not written a script on their own in a very long time. In fact, some shows have to have the writers' assistant or PA sit with those writers and type their scripts for them. . . if individual scripts are doled out.

As of late, the two worlds are starting to blend more. Because there are serious, emotional half-hour shows now, and really funny, joke-y hour-longs. And many hour-long writers are funny. There is no one-side-is-better situation, though many writers will lead you to believe so. Both have hardships and great moments.

MALE DRAMA SHOWRUNNER ON WHAT IT'S LIKE TO SPEND YOUR CAREER IN ONE ROOM

I was lucky enough to start off on a show that ran for a billion seasons, and I stayed on for almost the entire run. It was my first writing gig, and in the first season the showrunners were hesitant to delegate anything. It was very discouraging to feel on the outside, but as seasons passed, I learned the show (and them), and they started including me more and more. Learning to produce influenced how I pitched, which influenced my pitches making it in the show, which led to more opportunities to produce.

After a few years, a new problem cropped up: In the back of my mind, I was worried that I wasn't getting exposed to enough other writers and other rooms and other genres of TV. But I stuck around, and in retrospect, the breadth of experience breaking hundreds of episodes of TV and learning to produce them outweighed any creative stagnation.

If you are lucky enough to get the opportunity to climb the ladder on a long-running show, stick around and make sure you take advantage of it. Showrunners are busy and tired. Offer to do the things they don't want to do or find tedious. Ask to be included in edit notes and sit in on Production / Tone meetings. Eventually they'll have you cover those same meetings for them. And they'll have you do an early edit pass before them.

Everything you do on staff for somebody else's show is training for when you have your own show. And the longer you're on a show, the more opportunities you have to train.

A big caveat with all this is that this was a broadcast show. I know those aren't around much anymore, which leads me to one last piece of advice: If you have a chance to work on a broadcast show, do it. There is no replacement for the grind of breaking, writing, and producing twenty-two episodes a year. TV is a craft. Learn your craft. It will pay dividends when you get your own show.

Everyone in the room has a role, from the PA to the co-EP. Some roles are not well-defined; some are better so. There's the Punch-Up writer. The Writer with 1,000 Ideas. The Problem Solver. The one who knows the best restaurants to order lunch from. Personally, I'm a Problem Solver with a minor in Keeping the Room on Task. My advice when starting out is to figure out what role suits you best, and then use that in pitching yourself to the showrunner in your meeting. It shows that you know what your strengths are, and most showrunners will be relieved to find someone to fulfill that role.

15.

Now That Your Career Is on the Rise

**You've broken in; you survived
your first few rooms. Now what?**

J UST WHEN YOU START TO FEEL like you know what you're
doing in this crazy business, a new challenge drops in front
of you and you're right back to, "Oh no, I have no idea what
I'm doing." That's why you need your writer community
around you. This section is about two ways to utilize that. . .
by building a relationship with your union and by relying on
your fellow writers to help you navigate the spin cycle that is
TV development.

The WGA: how can they help you

Aside from the obvious — helping you get paid fairly and on
time, providing health insurance, and negotiating our union
contract with the studios — the WGA has developed a few
programs to help writers build their skill sets and push their
careers forward.

New member mentorship. When you join the WGA, you'll be
asked if you want to participate in the New Member Mentor Program. Say yes. You'll be assigned a mentor, usually on
the day that you attend your official new-member orientation,

where you'll learn how all your union benefits work. Your mentor will have a small group of writers, and you'll have a dinner and get together to ask questions, share stories, and start to build that community. P.S., Orientation day involves breakfast and a chance to socialize with the other incoming members. So it's also a great opportunity to build out your writer tribe.

Staff Writer Bootcamp. This program is one of the newer ones at the WGA, but it's invaluable. Every year, they invite newly hired staff writers to attend a full-day seminar with experienced writers sharing tips on how to handle the room, ways to make yourself invaluable, ways to handle set and post responsibilities. . . all the good stuff. And again, because you're in an environment with other writers starting out just like you, this is another great chance to form connections and develop your community.

TV Writer Access Project. The mission of this initiative is to identify and provide increased access to WGAW members from groups that have been historically underemployed in TV. The goal is to help members who have been unemployed for six months or longer get back in the staffing mix.

Networking through the WGA. Once you join the Guild, there are a few ways to get more involved right away. There are numerous committees you can join. Your participation can be as great or as little as you like, but the idea is that you will have the inside scoop on what that committee's doing in terms of educational or craft-building events, and you have a place to take your ideas when you want to propose a new event. What kinds of committees? There are a lot of options:

> *Genre Committee, Writers Education Committee, Activities Committee, Committee of Black Writers, Disabled Writers Committee, Native American & Indigenous Writers Committee, Latinx*

*Writers Committee, LGBTQ+ Writers Committee, Commit-
tee of Women Writers, Middle Eastern Writers Committee, Asian
American Writers Committee, and Career Longevity Committee.*

Showrunner Training Program (SRTP). Created by Jeff Melvoin
and co-run by Carole Kirschner, SRTP is a recommendation-
only application process. Existing showrunners and upper-level
writers can recommend writers who have pilots in development or have a show that's already been greenlit without the
writer having prior showrunning experience.

This six-week program features day-long workshops on
Saturdays with guest speakers from across the industry —
showrunners of varying experience, studio and network execs
— and relays information about how to handle studio and
network processes, budgets, hiring, running writers' rooms,
wrangling actors, and just about anything else you can think of.

Development: What is it? How to deal with outside meetings when you have writers' room obligations

Development is a strange beast of TV writing. It's often a lot
of work for just the hope of getting the gig to create a show,
meaning you've usually created 50 to 75% of it by the time
you actually get the gig.

Why is that? There's this heinous thing that happens to writers just starting out called a "bake-off." *This happens on what's
called open writing assignments, or an OWA* — an original idea
or piece of IP that a studio or POD is looking to develop but
they need a writer. So a call goes out for writers who seem like
a good fit, and if that's you, you'll read what material they have,
you'll meet with them, you'll talk about what you like, and if
they like you, they'll ask you to create a take.

And that's how you end up creating so much of a show because you already developed a whole pitch to try and get the job of pitching the show.

Yeah, that's a lot, I know. And it's free work, which the WGA is trying to push back on. For now, it's reality. But once you develop a few projects, you should definitely refuse to do this anymore unless it's a project you love.

But let's say you get the gig. You're going to create a studio/network pitch. . . but you also have a day job. And you're going to need to do notes calls and meetings in order to develop this new show. So how, exactly, do you squeeze that all in around your room hours?

There are writers who don't like for their bosses to know they're developing, and so they'll have "doctor's appointments" or "family stuff" to take care of when they need to be out of the room for calls or meetings on their own projects. I'm of the mindset that I am bad at lying, so if I get caught by a weird question about my appointment or emergency, I might blow the whole cover story anyway, so here are my strategies.

1. Request calls and meetings before or after room hours. Even if you're developing with fairly successful people, you get to say that you can't leave the room because that's your job — trust me, they wouldn't want you leaving rooms on shows they were producing to take meetings on other things, so it's fine to put up a boundary here.

2. Ask for feedback ahead of time via email so that you can shorten the length of notes calls. Often the execs/producers have written their notes down anyway. Ask if they can type them up and send them over so you can have time to absorb, problem solve, and save everyone

time on the actual call. Then maybe you can fit it in over your lunch break.

3. If you need to leave the room to go pitch in person, especially when you're talking with more than one outlet, try to consolidate your pitches into one or two days. It's much easier to go to your showrunner and say, "Hey, boss, I have this thing I'm pitching, and if you're cool with it, I got them to block everything into X day or into these two mornings so that I'm limiting my time out of the room." My bosses have been good about this because, let's face it, they all had to do it, too, at some point. And they appreciate that you're not dropping out of the room five or six times to go pitch on different days.

4. If you're scared to tell your boss you're pitching for fear that they will think you're not invested enough in the show or because they've just generally shown themselves to be not generous in this way with other writers, then refer back to my earlier comment. Have a doctor's appointment you can't reschedule, go pitch, and then be better at being able to lie about it than I would be.

Some tips to remember

Pitching, and the whole development process, is a book of its own, really. But there are a few things I want to pass on here:

1. As you start booking meetings to pitch producers, studios, and networks, if you know people who have done shows with those folks or at those outlets, this is another place you can reach out to your fellow writers and mentors and get inside info that may help you succeed. Some studios have a specific format they like

you to pitch in. So someone else who's already pitched there can clue you in. Some execs have particular things they like and don't like, and a writer who's already run into that issue can let you know what to do and what to avoid.

And if you're really lucky, someone you know is great friends with producer X or exec Y, and they will reach out and say, "Oh my gosh, you are going to love Niceole's take on this thing," and hype you up a bit before you go in to deliver your brilliance.

2.   Pitch pages and outlines are sales documents. You may get really specific producer, studio, or network notes on these pages, and you may want to scream at some of them. But if it doesn't fundamentally change your story and it gets you to the next step, take the note. You can find a way to try to write the note-giver out of that POV when you get to script. Right now, you want to sell your show.

But if it's a note that does upend your story in a way you can't live with, then you have a choice to make about how you want to handle it. I went round and round on a project in outline and finally had to say, "I promise, I know this structure works. Please just let me write it." And the studio said okay, and they got it so much better in script than they did in outline. So sometimes you just need to stand your ground and have a conversation.

There may come a time when you have to walk away from a project, even though you love it. It may be that you and the producers can't get on the same page about the tone or that the studio or network wants a different version of the show than you want to make. Or maybe something comes up with the talent or director attached and it's just clear you're working at cross-purposes. It won't feel good, and you'll be terrified... but leaving is better than making a show that will make you miserable. You have more ideas, I promise. Go develop and try to sell one of those.

3. If your producer/studio/network wants you to pitch with a deck (a set of images to support the pitch), try to get *them* to build it and have someone else run the visuals. Writers are not performers by nature, so we have to put a lot of energy into getting the story right. Having to manipulate tech in it as well can be daunting. So it's fine to utilize the support you have from your partners. If you have a director attached to the project, they may happily take on building the deck so they can curate the images to match their vision of the show. But you still have final approval on everything!

4. Only say yes to things you feel really passionate about. If you are successful, you'll be working on this project for the next three to five years. Be sure you want to spend that much of your time with the characters and in the world.

5. If you're developing at mid-level or in your first years as an upper level and someone says you need a supervisor (someone with more experience than you who can help you run and produce the show), make your own list of who you'd like to work with. Maybe it's mentors from your early days or an EP or showrunner you have a great relationship with. Maybe it's people whose work you really respect and admire. Whoever it is, bring your own names into the conversation so you aren't only meeting with people the producers/studio/network like and trust... because you have to trust them, too.

If you don't know anyone personally, talk to your friends about the types of things you should ask prospective supervisors or co-showrunners, and ask those questions in the meeting. Mostly, you want to be sure you're working with someone who wants to help your show succeed, teach you to run it on your own, then go back to their own development.

6. Development is a marathon. Most of your pitches won't make it to script, and most of your scripts won't make it to series. But the only way to get that magical "created by" on TV screens across the world is to stay in the game. So keep developing new ideas, keep pitching, and keep writing.

True Tales of Life Inside a Writers' Room

Female drama writer on developing while working on a series

I think developing while writing on staff really depends on the circumstance. The first time I did it, my boss had agreed, but I knew he was stretching the rules for me and so I never *ever* mentioned it during the workday, although I did take advantage of the quiet office and stay late at night to work.

As I moved up in my career, I felt more comfortable mentioning it in public, but I also was always mindful not to dwell on it too much. When you're in the room, you're on the show's clock and unless your boss is asking follow-up questions, no one really cares how your notes call with the studio went. As a mom, though, I found having a room where the door closed (not something I have at home) was incredibly valuable, and I almost always would pick a few days a week to stay late and work. I would tell myself I'd work from home, but I never did.

I've also worked on projects outside of TV (plays and essays, etc.), and for those, it's the same rule. I don't keep things from my boss because I'd hate for them to think I'm deceitful, but I tell the bare minimum and wait for follow-up questions.

The hardest part is maintaining creative energy, but I find that especially if you're in a room where you feel like a bit of an odd fit, it can be a relief to have another outlet.

FEMALE DRAMA WRITER ON DEVELOPMENT
BEFORE YOU EVER STAFF ON A SHOW

Coming from journalism, I went straight into development and had sold nine pilots by the time I landed a full-time role as an upper level in a room. That may sound like an unusual route, but it may become less so as more writers — especially those from marginalized groups — step sideways into TV careers. Many women, people of color, and other underrepresented folks are simply unable to take the traditional route of moving to LA after college and working our way up the assistant ladder. But we can use that to our advantage. I was hired not despite but because of my unusual background and experience. Now, having run my own room, I look for candidates who have taken interesting paths in life. I know they'll bring character, flavor, and stories from outside the Hollywood bubble.

16

ON YOUR WORST DAYS

Remind yourself: Someone is paying you to make TV.

T HIS IS THE MANTRA THAT WILL keep you sane. Learn it and remember it.

When I was thinking about how to wrap up this book, I realized I had to pass on the best piece of advice I've ever gotten. And it's this:

On your worst days, remind yourself: someone is paying you to make TV.

You'll need it. Because even though this is the greatest job on the planet, it's still a job that involves working with and managing other people.

You will have days where everything is falling apart. . . where a picture car broke down, there's weather warnings that could shut you down, an actor doesn't want to come out of their trailer, and oh, you're also over budget, which means you need to somehow cut a half-day of shooting by the end of today.

When that happens and you want to cry or scream at someone, that's when you remind yourself. . . *checks*. . . to make TV.

Think about all the jobs you had to get you where you are. . . the struggle to pay your bills and student loans or that time you really thought you were going to pack it all in and leave LA because, holy hell, how were you going to make it one more month?

Then look around you. . . you're in the room or on set or in post and yes, things suck right now because TV is still a business and sometimes it's hard to keep the train on the tracks and get the work done.

But then you get it done. TV gets made, and your friends and your parents get to watch it, and your name is up there on the screen. . . written by, produced by, created by. . .

When I thought about giving up writing back before I got into the ViacomCBS Writers Mentoring Program, I realized that I would write for the rest of my life, even if I never got paid, because I am a writer and I love it. I have thousands of pages of material on my computer that no one is ever going to see or pay me for, but I got such joy from writing them, and every word made me better at my craft.

So if I wasn't going to quit, then I might as well keep trying to get paid to do the thing I love, right?

So I kept trying. And now I get paid to do the thing I love.

I hope you will, too.

FREE TO BE YOU AND ME

a.k.a., Ageism in Hollywood is a pain in the ass.

"Post four movies released the year you were born."

"What was the number-one song from the year you were born?"

"Without saying your age, what's something you remember from your childhood that a younger person wouldn't know?"

"I was X old when I got my first writing job. Never give up!"

Twitter prompts like these have become the bane of my existence. Not because I mind them in general — I often get a real kick out of seeing my writer friends' responses. No, they're annoying because of what the responses to them reveal. . .

The majority of the respondents are male writers, with the rare exception of a high-level, firmly established female writer, or women who are obviously under the age of thirty.

Why do I find that annoying? Because I know that I can't respond to these memes because any of my answers will reveal a deeply held secret to anyone paying attention and willing to do the math.

I am fifty-two years old.

Yep. . . you read that right.

Not that more than a handful of people in the entertainment business know that factoid. Most people guess my age between thirty-five and forty, and that's been true since I got my first job in 2013. Like, the window kind of never changes. But I have taken a female writer or two who I became close with into my confidence, and the assistants who had to book my travel definitely know the truth. When I sent one my birthdate, I prepped her with "Don't pass out." She promptly walked down to my office and was like, "That's not real." But yes, it's real.

That wasn't the plan, of course. . . for me to be a late bloomer. I came to LA in 1989 to study acting and realized soon after that I was meant to write, not perform. I studied at a local junior college to cut my tuition costs down, transferred to University of Southern California, got a BA, got a Master's, and went out into the world with my writing.

And was met with a deafening silence.

I made some connections. Even got introduced to a few agents. But the refrain was the same. "We're just not taking on new writers." "We just need you to get some experience." And so it went, year after year.

So I kept writing. Kept trying to supplement my own education by buying scripts at local shops (yes, before the internet made scripts easy to find online, *we used to have to buy them from memorabilia shops in Burbank and Hollywood*), and I watched every TV show and movie I could get in front of my eyes.

I worked a bunch of jobs during those years. I was a hotel receptionist, a police dispatcher, newswire service typist/proofreader, office manager, closed captioner, assistant magazine editor, and freelance transcriptionist, and then I went back to closed captioning. P.S., The hardest thing I ever captioned was the musical episode of *Grey's Anatomy*. So, so, so hard.

I kept writing. I wrote specs. I wrote fanfic. I wrote short stories. *I wrote.*

I got a play I started in grad school produced and made it to the finals of the Disney General Entertainment Content Writing Program, but I didn't make the final cut. I got a manager who didn't do much for me, so I cut him loose. Everything was start, stop. Start, stop. Start, stop. And for ten years, I just kept trying and kept running into brick walls.

And then I started to think, well, damn, maybe this writing thing isn't going to work out. Maybe I should be thinking about a Plan B. So I started a baking business — and I was ready to devote myself to baking as my career *after* I applied to the ViacomCBS Writers Mentoring Program one more time.

And then. . . I got the fellowship.

I've talked a lot about how my career took off after that on various podcasts and panels. But what I haven't been able to talk about freely was the wonderful people who cared about me enough to have the terrible, uncomfortable conversations someone had to have with me. They told me the inside baseball stuff of Hollywood I had no way of really knowing yet. . . like the gray already showing in my hair would age me to people; like my "style" was a little old and I needed to young it up.

Those things were hard to hear. And let's be clear, it's not fair that someone had to say them to me. But it was honest. . . and real. Because for some reason that still makes zero sense, there's this perception that women over forty are somehow done. They don't get youth anymore, they don't know how the kids talk, and they aren't hip or funny. Which is utterly ridiculous, because *men* over forty get hired routinely to write teenagers and young women, and no one ever seems to think they're too old to do their job. But some execs and showrunners find out a woman is in her forties, and they think all she understands is cooking, raising kids, and being bitter at men who sleep with younger women or that they're hardened and shrewish and so they can't write ingenues anymore.

The thing that makes it all so ridiculous is that from my first job to my current one, *the reason I got hired was my experience. . .* the years I spent as a police dispatcher (four), the time I'd spent researching and writing about topics ranging from kidnapping cases to true crime murder tales, the maturity I brought into the room, especially my "Hey, no one's going to die here" mantra. . . because I had worked a job where people *could and did actually die*, and I knew the difference between a tough situation and a true crisis. The time I spent worrying over my aging parents, helping to raise my nieces and nephews, dealing with friendships and relationships that ran their course and ended. . . all of that fed the pages I wrote — that I write now —and what the hell would I write about without all that experience?

My life was the reason I was as skilled, calm, adaptable, and resilient in the room, on set, and in all phases of being a writer as I was, even as a newbie. Yet I knew there were people who would hear my age and think suddenly I was too old. . . not because I was, but because the number would become my defining characteristic.

After I started rinsing the gray out of my hair. . . after I picked up some great t-shirts and jeans. . . people started guessing my age closer to thirty. I was forty-one. And the truth is, my love of TV and comic books, and movies, and toys, and football, and so many other things, comes from such a joyous, pure place inside my soul that it tends to make people see me as younger anyway. So once I added on the hair rinse and the new clothes, I didn't even have to lie about my age to anyone. People just decided I was younger, and I never corrected them. And most people in this business won't ask your age directly. When it has come up over the years, I've been able to have a little fun with it, saying things like, "Old enough to know not to answer that question," or "I was raised by a Southern woman, and we don't discuss things like age." Or I ask people to guess how old they think I am. When someone says something like "Thirty-five?" I'll usually say, "A little older than that" and then change the direction of the conversation.

To this day, I still have people say to me, "You'll see when you're older and have kids, Niceole. . ." and I just laugh internally because that ship has *so sailed* . . . yet I hear it constantly. But I'm grateful for my parents' good genetics and that "Black don't crack" truism that has kept me flying under the age-ism radar.

I did actively lie about my age once, and it made me feel sick to my stomach. A thirty-something comics executive asked me point-blank how old I was, and I was caught off-guard because we were at a social gathering, and I just didn't expect it. So I said thirty-five. I was forty-three or forty-four at the time. And it made me angry that I thought this person would suddenly think I was too old to develop with him if he knew the truth. Because clearly if he was asking, it mattered to him. And screw that. I am a mega-nerd. You definitely want me to develop your comic book things. Age has nothing to do with my ability to nerd all day and night. In fact, it just means I have more experience nerding than your new, shiny twenty-somethings coming right out of film school.

I lost a friend over this issue, which was astonishing to me. This was a man I met my first year in LA and went to acting school with, who also wanted to be a writer. He made a joke about my age on Facebook, and I deleted it and asked him not to do that. I am friends with mostly TV people on Facebook, and again, while I try not to actively lie, I didn't need to broadcast it either. But my friend's response was abject outrage. He went off on me about how "only one of us was working," implying that somehow my opportunities had come at his expense and my lie of omission was the reason. Not the thousands of pages I'd written, not the two network writing programs I'd gotten into and finished. I was only succeeding according to him because I was lying about my age. So I told him that if he thought it was okay to criticize me for hiding my age when I was already dealing with being Black and female in a business dominated by white dudes, then he could kiss my Black ass. (I'm pretty sure there were some F-bombs in there, but I'm trying to be more PG-13 here.) We haven't spoken since. Because honestly, having a man belittle my hard work, to ascribe my success to just this one thing I had the power to erase as a limitation, something I couldn't do with my race or gender, it was infuriating to me in a way little else has been.

I have joked repeatedly with my inner circle that once I have three shows on the air, I'm going to publicly out myself and say, "So I'm X years old. I'm tired of dyeing my hair. And if you don't want to work with me because you think I'm old, well, that's fine. I'll go work with people who know how great I am."

But then I sat down to start this book, and I realized that one of the most important things I could say to people reading this who aren't twenty-something but are still dreaming about starting their careers is. . . *there's still time.* Age doesn't have to be a reason you can't break into TV writing. You just have to know what you're getting into. Know that if you can't hide your age, you have to love it. Be proud of it, and don't let anyone make you feel bad about it. And if you can hide your age but you don't want to, *then don't.*

And if you're going to take my route and let people assume for themselves, just know that it gets frustrating. There are things I just can't reply to in the room because to do so would give me away. Recently we had a conversation about the LA riots, and I couldn't talk about my experience because it would have clearly identified me as a person in college at the time, putting an age to me with my fellow writers. And honestly, I am so sick of it. I'm sick of worrying about the thing I'm going to say that is going to scream, "Yes, I'm old!" So I decided I was going to sit down and write this.

I'm not going to lie. . . the idea of including this in the book is terrifying. And I may not decide if it's really going to make it in until the day I have to send this thing off to the publisher.

But for now. . . it's written.

So now you know. . . I'm fifty-two (at the time I'm writing this). And I can *finally* answer these damn questions without being afraid of being outed because I have outed myself.

"Post four movies released the year you were born."
Butch Cassidy and the Sundance Kid
Pippi Longstocking
On Her Majesty's Secret Service
Bob & Carol & Ted & Alice

"What was the Number One song from the year you were born?"
"Sugar, Sugar" by the Archies

"Without saying your age, what's something you remember from your childhood that a younger person wouldn't know?"
The Commodore 64 computer

"I was forty-three years old when I got my first TV writing job. Never give up!"

Writers' Room
Lingo Glossary

What the heck does that mean?

Some of these I use, some I've heard, and some I've never come across in my career. But hopefully this list will give you some shorthand for the weird terms that come up in the room.

Additing. an attempt to edit or shorten a script during which you end up adding an unhelpful amount of extra material

Alt. a different take on a scene, action, or character reaction than what was just pitched or what is on the board

A side/B side. figuring out what to lay out before vs. after a pivotal piece of information, important scene, or plot point is revealed

Baby writer. a term used to describe new/lower-level writers — preferred term is "new writer" since people can start their careers at any age.

Barrel. when you have an overload of jokes in a script in a similar area — so if you have a lot of jokes about shoes for instance, you're in a shoe barrel.

Beat the pitch. Can anyone come up with something better than what's on the board?

Big-lipped alligator moment. a very bizarre scene in a normal story that veers off into the surreal or strange — upon exiting that scene, the plot continues on like it never happened.

Birdbrained nincompoop. used as an adjective to describe dialogue in a script intended for children, where the insults being thrown between the characters are clichéd and unconvincing — when you're writing for kids, there's a limit to how rude you can be, which can be a problem when characters need to argue.

Bit. the joke or concept a scene is built around — sometimes this also becomes the show set piece.

Blow. a funny joke that can be used to end a scene — in a drama room, this is also a "blow line" to get to the act out.

Blow your load. means why wait, do the big story point, joke, etc. right now — often used as an expression of positivity, saying don't hold back on a story you think will come down the line in the season. Impress everyone now.

Blue sky. when any idea goes because you're throwing everything out there, trying to find what sticks, usually a set period of time in the room at the start of the season or when an episode isn't working

Boathouse story. when one character takes another character down to the boathouse (or another remote location) to tell them a deep, dark secret

Bottle show. an episode that takes place only on standing sets and preferably uses only the main cast

Broom. an exit for an episode or a show

Building a front porch. when you want to add something to the top of a scene to help you get into the meat of it (or just throw in some exposition on the way)

Bump. "I'm bumping on this beat" means someone has an issue with the beat or moment and is looking for a slight adjustment.

Button. end of a comedy scene, often the last joke — it buttons up the scene, meaning ends it cleanly and sets the tone. Also used in dramas. What's the emotional button on the scene?

Callback. referencing something specific that was done or said in an earlier scene or in the same scene

Can I give that a haircut? as precursor to tweaking or punching up someone else's pitch

Cards up/cards down. used for storylines where one character might be hiding their true motives and has to conceal what they're doing

Carrying the idiot ball. where a character's stupidity fuels the story line

CBA. meaning "could be anything," a joke where a key component is interchangeable with many other options

CBB. usually formatted as "xxCBBxxx," it means "could be better" — I usually glare a lot if people use this in their script notes. Don't do it. You can say "beat this line" if you want to push for something better.

The chair. the physical chair or object in the room that represents an absentee showrunner

Chuffa. the random dialogue characters say at the beginning of a scene before getting into the storyline — also the action that can play at the top of a scene. . . you often want to cut through this to speed things up.

Chowder spout. a bad, gloopy, thick chunk of exposition, a.k.a., an "info dump" or an "expo dump"

Connective tissue. the stuff that gets us from logic point A to logic point B so the audience understands how the characters figured things out

Couch moment. sweet moment or lesson in a sitcom, like they are sitting on the couch to have a heart-to-heart — some rooms just call this the "heart moment."

Counterpoint scene. a privileged scene between guest stars that furthers the story, for example, your bad guys executing their crime, a cross between two people that will play into the A story later on

Detonator word. the key word that reveals the joke — which should be as close to the end of the punchline as is linguistically possible

Ding-dong. came from Laverne & Shirley. "Could we find someone dumb enough to _____?" Ding-dong, it's Lenny and Squiggy.

Double beat. when you have two redundant scenes that cover the same information or when you have one character/two characters repeating the same action in the same episode

Dramageddon. too serious for too long; lighten the mood

Expo fairy/exposition fairy. the evil little sprite that drops a boatload of exposition into a scene — actors hate being the expo fairy in scenes.

Evidently chickentown. If a rewrite requires lots of small but significant changes, and it all adds up to a big pile of work, then it's evidently chickentown.

Feathering the fish. when you keep adding and adding to a beat to make the logic work

Fighty, punchy. the obligatory third-act fight scene

First-thought theater (a.k.a., bad-pitch theater or first-take theater). a way to frame an idea that just popped into your head as the room conversation was flowing and may solve the problem — "first-thought theater, but what if we. . ."

The flip (or flip-it-and-dip-it). From "flipping the tables," it's when a story takes an unexpected turn in the opposite direction for a joke. Can also refer to a character who makes an unexpected move, out of character. The character "flips the script."

Flip the dolphin. changing the order of words/phrases — instead of "I love dogs. Is that a mutt?" someone changes it to "Is that a mutt? I love dogs." Legendarily birthed in the Cougartown writers' room.

Frankenstein (verb). joining already-written scenes together in a highly inelegant way — You know it's not pretty, but it's a temporary tool that might give you some idea how the completed sequence might work.

Frankenstein draft. preferred term for a script written by multiple writers where each writer takes a single act and a high-level writer then stitches it together. "Group-write" is also a common way to describe this. *Do not use or tolerate the usage of the old, overused term that starts and ends with a G — the one that references a violent assault.* That phrase needs to be banned for all time from writers' rooms. If someone uses it, call it out immediately and make it stop.

Fridging. when a female character is killed to give purpose to a man's journey

From there, it's a mad dash to the logo. We solved the thorny plot and character dynamics of the middle of the third act and are clear to race to the ending.

Front porching. excusing something before you even explain it or pitch it

Future us problem. a way of saying, let's just do the cool thing now and we'll deal with the consequences when we get to that point in the show

The f***ing crowbar. cramming in an F-bomb before the final word(s) of a punchline for added pizzazz — normally effective, but a soft indicator that the joke isn't one of the best

Gag desert. the bit of comedy script that goes on for too long without a joke

Gack. stuff, like the "gack" cops use in procedurals (guns, stun grenades, etc.) — usually stuff that's a staple on the show

Game. the joke that builds on itself/escalates from scene to scene — this is a big UCB Theater term and refers

to improv games when people "yes, and" a joke to make
it bigger.

Gilding the lily. piling on more beautiful to a moment
that's already beautiful and working well

Gilligan cut, a.k.a., a Gilligan. a cut that reverses or
undermines what's been set up in the previous scene

GOM. short for "Gift of the Magi," used instead of deus
ex machina

Gorilla. a plot point or joke that the audience will
remember after the show is finished

The Hammer. On a comedy, "The Hammer" is the funniest
one at the table.

Hang a lantern on it. lean into the thing you know is
obvious in a scene rather than try to avoid it: "Yes, what
he's doing is suspicious, but let's just hang a lantern on it."
Also "leaning into it."

Hard joke. a joke that is set up a few lines before and
is just funny on its own. . . not necessarily due to the
character's voice

Hat on a hat. something added to a beat that isn't needed
because something is already there to do the job in
the scene

Heightening. The process in which you make sure each
of your beats in the scene has a higher impact, and is
naturally funnier than the preceding one

Hide the ball. keeping a clue/character/motive/plot point
hidden until later in the story

Honey trap. again a super-dated term, often used in drama
when a man or woman tries to seduce someone else
for intel

House number. not the pitch per se, but the general area of
what you want it to be

In my brain/in my head. generally a backhanded way
of explaining an unfavorable opinion, like saying "In my

opinion" — as a showrunner once responded, "I don't care what you think. It should be about the characters."

Info dump/expo dump. that point or points in the episode where a lot of facts, clues, or details need to be explained to the audience — "here's where we put the obligatory top of act two info dump."

Irving the Explainer, a.k.a., Morris the Explainer. the guy who explains all the mysterious bits of the plot, usually about two-thirds of the way through the episode/season

Inside baseball. whenever a storyline is considered to be something that would only appeal to those who live and/ or work in a specific area/industry, usually Los Angeles or the entertainment industry

It's sixes. shorthand for "six of one, half a dozen of the other," a.k.a., I can't decide which is better

Jengags. as in "Jenga gags," i.e., too many gags piled on top of each other

Joke motel. an actor/actress who isn't funny — jokes check in, but they don't check out.

Jumped the shark. the nice way of saying the joke/ story could ruin the show — this is based on a *Happy Days* episode when The Fonz literally jumped a shark in water skis.

Kill your gays. a thing to not do; a well-known trope where gay characters are often killed off just as they finally achieve some sort of romantic happiness

Killing kittens. removing jokes that you really love because they're getting in the way of the story

Lamb chopping. when a character eyeballs someone or something they deeply desire but know they're not allowed to have (like in a cartoon wolf's thought bubble)

Lampshading. addressing a flaw, recurring trope, or plot hole by having a character point it out

Last man standing. the line that made everyone laugh like crazy at every read from day one, but, with enough people reading it over long enough time, gets taken outside and shot in the end anyway

The lateral punch down. when someone pitches joke or story changes that do not boost the jokes or story — like, they just make the script different. "Instead of Carol-Ann falls into a pie. . . make it Carol-Sue falls into a pie."

Launching grenades. when a writer on staff continually blows up other people's pitches without offering any alternative ideas. Don't be this person.

Laying pipe. planting the exposition that is necessary for the audience to understand what's going on — how did we get here? Is it clear?

Let's order dinner. words you never want to hear in a writers' room because you are going to be working late

Let's put a girdle on that/let's put it in Spanx. Let's tighten this shit up.

Let's Thanos snap the room. splitting the room in two so you can work on two different episodes/stories simultaneously

Lightning rod/purple goat/clay pigeon. a joke put into a script that is deliberately controversial, tasteless, or offensive, and designed to attract discussion and worry from producers, executives, and (in the United States) the Standards and Practices department — the lightning rod will be fretted over and eventually dropped, which is fine. . . because its true purpose was to deflect attention from another, only slightly less offensive joke that you really want to make it through

Logic police. When there is a logical flaw in a script that is significant enough to cause problems, somebody — an actor, producer, director, script editor, or the writer him/herself — must appoint themselves the "logic police" and point it out.

Make a meal of it. build an action or moment to really get every ounce of story and emotion out of it

Mary Sue. usually refers to a female character depicted as perfect and generally lacking all flaws (a.k.a., boring)

Monkey tennis. comes from a skit where Alan Partridge is pitching ideas to a commissioner, then after many failed attempts he just goes "Monkey tennis?" — so sometimes if you pitch an idea and someone goes "It's a bit monkey tennis," they mean it's odd.

More mouths to feed. This is when you have a large number of characters who need lines and story beats in an episode or scene.

Moustache-twirly. a villain who is so on the nose and evil, you expect him or her to twirl his or her moustache

Move it to the right. starting the story later (and, effectively trashing the earlier "slow burn" beats of a story on the board). Conversely, **move it to the left** means pulling a story up, forcing you to rebreak new beats later in the episode.

Mushy. as in, "this dialogue is mushy," meaning it's not as clear as it can be

The Nakamura. where you have a joke that you have several "callbacks" to during the episode. The first joke dies, and you realize you have several more references or "Nakamuras" ahead waiting to die a miserable and painful death.

Narm. essentially, "never mind," when you want to eject from a pitch — "what if we end this scene with — wait, narm."

ND. nondescript: specific mentions that are necessary to location/background/casting but require no special detail. "Two ND OFFICERS" = two police officers, no special requirements.

Needs a chiropractic pass. story *nearly* works but something structural needs adjusting — it usually means things are a bit too complicated.

Noises Off. Any time a writer pitches a chaotic story with multiple characters miscommunicating with each other, regardless of whether or not it makes any sense, he or she compares it to the 1982 Michael Faryn play *Noises Off.* It's a lazy way of justifying a series of chaotic events with no thesis or logic as grounding narrative anchors.

Noodling. another way of saying, "I was thinking on it." "I was noodling that act out, and. . ."

Not this but. when you suggest something obvious, crap, or half-formed, hoping that it'll get the idea ball rolling and lead to something better

On/off switches. writers who do nothing in the room until the showrunner comes in and they "turn on" — *don't be these people.*

On the nose. a line that is just too clumsily obvious and too direct, and lacks subtext

Opening the kimono. similar to peeling an onion, this is a dated term used all too often (still) to describe when a character reveals something personal — they "open the kimono" like a geisha.

Opposite, opposite. right ideas but flip the order

Out over his/her skis. a dated term to explain that someone is in over their heads, rarely used in a room, often used in executive meetings

Pigeon lands on center court. something impossibly basic that everyone laughs at

Piggyback off that. adding/building on someone else's pitch

Pile of skulls. shorthand for "the thing your showrunner is saying is optional but is actually mandatory," for example,

"What if it's a pile of skulls?" said as a joke, but it keeps coming up. Just make it a pile of skulls.

Pitcheroo. anything that reads well in a pitch document or story outline that you know won't quite hold water when you are writing the actual script

Poke holes in it. pointing out flaws in a story — don't do this unless you have a fix for it or unless you frame it with, "I don't have the solve, but. . ." then point out the problem.

Problemtunity. when the room looks at a story problem as an opportunity to come up with a cool character bit or clue to fix the problem

Pull a waternoose. This is when, in your climax, you have the villain unwittingly confess his crimes on live TV.

Pull up the story. another way of saying, "this needs to happen sooner"

Punch/punch-up. when writers are asked to make the current jokes in a script funnier — for some comedy writers, this is their only job (often shows have a break-off "joke room" with a small group where those writers only do punch-up). It's a true skill to know not only how to pitch on a current existing joke, but to also fit in new ones.

Put a pin in it. when a room is stuck on something and decides to come back to it because they can continue to work elsewhere in the story — also "table it"

Putting it through the blander. the implementing of network notes

Queerbaiting. where a show hints at but doesn't actually depict an LGBTQ+ relationship. Also "gaybait."

Ratings gold. a character moment that you know the network is going to love and promote the hell out of because they know people will watch the show for it

Real estate. Time in a comedy show is like land in Manhattan: There's only so much of it. If the episode you made runs really well at thirty-four minutes, not the intended twenty-eight and a half, it's no good and it's like asking the BBC to move the news; you've got to edit it down. True in dramas as well. . . most scenes get limited real estate. . . if you get to write a three- or four-pager, you're getting a dramatic gift.

Refrigerator logic. Something in a story that makes no sense but that the writers blow past it, assuming the audience won't notice until they go to the refrigerator; also called an icebox moment

The restaurant on the corner. a bit in a script where no matter what joke you put there, it still never quite works

Roll up the windows and drive by fast. an acknowledgment that there's a potential weakness in a moment/beat but we think we can get away with it, so we're just moving on — also "hand waving" our way past something

Root beer scene. a scene added to fill out time in an episode that ends up short — can apply to episodes created to pad a season order as well

Row of kettles. a plot point so contrived that its chances of working are exactly zero

Route one. an obvious, unsurprising, or unimaginative choice

Say-and-see (also known as a show-and-tell). a section of the script where we see what we are told. . . *often used in montages for dramas, especially spy shows.* While great in *Ocean's 11* — as they are explaining how a heist will go down, we see it in action — this is more of a no in comedy. Don't tell us in the next scene what we just saw in the last, unless the joke is that this is happening.

Schmience. fake, jargony science talk or idea ("We have to modulate the frequency to overload the buffer," etc.)

Schmuck bait. a story choice that is clearly *not* going to have dramatic value because it will *never happen* (like putting your lead's life in jeopardy when the show is named after her. She's definitely not dying.)

Script-saving note/script saver. often used as a fun joke for a note that is tiny and useful but not dire to the success of the script, such as a typo or likes

Scud. a joke that ends up getting the wrong target, for example, "The energy companies have done some truly appalling things — one of them based itself in Newport." The punchline is saying that Newport is shit, and not saying anything about the energy companies. Named after the outdated and inaccurate Soviet missile used by Iraq during the 1991 Gulf War.

Send that through to wording. when you're writing in a room and you've collectively got the shape and structure and comic idea of a gag or scene in place, but it needs writing up/rewriting

Set piece. the big funny concept the episode might be built around — usually there are two in a comedy half hour. They are big stunts or big belly laughs. Often physical and filled with spectacle. More for multicam. In drama, this is usually the big action/stunt piece or a piece that requires a lot of shooting choreography, like a huge party scene in a special location.

Shimmy. an add-on or slight adjustment to someone else's pitch — "a shimmy on that, what if we also did. . ."

Shave the monkey. describes tightening or streamlining a storyline or pitch — "I think we can shave the monkey if we. . ."

Shit fairy. when the room comes in after an evening off and goes through the board again to see if any story holes came to mind — "Let's see if any shit fairies showed up."

Shoe leather. the physical traveling or action of a character that is used to piece together clues or pieces of information in a story

Shruggo. dialogue that a character speaks while shrugging

So stupid. If said while laughing, this is normally a term of endearment for a joke that is so funny it is stupid, or so in character it is funny.

Small/tiny thing. Okay when not used in excess, this is a tiny note and a way to set up giving that tiny note if you are not the show or room runner. It will grate on people if used too often. "Small thing, there is no R in found."

Sport the sport. writing a scene dealing with athletics

Story armor. because we need this person for the story in episode/season X, nothing fatal can happen to them

Straight reversal. a joke construction that's very useful in topical comedy, where the premise of the gag is more or less a comical inversion of a real news story

Stress test. troubleshooting a story or idea, checking for plot holes

Taffy it out. When you take a conflict, or mystery, or any piece of story and stretch it longer than it needs to be (usually hoping to maximize tension or suspense)

Take the stink off. How can we make this obvious plot move a little more palatable because we need it, but we also know it's obvious?

Technobabble. language used to try to make scientific terms less intimidating

Tee up. setting up a reveal for later in the episode/season

That's a flight plan we can fly. when a pitch solved a plot problem

Thirty-thousand feet. Let's pull back and take a look at this from a higher-level without worrying about the details.

Tiny town. something that feels too close as to stretch credulity, for example, if everyone in your story is connected in a way that feels like it closes the world up

Treacle cutter. a joke used to cut a sappy or sentimental moment

A truck full of ducks. when you chase something and catch it, but it turns out to be completely wrong

Turn joke. when you start off one way and then land another — the joke is the surprise turn in the line. Like, "wow this dance is everything: cheap decorations, bad punch, and Teen BO — I love it!"

The turn. the unexpected thing that happens in the story that no one will see coming

Two bites of the apple. when you're able to stretch part of a storyline into more than one scene/hit it twice without being repetitive

Unfunny Moon. the desolate, airless place that comedians and presenters go when a joke doesn't land

Universal. as in "can we make it more universal" — this is usually code for can we make it more relatable to white audiences. . . red flag!

Up and back. when a character goes to X location, then to Y, then back to X — usually used to say, "Can we simplify this action, because right now, it's an up and back."

Vil-lil-oquy. a villain monologue (I'm trying to make this a thing. Work with me, people!)

Vomit draft. the very first draft of a script, which is almost certainly not shown to anyone — it's invariably full of typos, misfired jokes, and logical flaws. Also "puke draft," "draft zero."

The whiparound. an end of episode montage that checks in on all the main characters and where they are emotionally as the story wraps up. Also "round the horn."

Written in yellow sharpie on the board. used to explain a character who has no real story or drive you can cling on to, so you kind of have to squint or step up closer to try to get it, as if someone wrote it on a whiteboard in yellow sharpie

"Who's Jackie?" usually shouted at the table when a writer pitches something that reveals he/she hasn't been paying attention

Yes, and. a good way to jump in on someone else's pitch by supporting it and building it out further. Also if you mean "but," then say "but. . ." You can disagree with a pitch.

Your case, my case, same case. where two cases/ stories converge

Zammo. a pop-culture-reference gag that works in the writers' room but plays to painful silence in front of a youthful audience

DOCUMENT SAMPLES

Story areas and outlines look like what?

Included here are story areas, a synopsis, and an outline sample. This is by no means meant to be exhaustive because formatting varies room to room. But it should help you get a sense of how these documents are formatted while on a TV staff and why they're useful in the process of selling the story to the studio and network.

Thanks to Jeff Rake and Amanda Green from The Mysteries of Laura for allowing me to include our work from our Valentine's Day serial killer episode, "The Mystery of the Dark Heart"!

The Good Wife samples were created from a spec script I wrote in the ViacomCBS Writers Mentoring Program in 2010 and aren't reflective of their actual document formats.

- *The Mysteries of Laura* story area
- *The Mysteries of Laura* outline
- *The Good Wife* spec story area
- *The Good Wife* spec synopsis

The Mystery of the Dark Heart

CHRISTOPHER STANTON, 25, sets a scene for romance in his stunning penthouse apartment with beautiful views of NYC. . . rose petals line the floor, a gas fire roars, Marvin Gaye plays on iTunes. . . then a GLOVED HAND appears behind him, driving a DOUBLE-EDGED DAGGER into his back.

As Laura and Jake arrive at the crime scene, he quips: It's Valentine's Day. . . and they get to spend it with a dead body. Laura, fresh off her break-up with Tony in 213, begins an episode-long mission: let Jake know she wants him back, a task complicated by the fact that he thinks she's still with Tony. Jake interviews Chris' NEIGHBOR. . . looked like Chris was expecting company. Does Neighbor know who? She mentions his new girlfriend, TRACY CONLEY. Laura's eagle eye detects a woman's glove behind the couch. . . overnight bag with Valentine lingerie hidden in a corner — Chris' date had already arrived! The team scours the city for Tracy, driving on the theory that a heated argument led to murder. Meredith, staring daggers at Billy, comments: Maybe Chris blew Valentine's Day and Tracy killed him for it. Laura shakes her head at the fledgling couple and announces: She's not convinced. She re-examines the crime: the methodology, the timing. . . and bam! Something clicks for Laura. She pulls up an old case. . . *St. Valentine*. . . a notorious serial killer who struck five times in New York City from 1989 to 1993. . . his MO: kill the male half of a happy couple on Valentine's Day with a brutal knife strike, hold the female for thirty-six hours, then kill her and dump the body in a park. Jake sees the connections, but GLEN WILSON, a.k.a., St. Valentine, was shot and killed by the NYPD as he fled his last body dump in '93. The squad's working theory: *It's a copycat killer.* That means Tracy's got thirty hours left to live.

Laura wants to talk to the detective from the original case, but per Max, that officer is dead, and his partner's retired to a fishing boat in Puerto Rico. But a member of the citywide task force who hunted St. Valentine is within reach. . . former captain DAN HAUSER. Laura races to Wakefield Correctional as the squad retraces every step of Chris' life for clues. Hauser's initial thought: *Maybe they got the wrong guy back in '93.* But Laura moves past that quickly. . . Wilson was seen with the last body. But the current murder *is* connected. . . details, like the knife used, a collector's blade with a center ridge, are too exact. A review of the original case leads Laura to a key fact. . . DNA collected from murders pre-1995 weren't tested unless a case was going to trial. In a case with a dead suspect? *Never.* A fast-track test confirms — DNA found at the new crime scene matches samples from the original murders. . . but it's from *an additional suspect.* Laura reaches a stunning conclusion: This wasn't a copycat. *Wilson had a partner.* The St. Valentine murders were the work of *two people*, a la the Hillside Strangler case.

Billy and Meredith score a partial license plate while canvassing Chris' neighborhood. It returns to a business — DCI SECURITY — but at a residential address. Instead of the killer, Laura encounters MINDY SIMON, 40s, a divorcee who lives alone. Mindy remembers the Valentine killings — that's why she got a home security system, and how she met her husband. Mindy fell for her alarm installer, WAYNE BURROUGHS, back in 1993. They were happily married for years but then hit a rough patch and broke up. Laura recognizes the name "Burroughs" from the old case file. Glen Wilson had a cousin named Burroughs who claimed his body. Laura's theory: *Wayne* was Glen's partner. He went dormant after Glen's death due to a happy marriage. . . but was triggered again by divorce. The team has ID'ed the *other* St. Valentine killer but finding him could be impossible — the task force was never able to figure out *where*

St. Valentine killed his female victims before they were dumped in the city's parks. Wayne could be anywhere in the city -- and Tracy is running out of time.

As the team brainstorms possible hideouts, an alarm on Billy's computer blares — it's a "Happy Valentine's Day" reminder set by Meredith, who's frustrated Billy hasn't mentioned the holiday once. The alarm keys Laura to a life-saving answer: Wayne works as *an alarm installer*. Clients alert his company — DCI — when they go out of town for security purposes. . . he has his pick of empty homes in proximity to the numerous parks — and one of those houses is where he's holding Tracy. Laura cleverly profiles Wayne's psyche to pinpoint a location near Riverside Park. In a dramatic showdown, Laura and the team rescue Tracy and end Wayne's reign of terror.

With Tracy safe and Wayne behind bars, Billy lures Meredith down to the holding cells and surprises her with a romantic Valentine's surprise complete with twinkling lights and dinner — he ignored her all day hoping to get her to admit that she wanted him to treat her like they're a real couple. Meredith accepts a sparkly R2-D2 necklace from her "boyfriend," and admits: Yes, they're a couple. Laura, meanwhile, sits at her messy dining room table at home, stress-eating conversation candy hearts as she waits for Jake to arrive. When he does, she realizes there's only one heart left, and she holds it up to Jake in an effort to finally tell him how she feels. Jake: "Email me"? Laura rolls her eyes and pulls him in for a kiss. . . mission complete.

[NOTE: The ending of this episode changed when we actually broke the episode, but this was our initial idea. Then of course, we made everything messier and more complicated by adding Jake's new girlfriend to the ending, which kept Laura from expressing her feelings. You'll see this reflected in the corresponding outline sample.]

The Mystery of the Dark Heart

Written by Amanda Green & Niceole R. Levy

ACT ONE

1.1) INT./EXT. LOFT — NIGHT

A beautiful balcony overlooking a sparkling view of NYC at night. PARKER HENSHAW, 25, shirtless, hot, puffs on a cigarette, then stubs it out, comes back inside. As he turns to lock the sliding door, his body JOLTS, as if he's been hit from behind. Pain and confusion on his face. Parker drops to his knees. He tries to spin around, but a LARGE KNIFE BLADE swings downward, wielded by AN UNSEEN ATTACKER. The knife drives through Parker's back, exits his chest, heart pierced by the blade. As he falls out of frame, we PULL UP to that stunning view and TIME LAPSE to sunrise. SMASH TO:

1.2) INT. LAURA'S HOUSE — DAY

Laura filling Dixie Cups with Valentine CONVERSATION HEARTS, then wrapping them in Saran Wrap tied with Christmas ribbon. Epic mom crafting fail. Alicia enters, offers to take over. As Super Nanny salvages the boys' Valentines, she quips: The twins have their party today. What's Laura got on the V-Day agenda with Tony? If it requires a babysitter, Laura's leaving it pretty last minute. Laura's not in the mood to celebrate in the wake of Santiani's death. And, she admits, she and Tony broke up. Alicia teasingly asks for Tony's number. . . but then, seriously: Does this mean Laura might give it another go with her ex-husband?

Laura: Yes. No. Maybe. . .We establish that Laura hasn't told Jake about her newly available status. And would he even want her back after she recently kicked him to the curb all over again? Her indecision is interrupted by her ringing CELL. Speak of the devil. . . it's Jake. Laura listens, then says she'll see him soon. Alicia: Date? Laura: Dead body.

1.3) INT. LOFT — DAY

Laura joins Jake, who comments: Some way to spend Valentine's Day, right? Working a murder. At least they get to do it together. Laura tries to gauge Jake. . . what does that "together" mean? She opens a box of conversation hearts swiped from home, pops one — stress-eating her feelings. But her attention is quickly drawn to the crime scene. . . she clocks VINTAGE MUSIC POSTERS, asks how old their victim was. Jake: twenty-five. Laura doesn't get why he was listening to music made twenty years before he was born. As they walk, she spots SCUFF MARKS on the expensive hardwood floors. Laura: Seriously, you get these floors, you should treat them like a newborn baby. They join REYNALDO over the body, and he downloads: Parker was found by his housekeeper at 7 a.m. She's at the hospital with heart palpitations. Cause of death: multiple stab wounds to the back; the fatal blow pierced the heart and exited the chest. Time of death: six to eight hours ago. Jake clocks the scene: Looks like the victim fought back but lost. Laura notices evidence indicating a female was in the apartment. . . wine glasses on the counter, one with lipstick, rumpled sheets on the bed, long hairs on one of the pillows. . . but no woman to be found. Laura suddenly crouches down by the body, gloves up, and opens the corpse's mouth, looking inside. Jake: Little late for CPR. Eye roll. . . Man stabbed the night before Valentine's, lady love missing. . . ring a bell? Clearly not. Laura explains: St. Valentine, a SERIAL KILLER who struck every year from 1989 to 1993. Only killed couples; men at the initial scene on Feb. 13th, then the female victims were found murdered in Central Park by midnight on the 14th. Laura was in college then, refused to go on a date on Valentine's Day. Jake: Didn't they catch the guy? They did, just this case is eerily similar. . . but the killer's signature is missing. He used to leave the GROOM from a wedding cake topper inside the mouth of his male victims. There isn't one in Parker's mouth, so Laura dismisses her own hunch and suspicion turns to the missing mystery woman. As Reynaldo finishes with the body, Laura and Jake scan the loft.

Whoever the woman was, she doesn't live here. . . no female clothes or toiletries. Jake finds a BOX OF VALENTINE CANDY in Parker's nightstand, opens it. . . in the middle of the chocolates is a PLASTIC TOY RAT. Jake has a theory: Maybe this guy blew Valentine's Day, and our mystery girl lost it and killed him. They've investigated heat-of-passion murders triggered by less. Laura sees: A FOIL CANDY WRAPPER on the floor beside the bed. Doesn't match the candies in the box Jake found. Laura tells CSU to dust it for prints. . . maybe their mystery lady is a chocoholic. Meanwhile, she and Jake will dive into the data on Parker's cell phone. Laura: As much as twenty-somethings like to overshare every detail of their lives on social media, it can't be hard to find out who he's been spending time with. . .

1.4) INT. 2nd PRECINCT — BULLPEN — DAY

. . .Except Meredith's got bad news for Laura and Jake: There's no evidence in Parker's text messages, social media posts, or emails, that he was dating anyone. Billy's still canvassing the neighbors, but so far, only a few vague descriptions of a woman seen with Parker recently: petite, brunette. Laura's stunned they can't find anything on the cell phone, but Meredith explains Parker was a big user of anonymizing — tools that allow apps like SnapChat to be used without leaving a digital footprint. All of Parker's messages have been erased. Jake: Maybe by Parker's mysterious date; she could be a con artist or a catfish. . . Parker found out, so she killed him and ran. Their brainstorming is interrupted by the CHIEF OF DETECTIVES, who motions for Jake to join him in Santiani's office. . . the mourning crepe marking her death still hanging over the doorway. As Jake peels off, Meredith suggests that whoever this girl is, she might have a noncriminal reason for keeping her relationship with Parker quiet — a topic Meredith suggests she and Laura know well.

Meredith: Me and Billy, you and Tony, though now you guys are official, you don't have to sneak around anymore. Big plans tonight? Laura: Why the hell is everyone so interested in my plans? Deflecting, Laura downs a few more candy hearts and turns the conversation to Billy. . . she knows what a romantic he is. What big surprise did he drop on Meredith this morning? Meredith: Nothing. Laura: Nothing? At all? Meredith thinks it's great that Billy gets it: Valentine's Day just isn't her. . . he even skipped making her café con leche this morning to downplay it all. Laura thinks Meredith is reading the situation wrong, and doubts Billy will be able to let the whole day pass without playing Romeo. Anxious to change the subject, Meredith motions to Jake and the Chief in the Captain's office. Meredith wonders about the conversation happening inside: Does Laura think Jake might take the Captain's job back.

1.5) INT. 2nd PRECINCT — SANTIANI'S OFFICE — DAY

"No, thank you," Jake offers as we join him and the chief mid-conversation. He likes being back out on the streets — and though he doesn't say it, partnering with Laura. He's not interested in being Captain of the 2nd again. Chief: Neither is anyone else. Based on what's happened to the last three captains — one in prison for murder, two shot, one fatally — people aren't exactly lining up for this post. The Chief asks Jake to temporarily take the lead, make sure everything runs according to plan. And how's the current murder case? Jake tells the

Chief the mystery girlfriend is still the prime suspect. They're hoping Parker's co-workers might be able to ID her.

1.6) INT. QUARK — DAY

Trendy, hipster environment. Jake and Laura with ANDREA CHAMBERS, the president of this cutting-edge branding company. Andrea tells us Parker was a gifted creative. . . he just helped a sneaker company rejuvenate a twenty-year-old line as "the new retro chic." She also comments on how down-to-earth he was, how everyone at work loved him. She can't believe he's dead. Laura inquires about Parker's love life, but as far as Andrea knew, he wasn't dating anyone. Laura clocks a nearby cubicle with a PLUSH TOY RAT on the ledge.

She wanders over, notes the name tacked up in the cube: RAQUEL ANN TOMAS. "R.A.T." "RAT" could be a nickname, explaining the toy rat in the candy box at Parker's apartment. Could Parker be seeing Raquel? Andrea: If he was, he'd never tell me. Raquel was Parker's intern, a clear violation of HR rules. Where is the intern? Raquel hasn't shown up for work today. . . they had to get someone else to make the Starbucks run this morning. Laura searches Raquel's desk, finds a MIXTAPE and a PLAYLIST with a note attached: "Happy V, P." The songs are by the same bands whose posters we saw at the loft. For Laura and Jake, that's confirmation — Raquel was Parker's girlfriend. But where is she now? Raquel is Brazilian — meaning she could be on her way out of the country. As the cops exit, they're interrupted by a call from Reynaldo. . . he needs Laura at the morgue ASAP. Jake will head back to the precinct, put a TSA alert out on Raquel and set up surveillance on her apartment. Laura peels off to Reynaldo. . .

1.7) INT. MORGUE — DAY

Laura backs in carefully. Is it safe for her to turn around? She isn't in the mood for any open bodies today. Reynaldo tells her the coast is clear. . . Parker's body is in the cooler, but he did want to show Laura his stomach contents. Laura grimaces. Reynaldo: Trust me. You want to see this. Laura turns, prepared for the ultimate gross-out, but instead Reynaldo reveals: A GROOM FROM A WEDDING CAKE TOPPER. Because Parker was alive for several minutes after the attack, he struggled and aspirated, swallowing the murderous memento — that's why it wasn't in his mouth when Laura checked earlier. But her hunch was right. . . the killer used the signature from the original St. Valentine Murders. Laura: Oh my God. . . we have a copycat serial killer. . . and chances are, he's got Raquel.

ACT TWO

2.1) INT. 2nd PRECINCT — BULLPEN — DAY

Jake, Billy, and Meredith spitball. Could Raquel herself be the copycat? Meredith points out that per Reynaldo, the wounds came from a high angle and petite Raquel would've had to stand on a footstool to match Parker's height. She didn't murder him. . . ergo she was kidnapped by their St. Valentine copycat. So what happens next? Jake: All the female victims were found OD'd on heroin in the park by midnight on Valentine's Day. If this killer holds to the original pattern, we've got twelve hours to find Raquel or she's dead. So what more do they know about the old case? Jake has sent Max to pull the old case files, but here's the basic outline: The cops never figured out where St. V held his female victims or how he targeted the couples. . . but they knew one thing: He'd dump the woman's body in Central Park. They staked out the park, and in '93, they got lucky. . . caught GLEN WILSON running from the body dump. Shot him when he pulled a knife — the one used in the killings— while trying to flee.

Max enters, pushing a dolly stacked with file boxes. Billy: This is all St. Valentine? Max: This is just the first of the five double homicides. UNIs enter the bullpen with four identical dollies. Meredith opens a box labeled "database," excited. . . and finds: tons of outdated 5 1/4-inch floppy disks. The technology to read them isn't even in use anymore — but she'll do what she can. The sheer volume of information is daunting; Raquel may be dead before they even come up to speed. They need a short-cut — someone who worked the original case. Max explains that the lead detective died years ago, his partner retired to Mexico, and most of the other task force officers are dead or unreachable. Jake scans the roster of every cop who worked the St. Valentine task force and realizes there's someone who might be able to help. He just needs to make a call. As Jake rushes off, he tasks Meredith with rebuilding the ancient database. ON the dusty files. . . MATCH CUT TO:

2.2) INT. CONFERENCE ROOM - DAY

The boxes now empty, the space transformed into a make-shift war room — whiteboards rolled in as Laura, Billy, and Meredith post old images and evidence to look for similarities between the original killings and the new case. One thing they know for sure — Parker doesn't necessarily fit the "type" for the male victims in the original St. V murders. So the copycat is making his victim selections based on his needs, not a direct parallel of the old killings. Right away, Billy notices that the current crime scene is much sloppier than the originals. Laura: This victim fought back, resulting in the swallowed cake topper. Meredith: wonders if the original male victims were drugged so they couldn't fight back. A man's voice replies: Impossible.

None of them had drugs in their system. Laura looks up: former captain DAN HAUSER in the doorway, orange jumpsuit and shackles, a Corrections' Officer escort, and Jake. Laura can't believe her eyes. Jake explains that when he saw Hauser's name on the original task force roster, he called a friend in the DA's office, got a writ, and wrangled a helicopter transport, no big deal. But it is. Hauser, happy for the day pass and the opportunity to help, tells Jake to stop bragging so they can get to work. And they do.

At Laura's prompting, Hauser quickly downloads the most pertinent details. He discusses the dread the cops felt after the 1990 murders, when it became clear they had a serial killer in the city. After Glen was killed in '93, they searched his house and found souvenirs from the original crimes, and it was clear he had an obsession with horror movies and the methodology of killing. Laura asks if they ever had a profile on the killer. . . maybe the insights reached will help them now. Hauser bitterly recounts how they got two reports from two different shrinks. One said the killer was full of rage at men; the other shrink said the killer was remorseful and fixated on the idealized woman. The inconsistent findings led the task force to disregard the profiles entirely. Hauser notices something in the photos from Parker's loft: the scuff marks. Hauser tells Laura that he noticed the same scuff marks on the floors of the original crime scenes back in the day. Billy: Not uncommon in places without carpet. Hauser explains why it matters. He always thought the killer moved the female victim in a suitcase, but the lead detective discounted the idea. And then the kicker: The theory was only in Hauser's case notes — never typed into the official report. Laura, catching on: Meaning their copycat killer must have had access to inside information. Could the killer be a cop?

2.3) INT. 2nd PRECINCT — BULLPEN — VIDEO AREA — DAY

Maybe, says Meredith, at her computer with Laura. But after twenty years, information leaks. The crime scene photos from the St. Valentine case were never posted online. . . but they were for sale. On murderabilia.com, a website where people buy serial killer swag, including the Son of Sam's letters, the handle from Jeffrey Dahmer's fridge. . . Photos of sold items are still posted — including from the St. Valentine case. While Meredith searches out the owner of this eerie business, she notices a deliveryman moving through the squad room with flowers. She groans. . . anticipating that this is Billy's grand gesture. But the roses go right past her. . . to Max. Laura instantly interrogates Max — who are those from? Max: No one. Laura presses but he's unusually silent. She warns Max: I will find out. Meredith gets a hit — the owner of the Murderabilia site has a brick-and-mortar antique shop. Laura can't wait to see what kind of a sick person would deal in serial killer memorabilia. HARD CUT TO:

2.4) INT. ANTIQUE SHOP — DAY

POLLY DELVECCIO, 70s, unassuming grandma, behind the counter of an overstuffed East Village antique shop. Polly explains that her storefront business selling clocks and vases can't pay the bills. The only thing keeping the lights on is the online store her nephew helped her set up. She ushers the detectives into her back room where she shows off her wares: John Wayne Gacy's high school report card, Ted Bundy's undies. Turns out people will pay a fortune for anything associated with a serial killer. Laura wants to know where Polly got the St. Valentine crime scene photos and paperwork. Polly won't reveal her source — but pressed, she admits she's sold a ton of St. Valentine merchandise to a man obsessed with the case. Name: Kevin Williams. Polly liked having a fellow "fan" to talk to and was generous enough to show him her personal collection. The bastard stole one of her treasures: Glen Wilson's — aka St. Valentine's — baby tooth, given to Polly by Glen's mother herself. Polly: "Some people just have no decency. . ." Laura, sotto to Jake: Sounds obsessed enough to pick up where St. Valentine left off. . . Does Polly have Kevin's address? She does, and Laura tells Jake to call his D.A. friend. They need a warrant. PRELAP: Hard knocking on a door.

2.5) INT. HALLWAY/KEVIN WILLIAMS' APARTMENT — DAY

No answer. Meredith gestures to a SUPER, who unlocks the front door. Billy and Meredith, enter. No sign of Raquel or the killer, but the apartment is unnerving: dim, hazy light. Bare bulbs. Stacks of newspapers on the floor. And on one wall. . . a display of photos, clippings, maps, and case files, all relating to St. Valentine. At the center of this bizarre shrine, Billy spots it: a baby tooth. Who is this creep? Suddenly, the sound of a key in the lock. Billy and Meredith take positions on either side of the door as KEVIN WILLIAMS, 40s, enters and is immediately taken down. Pinning Kevin, Billy asks where the girl is. Kevin says he doesn't know what Billy's talking about, but Billy pushes: "You're St. Valentine. Don't bullshit us! Where is she!?" Kevin grins. "*I knew* it. I knew he'd be back." OFF Billy and Meredith, more than a little creeped out. *Back???*

ACT THREE

3.1) INT. 2nd PRECINCT — INTERROGATION ROOM — DAY

Kevin, cuffed to the table, as Laura challenges him: Of course St. Valentine is back. You're his copycat! Kevin denies it, demands to be let go. He's done nothing wrong. Laura: You stole a tooth valued at $5,000. That's grand theft. Why should she believe he's not a thief and a killer? But Kevin's got an alibi for Parker's murder. . . he was out all night with an expert on self-publishing he met at a book fair. Kevin explains: He's an author, collecting all this memorabilia for a book on the St. Valentine's murders. And the tooth? A little financial speculation. When his book finally comes out, that tooth will be worth its weight in gold. Polly had a few; he only took one. Laura, almost afraid to ask, probes about the book, and Kevin is eager to expound. This book will exonerate Glen Williams once and for all.

According to Kevin, the cops got the wrong guy in '93, and rattles off his "proof": The same red- headed man appears in three crime scene photos, but he doesn't match the descriptions of anyone on the NYPD roster; chocolate wrappers were found by two bodies in Central Park, but Glen was allergic to chocolate — they couldn't have been his; a boot print found by the third female victim's corpse was two sizes too small for Glen; and, most damning of all, there was no DNA evidence linking Glen to the murders.

3.2) INT. 2nd PRECINCT — CONFERENCE ROOM — DAY

With Laura and Meredith, an incredulous Hauser rebuts each of Kevin's claims. The red-headed man in the photos was an M.E. technician. Not every tech wore a windbreaker back in the day. The chocolate wrappers at the crime scene were meaningless, like the boot print. It was Central Park trash, and footprints could've been left there by anyone at anytime. Meredith brings up the lack of DNA evidence — she hates to say it, but obsessive Kevin has a point. Hauser rolls his eyes. Of course the cops didn't test Glen's DNA — they didn't need forensics when they had evidentiary links and a dead killer. The cops saw Glen in the park near the last female victim's body, found the knife that killed the five male victims on him. And, oh yeah, after he died, the murders stopped. Meredith isn't quite sold. Didn't they want to test the DNA just to be certain? Hauser reminds the young detective that DNA testing wasn't common at the time. There was no CODIS to test against, it took months, and it was prohibitively expensive. Unless the test was for a trial and you had a suspect to compare samples to, it just wasn't done. Laura is frustrated — Raquel has so few hours left to live — did Meredith find anything in the old St. Valentine's Killer database?

Meredith confirms that she tracked down a floppy drive, managing to port and restore the old databases — but the NYPD's systems of cataloguing evidence and data back in the day left much to be desired. Info, suspects, tips — it's a gigantic haystack, and they don't know what needle to look for. Hauser counters: That was cutting-edge back then — they brought in a special expert to code all that information. Laura knows what their next step should be: They need to run Glen's baby tooth for DNA. Hauser's taken aback: Is she on Kevin's side? Does she think they got the wrong guy? Laura: Not for a second. But like Hauser said. . . none of the DNA evidence from the old crimes was ever run through CODIS because CODIS didn't exist. Now they can run it per regular procedure — maybe something shakes loose that helps with their new murder. And bonus, once Glen's tooth DNA comes back a match, the NYPD will have a ready defense when crackpot Kevin accuses the police of getting it wrong to promote his book. PRELAP Reynaldo: I hate to say it. . .

3.3) INT. MORGUE — DAY

. . . But the DNA from the baby tooth does not match the DNA samples from the original killings. A stunned Jake hears Reynaldo's news. That can't be possible. Reynaldo: Are they positive the tooth is Glen's? Jake: The antique dealer proved she bought it from Glen's mother — provenance guaranteed. Jake counters: Maybe the samples from the old cases were contaminated. But Reynaldo says they were pristine, despite years in storage. So maybe the cops really did get the wrong guy. But Jake doesn't buy it. Hauser's positive Glen was St. Valentine. In which case, whose DNA is this??? Jake: We're missing something — we need to go back to square one.

3.4) INT. LOFT (CRIME SCENE) — DAY

Armed with autopsy reports and crime scene photos, Laura, Jake, Reynaldo, and Hauser compare the original murders to the current homicide. The attackers' heights are the same, as is the type of knife. And both killers are right-handed. The scuff marks on the loft's floors match those at the old crimes, off which Reynaldo seconds Hauser's suitcase theory. . . the female victims had tendon tears consistent with being folded into odd positions. But that's where the similarities end. The stab wounds on the original male victims were precise, almost surgical. Parker's wounds were messy, and there were hesitation marks — this killer wasn't as comfortable with a knife as the original St. Valentine. Another key difference: The original male victims had deep bruises on their necks. The current victim had none, even though Parker fought for his life. Struck by an idea, Laura grabs Hauser and re-enacts Parker's murder, taking on the role of killer. Even cuffed, Hauser easily pulls a spin move and escapes. Laura pulls him to his feet, grabs his throat from the side, then tries the stabbing motion again. And again, Hauser's able to pull away. Not a foolproof restraint, so why did the original killer use it? Reynaldo: The original medical examiner attributed the bruising to the men being choked unconscious, then stabbed. But Laura recalls the "angry, rageful man" psych profile. . . that guy wanted to see his victims suffer. The gentle kills were for the women.

Wheels turning, Laura tells Jake to stand in front of Hauser and grab him by the throat. Hauser is stunned by the movement long enough for Laura to pull off the stabbing motion from behind. Laura: Taking into account the seeming copycat mechanics of the crime, the insider knowledge of scuff marks, and the mystery DNA, there's only one explanation: "Crazy Kevin is half-right, and Hauser, you're not wrong. Glen was the killer, but he didn't act alone. . . he had a partner. The copycat is really the second St. Valentine Killer. And he's only hours away from killing Raquel."

ACT FOUR

4.1) INT. 2nd PRECINCT — BULLPEN — DAY

Tensions are high, the team keenly aware that Raquel's time is running out. The makeshift war room has spilled into the bullpen as the squad races to identify the second St. Valentine killer. Who was he, what was his connection to Glen, and where the hell was he for the past twenty-two years? The detectives spitball theories — maybe he was killing in another city? Or he was locked up in a psych ward. . . or imprisoned for a separate offense and only recently released. While Max runs the MO against the ViCAP database of serial killers and checks prison records, Laura goes back to the two original psych profiles. What seemed contradictory makes perfect sense now that we know there were *two* killers. One profile painted a picture of a violent offender who was jealous of the male victims, stabbing them brutally and violating their bodies with the cake topper. The other suggested a killer who idolized the female victims, killing them "gently" with an overdose of heroin and delicately staging the bodies in a wedding dress. Based on the clinical sadism of the original five stabbings, it's likely the first psych profile was Glen, while the second is our present-day killer. While Laura continues to flesh out the new profile, Hauser, trailed by his guard, quietly excuses himself to the break room. Sensing something is amiss, Jake follows—

4.2) INT. 2nd PRECINCT — BREAK ROOM — CONTINUOUS

Jake finds a sullen Hauser getting coffee. Jake understands instantly, says this isn't Hauser's fault. Back in the day, they did the best job they could with the evidence available. But Hauser isn't hearing it. Parker would be alive; Raquel would not be in danger if they'd truly closed the case twenty years ago. Jake stops him — none of that matters. What's important now is finding Raquel in time. Looking for an opportunity to change the subject, Hauser asks Jake about Laura. Has she forgiven Jake yet? Jake dodges: "We're moving past it." Hauser nods as he finishes his coffee — he knew they would. After all, if Laura forgave Hauser, she could forgive Jake, too. Not wanting to correct Hauser's impression with the more accurate, depressing details, Jake leaves it be.

4.3) INT. 2nd PRECINCT — BULLPEN — DAY

Laura digs through original crime scene photos, looking for any detail she might have missed. Something grabs her eye — the candy wrappers found at the 1992 Central Park body finds. They're not just any chocolate — they're Mallo- Hearts, Laura's absolute favorite seasonal treat! Her then-boyfriend, Brad Smith, got them for her first real Valentine's Day back in eighth grade. Jake hates to interrupt her trip down memory lane, but what does that have to do with anything? Laura explains: The wrappers in the crime-scene photos are the outer red cellophane, but Mallo-Hearts have a silver inner foil wrapper — just like the one they found at Parker's loft. Crazy Kevin's theories might be off the wall, but he was right about one thing — Glen really was allergic to chocolate. His medical records confirm it. Meaning those wrappers belonged to our second killer. Jake isn't convinced — why leave chocolate wrappers behind? Laura: He probably didn't mean to. She proves her point by drawing her hand from her pocket. . . gum wrappers and stray receipts spill out onto the floor. There's one problem, though: They stopped selling Mallo- Hearts a decade ago. Is our guy eating ten- year- old chocolates? Max, already typing at his computer, says no. As it turns out, the Mallo- Heart brand was recently revived by a specialty candy distributor and can be purchased online by special order. Laura lights up: "If these are such a rare item, maybe we can see exactly who ordered them."

We TIMECUT as Max reports: He called the candy shop, but unfortunately, they had two hundred online orders in the tristate area in the last month alone. There's no way they'll have time to run down all the buyers before midnight. On the positive side, Meredith thinks Max's info is a needle to search for in the old St. Valentine database haystack. She takes the list of Mallo-Heart buyers and cross-references them against all the data input from the original cases — and, lo and behold, they get a match. Back in 1993, the cops were searching for a white van with a broken taillight spotted near the site of the '93 male victim's murder. Someone called in an anonymous tip was that a guy who lived at 233 Bowery St. drove a similar white van. But the police caught Glen Wilson that night and thought the case was closed, so the tip was never followed up. But there's a Mallo-Heart order addressed to W. Burroughs *at 233 Bowery*. Records show a Wayne Burroughs owned the house back in 1993, and he still owns it now. Could this be the second St. Valentine killer?

4.4) INT. 233 BOWERY ST. — DAY

Vests on, guns out, ESU in the lead, Laura and Jake breach the door and our detectives spill in hot — only to find a terrified WOMAN, 40s, afraid and confused about why the police just burst into her house. Jake shouts: Where's Wayne!? The woman says he doesn't live there anymore. Who is she? MINDY BURROUGHS — Wayne's ex-wife. Laura stops in her tracks. Stares at Mindy, wheels turning. She pulls out a photo of Raquel and holds it up to Mindy — Raquel is the spitting image of Mindy, only twenty years younger. Holy shit! Mindy turns to Laura, pleading. Mindy: Please, I don't know what's going on here. Looking up from the photo, Laura responds: I'm beginning to think I do.

ACT FIVE

5.1) INT. 2nd PRECINCT — CONFERENCE ROOM

Jake with a shocked Mindy, who explains that she and Wayne met because of St. Valentine. In '93, she was afraid of St Valentine like every other young, single girl in the city. Mindy got a security system for her apartment and fell for the quietly romantic man who came to install it. . . Wayne Burroughs. He made her feel safe, idealized her, put her on a pedestal. But time wore on, and Mindy couldn't live with his expectations anymore. She started noticing other men. She didn't want to cheat on him, so a few months ago, Mindy told Wayne she wanted a divorce. How did Wayne take it? Mindy: At first, he came around all the time, trying to convince her to change her mind. But recently, he seemed to accept it. Mindy breaks down, stunned at the realization of her husband's true nature. She can't believe the man she slept next to for all those years was the monster from her nightmares.

5.2) INT. 2nd PRECINCT — CAPTAIN'S OFFICE — DAY — INTERCUT

Laura and Hauser exchange a quiet look, both knowing what it's like to have a marriage turn disastrous. The story prompts Laura to crunch a few more candy conversation hearts as

Hauser notes that Mindy solves the puzzle of Wayne's dormant period. He stopped killing after he met her because he found what he was seeking: a woman who needed him. But when their relationship ended, he returned to his old ways. Laura agrees, saying that Wayne is a white knight who wants to be the hero, the rescuer. Wayne is trying to replicate that same situation again. Twenty years ago, a scared Mindy turned to him for security. Maybe in Wayne's mind, if Mindy once again feels threatened by St. Valentine — the abductor/murderer of a woman matching Mindy's own description, she'll turn to him for safety once more. We INTERCUT—

Back in the interview Jake, presses on. Did Wayne ever mention Glen Wilson? Mindy doesn't recall the name from anything but press. But Wayne did allude to a friend having died just before they met. She explains Wayne's job history — over the years, he transitioned from installing phone lines to alarms, now fiber optic cables. Mindy doesn't know where Wayne is living, but it seems to be someplace impermanent. He still comes by the house once a week to pick up his mail — that's why the Mallo-Heart order came to her house. As far as she knows, all of his stuff is still in storage. She got tired of Wayne's procrastination and moved it there herself a month ago, gave Wayne the key.

In the next room, Laura spitballs: A storage unit would be a perfect place to stash Raquel. They need to get to that locker, and fast.

5.3) INT. WAYNE'S STORAGE LOCKER — NIGHT

Laura, Jake, and Billy burst in. . . but no sign of Raquel. There is a camp bed and a kerosene lamp. . . and, ominously, *the bride's side of six cake toppers*. It seems that Wayne has been living here — and revisiting his trophies from his crimes. But where is he now? Meredith enters, having pulled the security footage. On her tablet, she displays footage of Wayne exiting his unit carrying a suitcase in one hand. Jake notes that Wayne lifts the suitcase easily; can't be a body in it. Meredith confirms that this footage is from yesterday afternoon, before the murder/abduction. Unfortunately, it's also the last time Wayne was here. Laura takes a closer look at the tape. . . Wayne is wearing his work jumpsuit. . . she can see the patch with the company's logo on his chest. Billy chimes in: He checked with Wayne's employers and Wayne's not scheduled to work this weekend. So why's he in his uniform? Laura has an idea. She calls Max and asks where Wayne's current assignment is. It's at COMPUTEK, installing and connecting their new servers. But Monday is President's Day, so the whole building is closed for the long weekend. Laura, wheels spinning, thinks Wayne might be there now, with Raquel. The building has decent proximity to Central Park, his preferred body dumping ground. And in his uniform, Wayne would have unquestioned access — if anyone is even around to see him given the building closure. She checks her watch — they're running out of time to save Raquel. OFF the team, racing out. . .

5.4) EXT. COMPUTEK — NIGHT

BINOCULAR POV: The CompuTek building — thick walls, windowless. Jake (O.S.): It's a fortress. Pull back to reveal: Jake, with binoculars and Billy with an ESU SERGEANT, surveilling the building from a tactically safe distance. Plans of the CompuTek building unrolled on the hood of a car. The ESU Sergeant confirms there's only one way in, no way to make a forced entry without detection. Aviation did a flyover in a helo equipped with FLIR (forward-looking infrared), and found two heat signatures on the top floor, the northwest corner of the building. Looking at the FLIR on a tablet, Jake and Billy see that while one of the heat signatures is a vibrant red orange, moving around, the other is fading out, yellow into greenish blur. Raquel is losing body heat — she's dying. ESU Sergeant:

We have a tactical team on the roof, trying to drill in for camera placement. Jake: We're running out of time. We have to get in there, now. PRELAP: We've got fiber optics online!

5.5) INT. MOBILE COMMAND POST — NIGHT

The NYPD's gacked-out RV, loaded with all the bells and whistles. Laura, Jake, and the ESU Sergeant gather around a monitor, on which we see the inside of the server room, in grainy black and white. ON SCREEN, we see WAYNE BURROUGHS, 40s, antsy, pacing. On the floor is RAQUEL, already clothed in a white wedding gown. She's not moving, and barely breathing. ESU Sergeant: It's worse than we thought. They're in the server room. It's basically a vault — climate controlled, only one door, no windows. Laura: We have to get in there, now. What's the plan? They could use knockout gas, and make an entry once Wayne is unconscious. Laura: We can't risk it; in Raquel's weakened state, she might not wake up. Then the only option is a tactical breach — using brute force to make an entry through the server room's only door. Laura nixes that too — if Wayne hears them coming, he'll kill Raquel immediately. Jake wonders what other options they have — there's no other way to get inside. Laura: Then I'll get him to come out to us. OFF Laura, eyes alight with a plan. . .

ACT SIX

6.1) INT. COMPUTEK — NIGHT

Dark, shadowy. FOOTSTEPS approach a heavy door, clearly marked "SERVER ROOM." Then from inside, WAYNE'S VOICE calls out, nervous: Who's there?

INTERCUT WITH:

6.2) INT. COMPUTEK — SERVER ROOM — NIGHT

As seen through the fish-eye lens of ESU's fiber-optic camera: Wayne stands by the door. He looks jittery, amped, and highly unpredictable. On the floor, Raquel lies unmoving in the wedding dress, barely breathing. From outside the room, a female voice replies: Wayne. . . it's me. Mindy. (We recognize the voice as, in fact, Mindy's.) The unexpected answer makes Wayne panic — he looks wildly from the door, to unconscious Raquel and back again, then replies: Mindy? What are you doing here? Mindy explains that she thought he might be at work. She needed to find him, tell him she made a mistake. She doesn't want a divorce. Mindy: "I don't want to be apart from you on Valentine's Day. Please, Wayne, let me in. . ." A beat, then on the fish-eye, we see Wayne cross to the server room door. Wayne: Don't. . . don't come in here. I'll come out to you. He puts his hand on the doorknob –

6.3) INT. COMPUTEK — NIGHT — CONTINUOUS

Still pitch black. The door of the server room opens, casting a thin beam of light. . . which slowly widens. A long beat, then Wayne's shadowy silhouette. Wayne: Mindy? Where are you? He steps forward into the darkness. . . and is suddenly TACKLED BY ESU. As the men in body armor wrestle him to the ground, the lights go on, illuminating Laura, cell phone in hand. She thanks Mindy on the other end of the line as she rushes into –

6.4) INT. COMPUTEK — SERVER ROOM — NIGHT — CONTINUOUS

Laura beelines to Raquel's side. As she scoops the woman's limp body into her arms, Jake roughly interrogates Wayne, demanding to know if he gave Raquel heroin like he did his prior victims. Wayne admits it, and Jake signals to arriving EMTs, who rush in to administer the Naloxone shot. An EMT rips open the sleeve of the wedding dress, injects Raquel with a hypodermic.

A beat. No reaction. Laura: Come on Raquel. Fight. Another long, agonizing beat — then Raquel coughs, sputters to life like a revived drowning victim. Laura tenderly hands Raquel over to the EMTs' care. Laura: It's over, Raquel. You're safe. A weak flutter of Raquel's eyes and a cough let us know she's going to make it. OFF Laura, finally able to exhale. PRELAP Hauser: Proud of you, hotshot.

6.5) INT. 2nd PRECINCT — BULLPEN — NIGHT

Where Hauser backslaps Laura — drained, but happy. Hauser comments that only Laura Diamond could finally close the St. Valentine case for good in just twenty-four hours. Laura shoots back: Actually, it was only thirteen hours since the maid found Parker's body. A uniformed WAKEFIELD CORRECTIONS OFFICER steps up. The rattle of the leg irons and belly chains tells Hauser it's time to go. He and Laura say a professional goodbye under the C.O.'s watchful gaze. On a personal note, Hauser tells Laura that he's happy for her. Off Laura's look, he explains: You and Jake belong together. I'm glad you're both putting the past behind you. As Hauser exits, Laura's lost in thought — could it really be this easy to put her life back together? Her reverie is broken by an "Awww. . . is it on?" and she turns to see Max eavesdropping. "Valentine reunion, after all? Cause that would be uber-adorable." Laura calls for silence from the peanut gallery. Then her gaze is caught by a BOX OF CANDY peeking out from an interoffice envelope on Max's desk. Eager to turn the tables, Laura announces that the box of chocolates is a bit much. She now knows Max sent it — and the flowers — to himself so no one would know he's alone on Valentine's Day. Max guiltily admits that she caught him. Laura asks if he wants to hang with her tonight. They could watch rom- coms and crush that candy box. Max balks, taunts Laura: Is she really not going to carpe the diem with Jake? Could the stars not be more aligned? OFF Laura, tempted—

6.6) INT. 2nd PRECINCT — HOLDING CELLS — NIGHT

Passing Billy finds an exasperated Meredith lying in wait. She corners him up against the bars of a cell. Before he can say a word, Meredith makes sure the coast is clear, then lays into him: All day long and not the slightest, secret acknowledgement of Valentine's? He responds deadpan: "I thought that's what you'd want." Meredith sighs, admits that's what she thought, too. "But you're my man and I'm your woman! This is a relationship! Which means we celebrate Valentine's Day!" A beat, then Billy: So you finally admit it. We're a thing. Yup, Meredith replies. . . A good thing. And now Billy cracks a smile. Follow me. Meredith, perplexed, follows him to. . . a door. Billy opens it, revealing —

6.7) INT. 2nd PRECINCT — COPIER/SUPPLY ROOM — NIGHT

The usually dingy and disorganized space transformed by mood lighting, flowers, and a picnic blanket on the floor, on which are a bottle of wine, two glasses, a plate of decadent chocolate truffles. Meredith smiles, ruefully tells herself she should've known Billy the romantic couldn't resist. . . Billy smiles back, presses play on an iPhone in a docking station. A Marvin Gaye needle-drop begins. The music carries us to —

6.8) INT. 2nd PRECINCT — LOCKER ROOM — NIGHT

The music continues as Laura stands at the open door of her locker, using a small mirror on the inside of the door to fix her hair, apply some fresh lipstick. She stares at her own reflection for a beat, then her gaze wanders to a family photo taped up beside the mirror: Laura, the boys, and Jake, in younger, happier times. Automatically her hand strays to her pocket, ready to stress-eat more candy hearts. But there's only one left. She reads the message: "BE MINE." She places the now-empty box in her locker, tenderly holds the candy heart, ready to let it speak for her. A deep breath, summoning her courage, then she closes the locker door. As it wipes frame, we are in—

6.9) INT. MEDICAL EXAMINER'S OFFICE — NIGHT

Still under the music cue, Reynaldo finds an INTER- OFFICE ENVELOPE on his desk. He opens it. . . and out slides the box of chocolates we last saw with Max. Reynaldo smiles. And just like that, Max's secret is revealed. . .

6.10) INT. 2nd PRECINCT — BULLPEN — NIGHT

And now it's Laura, at the door to the Bullpen. She takes a final glance at the "BE MINE" candy heart, ready to confess her love to Jake. . . She pushes open the door . . . only to find Jake chatting with a STRIKING WOMAN, 40s, bathing in the full charm of Jake's baby blues. And there's no way Laura Diamond could miss the romantic tension crackling between them. She looks familiar, but before Laura can place her, Jake makes the introduction. This is Jennifer Lambert, his pal from the DA's office who helped with the warrant yesterday. Jen reaches out a hand. Laura shakes, relieved to discover this is a professional visit (though she's too collected to blurt it out). Laura tells Jen she thought she looked familiar. Have they had a case together? Jen laughs, tells Laura that they've met in a different context. She's Ethan's mom. From school. Laura's wheels start to spin [We flash to Jake's previous mentions of interacting with Ethan's parent in Ep. 212/213]. Jake cuts in — Jen's been so great on the case, he's taking her out for a bite. Both of them found themselves untethered on the worst of all days, so why not? Whatever Jake's saying, the message is clear to Laura: This is a date. He asks what she and Tony are up to — Laura is speechless, hems and haws a vague something or other.

An awkward moment, but Laura smiles through it, telling Jen it was great to see her. ON Laura, as Jake and Jen exit, happy laughter slowly fading away. She looks down at the candy heart in her hand, the "BE MINE" message now painful. We end on Laura, dateless, shell-shocked, out-of-her-mind jealous, and not about to take this lying down.

END OF EPISODE

The Good Wife Spec Story Area — *Puppet Dance,* Niceole Levy

A singer who survived a violent attack by a stalker years ago seeks out Peter, the man who put her assailant away, when her imprisoned attacker plans to publish a book of photos that she knows but can't prove are of her. Peter refers her to Lockhart, Gardner & Bond. Because Illinois has repealed their "Son of Sam" statute without replacing it, they have to fall back on a prior judgment in a civil suit to lay claim to the income from the book and hope it dissuades publication. But is money the motivating factor behind the book at all? And Alicia finds herself suspicious of Peter's connection to the female victim, opening old wounds. Meanwhile, after Diane is hurt in a hit-and-run DUI case, Cary is assigned as prosecutor, and the two negotiate a fine line between respect and mistrust as they try to find a good resolution to the case.

The Good Wife "Puppet Dance"
Spec Story Synopsis 11/25/10
Niceole Levy

LOGLINE: *SYDNEY WALKER, a world-famous singer who survived a violent attack, turns to LOCKHART/GARDNER for help when her assailant tries to publish photos that she's certain are of her naked body. . . but she can't prove it. As the attorneys fight to protect their client from further victimization, the case puts pressure on ALICIA and PETER's tenuous relationship when she finds out he was involved in the prosecution of Sydney's attacker and spent time with her outside of business hours.*

Meanwhile, DIANE is injured in a hit-and-run accident and the other driver, big shot political reporter VIVIAN TALLY, is arrested. New State's Attorney employee CARY is assigned the case, and he and Diane must find a way to work together after she fired him from Lockhart/Gardner because they have a common goal: keeping a serial drunk driver from getting back on the streets again.

And as KALINDA does her detective thing to assist on both cases, she finds herself once again stuck in the middle of the FLORRICK marriage as Alicia suspects there was more to Peter's relationship with Sydney than either is saying.

Themes: trust, privacy, victims' rights, alcoholism

A STORY (ALICIA/WILL/PETER/KALINDA)

It's early morning in Chicago. We see PETER climb out of his parked car wearing gym clothes, dark shades, a scarf. He doesn't look like he's hiding, but he doesn't look like the Peter Florrick, State's Attorney candidate, we're used to either. He walks into a neighborhood diner and approaches a woman who *is* hiding -- she's seated in the back, her hair in a ponytail, a baseball cap pulled low. This is SYDNEY WALKER, early 30s, and she's visibly upset and nervous. Peter sits down and after he orders coffee, Sydney apologizes for coming to him, but says she didn't know who else to go to. He takes her hand and tells her that everything will be okay. Sydney's response is that she finally has the life she always wanted, and now she's afraid what happened then is going to ruin everything. Peter looks on with concern.

Later, as DIANE LOCKHART drives her silver Mercedes through the city, her cell phone rings. She's stunned to learn it's Peter Florrick calling. He has an old friend who needs help. When he mentions Sydney by name, Diane recognizes it and asks if this is related to the prior incident? When Peter says yes, Diane tells him to have Sydney go straight to the office. *Diane is barely off the phone when a car runs a red light and broadsides her. . .* but more on this later.

At the LOCKHART/GARDNER/BOND offices, Alicia arrives at work and sees Will in the conference room with Sydney, who has shed her ball cap and let her hair down. Will waves Alicia over and explains that Diane was supposed to meet with their new client, but she's in the E.R. after a hit-and-run accident, so he's taking over, and since Derrick is in D.C., he could use Alicia's help in the meeting.

Will and Alicia join Sydney, and their discussion reveals her history. Not long after she scored her fifth number one on the R&B charts, a man named JEFF CRAWFORD, who had been stalking her, turned violent. He kidnapped and tortured her for three days before police rescued her. He was arrested a week later. After eight years of surgery, physical therapy, and shrinks, she reclaimed her career, and has been back in the limelight for two years, is even planning her wedding. But now Crawford has struck again. . . *he's acquired a book deal to publish his photography as "a collection of artistic photos in a study of the human* body," only the photos are all of Sydney from his days stalking her and her imprisonment. Sydney hopes they can find some way to stop Crawford from exploiting her. When Alicia casually wonders why Sydney decided to come to their firm for help, Sydney replies that Peter sent her. Alicia can't hide her surprise. . . *why wouldn't Peter tell her he was sending over a client?*

The firm digs in but realizes that Sydney's case isn't an easy one. The "Son of Sam" statute only prevented criminals from profiting personally as a direct result of their crimes, it didn't bar them from participating in the project. And Illinois repealed their version of the law after the Supreme Court called the wording of several state statutes into question. Sydney's desperate to stop this, but Alicia explains that because her face isn't visible in the photos, it's impossible to prove they depict her without confirming testimony — meaning Sydney would have to testify in court and prove the intimate photos are of her body. Will adds that since the photos weren't used as evidence in the trial, the state can't argue that publication violates the evidence seal on the case. But there is hope. Since Sydney sued for and won a civil judgment against Crawford after her attack, they can ask the court to turn over the funds from the publication to her in fulfillment of that judgment, possibly taking away his motivation for the publication. Alicia adds that the bad press to the publishing house from the hearing might also help dissuade them from going ahead.

Later, Will, and Alicia discuss Sydney, and Alicia recalls how obsessed Peter was with putting Crawford away, but Alicia was busy with her kids and didn't pay much attention to it beyond what was general public knowledge. Will points out that it was great of Peter to refer Sydney to them, but as Will heads back to his office, Alicia looks more than a little worried that Peter's involved at all.

Once a hearing is set, Will explains their position to the judge. CRAIG HANSON, Crawford's lawyer reminds the judge that there is no legal bar from his client profiting from use of his private photo collection even if there was proof it was connected to his crime. SARAH FLEMING, the lawyer for publishing company *Resolution Press*, explains that Crawford has offered to donate all of his profits to a charity for families of victims of violent crimes. Will counters that the money is legally subject to the civil judgment from years prior and should rightfully go to Sydney. The judge calls the law on the topic "an unfortunate sea of legalese." He needs time to review the existing case law before he rules.

But Will and Alicia are leaving nothing to chance. . . they have Kalinda on the hunt for information. She visits Statesville Correctional and gets access to Crawford's visitor's log. She notes that an APRIL DAVIDSON has visited the stalker weekly for years.

Wasting no time, Kalinda goes to see April Davidson, pretending to be a reporter doing a story on Crawford's book. April says she met Crawford through an inmate pen pal website, and that he talked so much about his photography but was sad he'd never be able to share it with the world now that he was in prison. *When Kalinda asks if the book was already done when he was arrested, April reveals that it was not.* Once they fell in love, Crawford trusted her to put it together. When Kalinda asks how they did it, April gets nervous and ends the interview.

That night at home, Peter asks Alicia if she's on Sydney's case. She asks why he didn't tell her about it or mention he was referring a client. He explains that Sydney called while he was at the gym and he went straight to meet her, and by the time he got home, Alicia was already on her way to work. When he senses her suspicion, he gets defensive, telling her that Sydney was a victim he helped to get justice, and that's it, and if Alicia really thinks anything else went on, that he'd take advantage of someone he was trying to help, well, then maybe her opinion of him hasn't changed much since he came home. Angry, he stalks off to bed.

The next day Diane joins Will, Alicia, and Kalinda for a strategy session. She theorizes that Crawford's donation ploy isn't just about trying to get some good spin; he's set on victimizing Sydney all over again with the book, and if she's trying to stop a victim's group from taking money, then there will be jerks in the press who act like *she's* the bad guy. Then Kalinda arrives with an update: She's found some typical dirt on the publishing company owner, HENRY WELTSON: gambling, some women on the side, some disgruntled partners, but so far, nothing that will help them in court. She tells them about April and says she's found a pattern of car rentals that she's investigating to try to find out what the woman's involvement in the book deal was. Kalinda also has a phone interview set up with Sydney's former assistant, MARY, who had moved to Los Angeles a year earlier, to see if she remembers anything that can help them.

Meeting finished, Kalinda follows Alicia to her office and closes the door. She tells Alicia that while she was working on the background on Sydney, just making sure there were no land mines to be found, she came across something that she isn't sure Alicia wants everyone else to see. *She hands Alicia a copy of a hospital release record from a few weeks after Sydney's attack. Peter signed it as the responsible party, and Sydney was released AMA — against medical advice.* She has the copy because it was in the personal records Sydney gave to them to help the case. But the official medical file she managed to take a peek at? It's missing any record of Sydney being admitted to the hospital on that date. Kalinda leaves the document in Alicia's hands. Alicia's distracted thinking about Peter and what this means but snaps out of it and asks the P.I. to find something they can use as leverage against Resolution Press.

Eli Gold approaches and overhears Resolution Press' name and tells them they should get in touch with BENJAMIN AUSTIN JAMES. Kalinda recognizes the name from Resolution's authors list, and Eli says he's an old friend and that he thinks they might get a reaction from Benjamin if you tell him Resolution is planning to publish a book from a violent psychopathic woman-hater. Kalinda goes to track him down. Alicia eyes Eli with suspicion. What is he doing there? Eli says he just wanted to make sure she was fine, but it sounds more like a question than a statement. Surmising Peter told him about their argument, she assures Eli that yes, she is fine. He asks if it's possible she's ever going to be permanently fine. Alicia glances at the medical report bearing Peter's signature. . . and doesn't answer the question.

Alone in her office, Alicia gives in to her suspicions. She types "PETER FLORRICK SYDNEY WALKER" into the computer search engine. A series of links come up about the trial, and then she clicks on a YouTube link. A video plays of Peter standing next to a still clearly traumatized Sydney at the courthouse. A reporter asks Peter how he thinks the first day of the trial went, and he says they're confident that the jury will see through any phantom defense thrown at them. A second reporter asks Sydney what it was like to see Crawford again. She looks like a deer caught in a headlight, and Peter puts his hand on her arm. Sydney looks over at Peter, and Alicia pauses the video. She stares at the look on Sydney's face, then Peter's hand on her arm. But her expression gives us nothing on what Alicia's thinking.

In a luxury high-rise, Kalinda visits Benjamin James Austin, a prolific best-selling crime author who is also the head of a foundation to keep repeat violent offenders in prison. His son was murdered in his teens and Austin has been a victims' advocate ever since. When he hears about Resolution's publishing plans, he pulls out a contract and points out a clause to Kalinda. She asks if everyone's has this, and he says as far as he knows, and he's willing to make some calls to the other authors to find out.

At the office, Alicia is buried in paperwork when Sydney knocks on her door and asks if they can talk for a minute. Noting that she's felt Alicia being a little uncomfortable around her, Sydney explains that obviously she knows about what happened in the Florrick marriage, and she can't imagine what that's been like for Alicia to try to forgive. *She assures Alicia that her feelings for Peter are that of everlasting gratitude and little else.* He promised her while she was a bleeding mess in the hospital that he would put Crawford away, that he'd help shield her from the media as much as he could, and that he'd be there whenever she needed help, and he was, and *Sydney believes she'd have never recovered without having something. . . or someone. . . to believe in after what she'd gone through.* Alicia is pleased to be reminded of that side of her husband because she knows Peter *can* be that guy. She thanks Sydney for telling her. Then as Sydney leaves, Alicia is summoned to the conference room, where. . .

. . .*Kalinda has scored the holy grail* thanks to her meeting with Benjamin James Austin. *It turns out Resolution includes a character clause in all their contracts allowing them to be voided if the authors conduct themselves in a manner detrimental to the company's ability to sell their books* or in a way that causes Resolution's image to be damaged. Austin got the other nine of the top ten authors on Resolution's list to agree to breach their contracts in protest of Resolution's publication of Crawford's book. *And what was April's mysterious role in all this?* Crawford got her a fake ID that she used to retrieve the photos from safety deposit boxes all over Illinois, which she did using the series of rental cars Kalinda found records for. Kalinda also reveals that Austin got a copy of the contract Resolution signed with Crawford, and she gives it to Will, telling him to read the highlighted passage. He, in turn, smiles like the cat that ate the canary.

The next time we see Will and Alicia, they are back in the conference room meeting with Resolution's owner Weltson and his lawyer Fleming and telling them about the authors' pledge of protest solidarity. When Weltson says he'll just sue them all, Will advises him to go ahead, because Lockhart, Gardner & Bond has agreed to represent the writers in a countersuit claiming the company violated their own morals clause. They may lose, but the case will cost Resolution a fortune with no income coming in since these authors are willing to withhold their manuscripts for the time being. But, Will says, he does have another idea if Weltson is willing to listen. Fleming asks what they're offering. That question hangs in the air until we return to. . .

. . . The courtroom, where Crawford and his attorney wait, *the Resolution owner and attorney noticeably absent.* The judge rules that while he wishes he had the power to block the book entirely, the best he can do is fulfill the prior court's promise and award all the monies earned by Jeff Crawford be forfeited as payment of the civil suit judgment to Sydney. Despite losing the money, Crawford can't resist casting a smug smile in Sydney's direction, but it doesn't last long.

Will walks over to him and tells him that Resolution's been sold, and the new ownership has decided to stop publication of the book. He'll be paid in full, of course, with the money being forfeited to Sydney. . . who also happens to be the new company owner. And Will reminds Crawford about the fine print that Kalinda found in his contract. . . to get the original deal, Crawford had to swear he was turning over all of his photographs, which means if he has more hidden away and tries to publish them elsewhere, he'll be in violation of his contract, and Sydney, as owner of the publishing company, can sue him again. Triumphant, Sydney, Will, and Alicia leave Crawford and his attorney speechless.

As the firm celebrates their victory, Kalinda pulls Alicia aside and reveals that she finally spoke with Sydney's former assistant, Mary, who took care of Sydney for the six months following her kidnapping. When Kalinda starts to talk about Peter, Alicia tries to stop her, but Kalinda keeps going and explains that Mary said Sydney tried to kill herself three weeks after the attack, and Mary didn't know whom to call, so she called Peter. He convinced the hospital not to put Sydney on a seventy-two-hour hold because he knew the bad press would only hurt her more. He then helped Mary hire home-care nurses so Sydney wouldn't be alone, helped find her a top-notch trauma psychiatrist, and basically set up the support system that kept Sydney alive. While she doesn't know who made the original paperwork at the hospital disappear, Mary never saw anything that made her think Peter and Sydney were involved beyond his making sure she had a chance at reclaiming her life. Alicia smiles and lets this latest bit of news sink in.

That night, Alicia arrives home to find Peter waiting in the living room with a bottle of wine and two glasses. He tells her he doesn't care if she's suspicious of him and every woman he walks past because he knows he earned that. But it upset him when she thought he had been involved with Sydney because he remembers walking into her hospital room and seeing this broken, bruised, scared girl who was all alone, no family, and he knew if it was Grace and he wasn't there to fix it, he'd want someone to step up. Alicia tells him he did a great job by Sydney and that she's proud of him, and when he says it's been a long time since he's heard that, she says, "I know," and then leans back against his shoulder as they just sit there quiet, together. . . for now.

DIANE/CARY

Will dispatches Kalinda to the hospital to check on Diane after her car accident, and Kalinda reports back from the E.R. — Diane has a dislocated shoulder and a cut on her head, but she'll be fine. On her way out of the hospital, Kalinda runs into Cary, who tells her State's Attorney Childs sent him down. When she asks if they found the other driver, he says the police arrested VIVIAN TALLY. Kalinda's response: "Vivian Tally who spends every Sunday burning Childs at the stake on her polit- ical news show?" Kalinda tells Cary to be careful. Vivian has very important friends who don't like the people who mess with her, even when she deserves it.

Once she's released, Diane goes over the details of the accident with Cary. He reveals that Vivian had a blood alcohol level of .19 and has been arrested twice before for DUI, though her blood test results disappeared on the first charge, and it was dropped to reckless driving. Diane quips that considering the friends Vivian has in Illinois politics, it's amazing she was con- victed at all.

Cary ignores that and brings up Diane's admission of being on the phone just prior to the accident. She counters that she was using her hands-free device, which is legal. Cary says that it could still cloud a jury's thinking about Vivian being entirely at fault. Diane wonders if he's getting *his* defense ready in case Vivian pulls strings and slips through his fingers. Before he can respond, Diane laughs and points out that Cary can't win here — *he personally*, not he as a prosecutor. The media doesn't talk about Vivian's drinking because no one else will. Everyone who could talk about it is too afraid of her. Hell, Oprah's proba- bly afraid of Vivian. And so Cary gets this case. . . and Childs can blame *him* as incompetent or overeager if he loses. And if Diane's unhappy with how the case turns out, she could say he lost on purpose because of their past. "Like Will always says, it's Chicago." Cary knows she's right, but admits he likes his work, and he wants to be good at it. He agrees to do his best if she'll trust him. Diane nods her agreement.

Back at work, Diane reviews photos of the accident: it was a close call. Cary says his investigators have dug up the dirt he needs to go to trial. But he admits he thought about what Diane said earlier, *and he thinks Childs wants him to embarrass Vivian* because she doesn't support him as State's Attorney and because he can imply Peter somehow went easy on her past cases even though the push to go soft on the case probably came from over Peter's head. Diane asks Cary what he wants to do. As far as Cary's concerned, this is Vivian's third offense. He wants jail time *and to not get used*. Diane smiles and tells him to go do that then.

Later, Diane gets a visit from Eli, saying he just wanted to make sure his lawyer was still in one piece. She says she is, no thanks to Vivian Tally, who Eli points out likes Peter a lot more than she does Childs. He saw Cary walking out. Wasn't that the young man she kicked to the curb in favor of Alicia Florrick? Diane says yes, but not because he wasn't good. Eli asks if he's good enough that Peter might want to keep him around when he gets his old job back. Diane confirms that Cary is just the kind of protégé a man like Peter could make very good use of.

At the State's Attorney's office, Cary meets with Vivian and her lawyer. He points out that Diane's got friends on the bench who might give Vivian up to 364 days in jail between the DUI, reckless driving, and leaving the scene of an accident charges. Cary's willing to drop the charge for fleeing the scene if she pleads to the DUI and reckless charges and takes ninety days, a $10,000 fine, and a mandatory thirty-day treatment program. When Vivian hesitates, Cary plays hardball. He tells Vivian he'll call her son to testify — he was there for her first arrest; Cary will get her ex-husband to testify about her ramming her car into their house during a drunken rage. Once that's out there, does she really think the media won't run with it? Cary adds that if she doesn't take his deal and go get some help, when she finally does kill someone in a DUI, he'll do whatever it takes to make sure the judge locks her up and throws away the key. Cornered, Vivian takes the deal.

Later, Diane tells Cary that she hired him because she liked him, so she's offering him some advice — bide his time with Childs and steer clear the politics, because if he really likes what he does, Peter Florrick is a man who can get him where he wants to go, and Childs isn't. Cary files that way and maybe, just maybe, we know who just got his vote for State's Attorney.

ABOUT THE AUTHOR

After growing up near China Lake Naval Weapons Center in the middle of the Mojave Desert, Niceole escaped to the bright lights of Los Angeles. While studying acting at the American Academy of Dramatic Arts, she realized her true love was writing stories, not playing them out. She worked as a police dispatcher to pay her way through University of Southern California (USC) undergrad and then completed the Master of Professional Writing program, also at USC. An alum of the ViacomCBS Writers Mentoring Program, NBC's Writers on the Verge, and the WGAW Showrunner Training Program, Niceole has written on *Ironside*, *Allegiance*, *The Mysteries of Laura*, *Shades of Blue*, *Cloak & Dagger*, *Fate: the Winx Saga*, and *S.W.A.T.* She also co-wrote a feature, *The Banker*, with former *Allegiance* showrunner and director George Nolfi, available on AppleTV+. Niceole was recently a co-executive producer on *Graymail* for Netflix and is currently a co-executive producer on another upcoming Netflix series. She also has several TV and feature projects in development.

MICHAEL WIESE PRODUCTIONS

IN A DARK TIME, a light bringer came along, leading the curious and the frustrated to clarity and empowerment. It took the well-guarded secrets out of the hands of the few and made them available to all. It spread a spirit of openness and creative freedom, and built a storehouse of knowledge dedicated to the betterment of the arts.

The essence of Michael Wiese Productions (MWP) is empowering people who have the burning desire to express themselves creatively. We help them realize their dreams by putting the tools in their hands. We demystify the sometimes secretive worlds of screenwriting, directing, acting, producing, film financing, and other media crafts.

By doing so, we hope to bring forth a realization of 'conscious media,' which we define as being positively charged, emphasizing hope, and affirming positive values like trust, cooperation, self-empowerment, freedom, and love. Grounded in the deep roots of myth, it aims to be healing both for those who make the art and those who encounter it. It hopes to be transformative for people, opening doors to new possibilities and pulling back veils to reveal hidden worlds.

MWP has built a storehouse of knowledge unequaled in the world, for no other publisher has so many titles on the media arts. Please visit www.mwp.com, where you will find many free resources and a 25% discount on our books. Sign up and become part of the wider creative community!

MICHAEL WIESE, Co-Publisher
GERALDINE OVERTON, Co-Publisher

INDEPENDENT FILMMAKERS
SCREENWRITERS
MEDIA PROFESSIONALS

MICHAEL WIESE PRODUCTIONS
GIVES YOU
INSTANT ACCESS
TO THE BEST BOOKS
AND INSTRUCTORS
IN THE WORLD

FOR THE LATEST UPDATES
AND DISCOUNTS,
CONNECT WITH US ON
WWW.MWP.COM

 JOIN US ON FACEBOOK  FOLLOW US ON TWITTER  VIEW US ON YOUTUBE